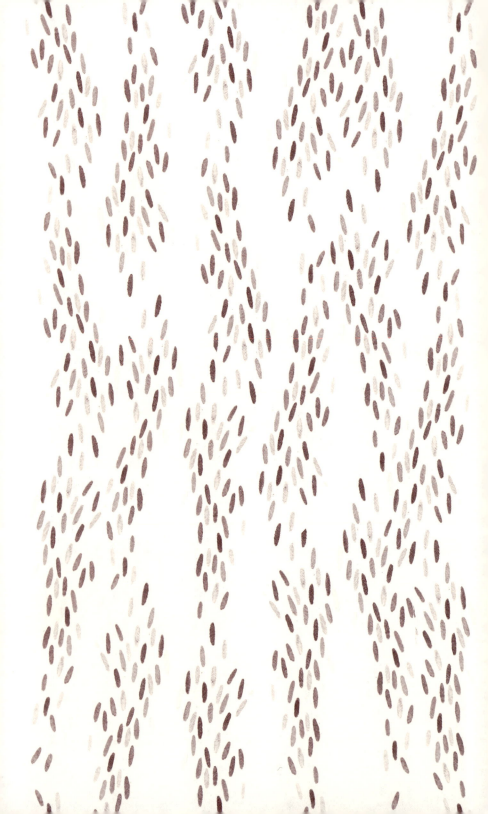

IN
WINTER'S
KITCHEN

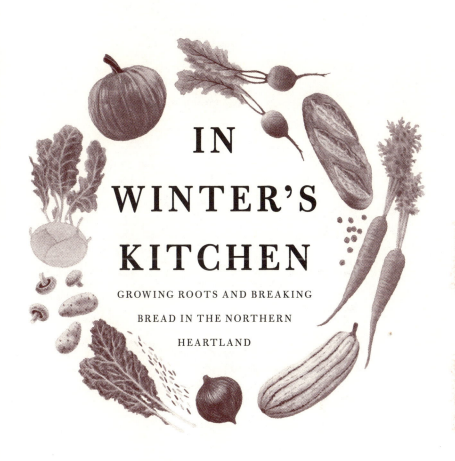

IN
WINTER'S
KITCHEN

GROWING ROOTS AND BREAKING

BREAD IN THE NORTHERN

HEARTLAND

BETH DOOLEY

MILKWEED EDITIONS

Published 2015 by Milkweed Editions
Printed in the United States of America
Cover + interior design by Mary Austin Speaker
Cover illustration by Josh Birdsall
Author photo by Mary O'Brien

15 16 17 18 19   5 4 3 2 1
First Edition

Milkweed Editions, an independent nonprofit publisher, gratefully acknowledges sustaining support from the Lindquist & Vennum Foundation; the McKnight Foundation; the National Endowment for the Arts; the Target Foundation; and other generous contributions from foundations, corporations, and individuals. Also, this activity is made possible by the voters of Minnesota through a Minnesota State Arts Board Operating Support grant, thanks to a legislative appropriation from the arts and cultural heritage fund, and a grant from the Wells Fargo Foundation Minnesota. For a full listing of Milkweed Editions supporters, please visit www.milkweed.org.

Library of Congress Cataloging-in-Publication Data

Dooley, Beth, author.
  In winter's kitchen / Beth Dooley. -- First edition.
    pages cm
  Includes bibliographical references.
  ISBN 978-1-57131-341-6 (alk. paper) -- ISBN 978-1-57131-881-7 (ebook)
  1. Cooking, American. 2. Local foods. I. Title.
  TX715.D6872 2015
  641.5973--dc23

                                        2015033774

Milkweed Editions is committed to ecological stewardship. We strive to align our book production practices with this principle, and to reduce the impact of our operations in the environment. We are a member of the Green Press Initiative, a nonprofit coalition of publishers, manufacturers, and authors working to protect the world's endangered forests and conserve natural resources. *In Winters Kitchen* was printed on acid-free 30% postconsumer-waste paper by Edwards Brothers Malloy

For Kevin
Matt, Kip, and Tim

IN WINTER'S KITCHEN

Introduction

DO YOU KNOW WHERE YOU ARE?

I n late summer of 1979, my husband, Kevin, and I loaded a U-Haul in Princeton, New Jersey, and headed to Minneapolis. "Why?" friends wondered. Didn't we already have plenty of great prospects in our hometowns? What about our families, the bustling New York metro? They could understand Los Angeles or Chicago, sure, but "Mindianaolopis," as my dad called it, was flyover country, land of interminable winters and a lot of corn. Kevin, a fresh-out-of-law-school attorney, was drawn to the Twin Cities' vibrant business economy and lack of big-city commute. And we were both attracted to Minnesota's lakes and trails, the piney woods and big rivers. I had already left my job with a large New York publishing firm to take on freelance writing assignments, work I could do anywhere.

So, like generations of women before me, I went west with the man I loved to create a new life and make a home. I'd loaded up our starter furniture and wedding gifts as well as my grandmother's worn bread trencher and dented copper bowl, familiar tools of my past that seemed essential to my future.

In my beloved grandmother's kitchen, with its chipped blue cabinets, rolling wooden floor, and smells of coffee, oatmeal, and cooling pies, I'd learned to knead bread dough until it was soft as a baby's bottom and simmer raspberries into jam thick enough to coat the back of a spoon. When I was small, we'd drive Route 35 to her home on the Jersey Shore and at each farm stand she'd chat with Dolores, Bonnie, or Joyce; sniff peaches; thump melons; and check the princess corn, pulling back a few leaves to inspect its pearly kernels. While she shared recipes clipped from the *Newark Star-Ledger*, I'd toe at the dirt with my sneaker, pet a scruffy dog, and lug the basket back to her blue Cadillac, seats sticky from heat. My reward was a sun-warmed peach so ripe its juice dribbled down my arm. When finally we crunched over the stones in her driveway and stepped into the soft briny air, our evening hungers surged. She'd sizzle meat patties from Arctic Meat in the black cast-iron skillet and steam Spike's Fish Market's blue crabs in the red enamel pot; I'd peel the fuzzy fruit to top with sweet cream delivered to her back door by Jeff of Borden. Every ingredient came from a person and place with a name. Just before sitting down, I'd carefully slice those blowsy, delicate Jersey tomatoes into fat wheels: tomatoes that remain, for me, the taste of summer itself.

The year before we moved, I'd been writing for the weekly *Princeton Packet*, covering home and garden features like the Baptist church's hundred-year anniversary potluck, as well as the beat no one wanted, the Planning and Zoning Board meetings. These civic gatherings, focused on land-use issues—water drainage, setbacks, building codes— were long, contentious, and fascinating. Residents fought to hold development at bay in an effort to save lush farmland while the real-estate lawyers, with flip charts and projections, promised increased tax revenues, new schools, and community centers. I watched as, quick as a cold snap in autumn, the bucolic landscape gave way to malls and condos for New York and Philadelphia commuters. By the time we left Princeton, the farm stands along Route 35 were gone. To find a Jersey tomato you'd have to grow your own.

As we fit the last box into the trailer, delaying our goodbyes, I offered to host Thanksgiving. My dad's favorite holiday involved our extended family and assorted friends and, for as long as I could remember, had been held in my parents' home. But Dad squared his shoulders and gamely said, "Sure. Why not?" When he promised to fly everyone out, I sighed in relief and excitement. I had a date and a focus to frame this adventure, a purpose and deadline by which to get my turkeys in a row; Thanksgiving would be my guide star to a new place.

Kevin and I barreled into the land of the "Jolly, ho ho ho ... Green Giant" with a bouncy, week-old brown Labrador pup, Hershey. Through Ohio, Indiana, and Illinois, acres of monotonous neon-green corn rolled by. These large tracts looked nothing like the uneven patchwork of crops on the small farms in NJ. In fact, what was growing here was not edible corn but the ingredients for sodas and food products. Where were the people? Where was the food? We pulled off the highway in search of a diner, and drove along ghostly main streets of empty storefronts, anchored by gas-station convenience stores. The only produce—apples individually wrapped in plastic, bruised bananas, and shriveled oranges—was tucked on a back corner shelf. White-bread sandwiches in clamshells and hot dogs spinning on heated rollers: all looked pretty grim.

Eventually, as we cleared Madison, the countryside began to soften to more natural shades of gold and pale green, and we wound up I-94 through central Wisconsin's rolling fields, under wide skies and tumbling clouds. Cattle grazed on greening pastures and horses wandered near big red barns. When we finally crossed the St. Croix River into Minnesota, my heart, opened by such expanse, was humble and hopeful.

Soon as we unpacked the last box in the lower level of our Minneapolis duplex rental, we met up with a classmate of Kevin's at Becky's Cafeteria for what he called the "true Minnesota lunch." On the corner of Hennepin Avenue, one of the city's main arteries, Becky's was a huge, dim space of velvet curtains and soft organ music. On a table near the cafeteria line, a Bible was opened to Jeremiah, chapter 31, for casual reading. Becky's offered a "four-square" selection cucumber and sour cream salad (eighteen cents), beef loaf (seventy-two cents), potato hash (thirty-five cents), and a slab of Jell-O, plus warm, soft potato rolls just out of the oven and apple pie with a crust so rumpled and uneven, it had to have been homemade. Every seat was taken—by bearded students, business suits, blue-haired women. The meal was honest, but I had to wonder: *Do people here really eat swampy broccoli, iceberg lettuce, and fried chicken for lunch everyday?* Not far from our home, the Red Owl grocery stocked disappointing soft apples and wimpy carrots, aisles of frozen dinners and shelves of packaged mac and cheese. We had landed in "the nation's breadbasket" only to find it filled with tasteless white bread.

But on a tip from our neighbor Bettye, a chatty retired teacher who had delivered a batch of fresh blueberry muffins to our front door, I ventured off one Saturday morning to find the Minneapolis Farmers' Market. There, I was swept into a whirlwind of colors and aromas—brilliant red tomatoes, glossy eggplants, crimson crab apples, wrinkled tiny hot peppers—aromas of damp earth, wet wool, coffee, sweat, and sweet cider—jolly laughter and shouts in languages I couldn't understand. I stopped at a mound of orange carrots with frilly green tops and handed a dollar to the grower, Eugene Kroger, for a bundle of roots that resembled his gnarled fingers. He rubbed off a little bit of dirt and gave me a carrot to taste. With a delicious crunch, and for a bittersweet moment, I tumbled back to my grandmother and those New Jersey farm stands.

Registering my delight, Kroger smiled. "These are plenty fresh, I picked them at 4:00 a.m. this morning," he said, and bit into a carrot, too. This exchange between cook and farmer is as familiar to me as my childhood and as ancient as civilization.

So began a Saturday ritual and unlikely friendship between this rugged back-to-the-lander and me, the curious ingénue, connected through our love of sweet carrots. I'd bring him a coffee and he'd slip me an extra carton of raspberries or a melon or two. This Vietnam vet, missing a leg, did not look as though life had pummeled him into the ground. "Working the land," he said, "I figured it out." On Saturday mornings, I rose early and left our quiet house, drawn to the jostling, shouting, and tasting, the aromatic life that brimmed in those stalls. Each week served up a surprise as the season built to the crescendo of harvest. Gritty and colorful, chaotic and coded, the market was seductively real. Through the months, I began to get a sense of this place, its food, and the people who grew it and bought it. And I knew that here, in the market, I might find the life I wanted, guided by memories of those I loved and all that I'd left behind.

The farmers' market was more than the source of a week's fresh produce; it was a wellspring of inspiration, a weekly calendar of the land's bounty. There, I also met Pakou Hang, an energetic Hmong teenager who explained how to steep fragrant lemongrass in soup, toss Thai basil in salads of chicken and beef, and roast and mash her farm's ruddy sweet potatoes with fish sauce. As she dug into the cash box to make change, she'd translate my questions for her grandmother, who sat in a lawn chair next to the family's van. The grandmother answered in Hmong, smiling and gesturing with her hands, chopping vegetables, stirring a pot, and warning me about her fiery leghorn peppers, named for a chicken's ankle. As I carried home my market basket of bok choy and bitter melon, Kroger's carrots and tiny strawberries, I could almost feel my grandmother's hand in mine.

My mom had slipped her copy of *The Joy of Cooking* into one of our moving boxes and when I unpacked this unexpected gift it greeted me like an old friend. As a teenager I'd tucked it into my book bag to read like a novel when I should have been studying. All through college, when I'd felt lost or homesick, I'd turned to cookbooks to soothe and entertain.

And cookbooks, too, had introduced me to agriculture's environmental issues back when I had been a graduate student living in a shared house, cooking with friends. *Diet for a Small Planet* and *The Moosewood Cookbook* had been our Bibles of food awakening. Fueled by nicotine and cheap wine, we'd lingered for hours at our table, an old door propped on cinder-block legs, discussing farm issues and claiming "the personal is political"—talking over Cesar Chavez and workers' rights, Rachel Carson's *Silent Spring*, the dangers of Alar and DDT.

So, as I sat at the table my brother had built for our first Minneapolis kitchen, turning those sticky, dog-eared pages, I began to feel more at home. Beneath a cookbook's lists of ingredients and steps to follow lie tales as rich and deep as any to be found in fiction. They are forays into families' homes and glimpses into far-off lands redolent of garlic and rosemary, saffron and cardamom. Recipes are stories with happy endings, of being sated and cared for in a way that feels gentle. I'd even suggest that the intentions of a cookbook author are the same as those of a novelist: to use both creativity and format to transmit an experience to the reader. As I revisited the old *Joy*, I realized I wanted to learn this language and translate the sounds, scents, and tastes of cooking onto the page, just as a composer writes out a score. I've always been happiest in the kitchen—chopping, sizzling, stirring—creating beautiful, flavorful food that nourishes and delights. As a reader of cookbooks, I loved the instructions that helped me imagine a meal. I wanted to know how to document such steps to pleasure, to both capture and share them. And I hoped such work would guide my search for the hearth, the heart of the home.

Despite all my reading, however, I had never stepped into a farmer's field. At the Minneapolis market, I could finally get answers directly from working growers about what it takes to cultivate delicious, bright-green lettuce and why the local varieties I used in my salad cost more than the pale heads sold in grocery stores. I began to understand local food.

Innocent and ambitious, I wanted to share with my family these new discoveries when they arrived in town. Hosting Thanksgiving for the first time is a rite of passage for any cook. Like that first bike ride without training wheels, it is both daunting and liberating. I got to choose which traditional foods to serve and which to scratch. I wanted to showcase those carrots—as well as ruffled kale, cranberries, sweet potatoes, and a small free-range turkey—and I wanted to make all the pies, bake all the bread, and create all the condiments by myself.

We didn't have a single table big enough to seat everyone, so I simply duct-taped together three different tables and smoothed my grandmother's lace tablecloth over the odd assembly. My dad told me over the phone that he'd ordered special cheese to be delivered and that he planned to bring the "good carving knife." I could picture this bone-handled beauty, snuggled in its velvet-lined, rosewood case and folded into his suitcase for a trip into an unknown place so far from my family's comfortable home.

It's not that our traditional Thanksgiving fare was all that special. Sometimes the gravy was gloppy or the turkey dry. But in my parents' sprawling dining room we'd always played out our vision of what a family might be if we didn't have to live with each other all the time. No uncle's divorce, no cousin's odd girlfriend, not even differing views on the Vietnam War could spoil the fun. We were open, joyful. The lights of Thanksgiving past would glow warmly as my father held court at the head of the table. Having sliced the breast meat to the bone with exquisite thinness, he would raise his glass to toast the guests and the bounty before us. More than any other day, Thanksgiving brought out the essential nature of my dad. He showed us that one could live both loud and gentle, both hungry and whole.

So now, with that *Joy of Cooking* spine cracked flat open on the counter, I rolled pie dough, kneaded bread, and scored and roasted chestnuts for stuffing. I scrubbed the counters and floors, ironed napkins, polished silver, and, as fatigue set in, began to wonder why I'd thought this was such a great idea.

The night my family flew in, the Twin Cities were hit with the season's first storm of wet, sloppy snow. My family was delayed several hours in Chicago and it was near midnight by the time I picked them up. The driving had been slow, the roads treacherous.

After heartfelt airport hugs, all six of us, sitting on luggage, squeezed into my Datsun and crept onto the highway.

Icy clumps pummeled the roof and glazed the windshield, making it difficult to see as freight trucks barreled by. The giddiness of our reunion soon congealed into uncomfortable silence. I missed our exit, circled up over the highway, and retraced our route, not once but twice, and on the third try, as we passed the grain silos on Hiawatha Avenue . . . my father could hold back no longer and asked me in a whisper, thin with impatience, "Beth, do you know *where* you are?"

What I *knew* was that change is hard. But while I realized that this was going to be a different Thanksgiving in location as well as food, I was naively unprepared for its emotional impact. Applying my grandmother's early lessons and my understanding of Rachel Carson to the fresh, beautiful food from my new local market just wasn't playing out quite as planned. I had a lot to learn.

Thanksgiving morning my mother, looking askance, asked, "No creamed onions?" Even though none of us had ever actually eaten the Birds Eye Pearl Onions in a Real Cream Sauce, they were my absent Aunt Ruth's favorite. Aunt Ruth adored fake pearls and Scotch and doused herself in Shalimar, and though she was not present, the missing onions seemed like a slight.

"Where's the big bird?" my dad asked as I trussed the local, organic, free-range, but admittedly undersized turkey. My brother, digging a bag of Cheetos from his backpack, paused long enough to say, "Looks like Beth went with a fat chicken instead." In our tiny living room, sibling rivalries, unspoken resentments, and secret rages, fueled by the exhaustion of holiday travel, threatened to boil over. "Oh God! Not more weeds and seeds," moaned my sister as I trimmed the kale. "Eeew," she said, spotting the yogurt curing on top of the fridge. "Stinky milk!"

My hopes for fluffy mashed potatoes were dashed, for I'd chosen the wrong spuds—waxy yellow Finn and red bliss—a mistake compounded when I tried to whip them up in the food processor and churned out a gluey and gray mass. That little turkey had a teeny lean breast but huge thighs and might have provided delicious dark meat, if it hadn't been overcooked (no pop-up thermometer).

The kale, however, was a surprising hit, thanks to my friend Atina's advice to sauté it with garlic and douse it with dark sesame oil. ("Cooked that way, even gravel tastes good," she quipped.) The gnarled sweet potatoes were wonderfully and naturally brown-sugar sweet, and the Haralson apples for pie were tart, juicy, and crisp. As we peeled and sliced them my mom asked me to ship a box back east. My valiant failures had elicited sympathies and inspired engagement as my brothers and sisters chipped in to help with the meal. Being in the kitchen knitted us together in ways we didn't know we'd forgotten.

At the rickety makeshift tables, my dad did the best he could to carve the little turkey with the beautiful knife he had bequeathed us. We lit candles as the day darkened and the mood shifted. In the making and partaking of this dinner we'd renewed our relationships, to each other and to a different tradition.

Though my father is long gone now, that knife still helps me cut through all my doubts about the importance of cooking, of gathering in the kitchen engaged in simple, joyful tasks. Sharing time, working with our hands, and chatting keeps these traditions relevant, no matter the distance and differences.

Thanksgiving is the finale for the farmers at market, and on Black Friday, Christmas-tree vendors take over the stalls. But my journey into this place, Minnesota, through its food and its people, had just begun.

I discovered the Wedge Community Co-op, just a block from our home, one of the country's first. In the early 1970s, the People's Pantry, a food-buying club located on a University of Minnesota professor's back porch, had grown into a neighborhood co-op that inspired the area's next thirteen independent member-owned stores. Organized around "cooperative principles" of education, sustainability, and fair wages, they became centers of food advocacy. I was drawn to the produce, the brightest and freshest available, as well as the information the Wedge provided. Everything on the racks was labeled with its source as well as how it was grown—conventional, transitional, organic. The Wedge's newsletter and its flyers addressed every concern.

To work off my forty-dollar lifetime membership, I stacked organic apples and spritzed lettuce on early Saturday mornings, and learned from Edward Brown, produce manager, about his innovative financial agreements with farmers. Brown would guarantee a price for carrots or apples in advance of the growing season instead of looking for the lowest price posted by distributors each week. Sometimes this worked in the Wedge's favor, as when there was a shortage of an item and prices soared. In other instances, the farmer got a bonus, if the Wedge had promised more than current market price. Volunteering at the Wedge was like taking a course in food policy as well as ones in nutrition, cooking, and environmental studies. Mark Ritchie, former Minnesota secretary of state, once said, "Anyone in DFL [Democratic-Farmer-Labor] politics probably got their start at a co-op." For me, the Wedge was a source of more than good-tasting carrots and bulk oatmeal.

I'd found a job with a large advertising agency, writing promotional copy and brochures for food companies (Land O'Lakes, Jerome Foods, and Snoboy produce). I had wanted to write about food for a living and while this was not the kind of food I'd anticipated covering, it was the closest I could get at the time. I hoped the professional experience might fill out my short résumé and lead me to the kind of work I yearned to do. On weekends, I was at the Wedge or cooking for an ever-widening circle of friends. In those years, with no kids, I had endless hours to plan and shop for dinners of osso buco, potatoes Anna, tarte tatin, and home-made bread. And it seemed—in Minneapolis, anyway—that a good invitation was often returned in kind.

One evening, at a formal affair in a tony Kenwood mansion, I was dreading a meal of catered overcooked chicken. So I could hardly contain my delight when we were served honest home cooking: rosemary lamb stew with olives and buttered noodles, simple green salad in mustardy dressing, and a runny Wisconsin cheese with tart chutney and baguette, all followed by dark-chocolate truffles.

To my happy surprise, my tablemates, Meg Anderson and David Washburn, did not want to talk about the Senate race or the theater. Instead, they shared with me their newest project, an organic farm, Red Cardinal, the first community supported agriculture (CSA) in the state.

In answer to my rapid-fire questions, Washburn patiently explained diversified crop rotation, pest-eating ladybugs that replaced pesticides, and intensive composting practices in lieu of chemical fertilizers. He relayed the intricate calculations made to plant crops so that each week's delivery contained an interesting assortment for the member's boxed shares. Before I sipped the last drop of champagne, I'd written a check for a piece of the farm.

Washburn had just sold a chain of successful fitness

studios and was no stranger to the challenge of starting a membership-based business. Anderson had left her job as a buyer for a department store. The couple, backed by family resources, was committing their entrepreneurial and artistic talents to this new endeavor. Neither Anderson nor Washburn came from a farming background, but their knowledge of health and wellness, the environment, and social justice issues ignited their mission. Plus Anderson, a master gardener, could now devote more time to growing her grandfather's heirloom peonies for sale to restaurants and shops.

The third partner, Everett Meyers, grew up on the farm next door to Red Cardinal and was working as an agricultural technical trainer for the Peace Corps in Ecuador. He'd envisioned starting a farm on his family's land when he returned home, and so brought to the partnership an experience with small-scale agriculture and a knowledge of the land that became crucial to Red Cardinal's success.

That first season the pick-up days at a neighbor's home became the social highlight in our week. By that time, Kevin and I had three young boys—Matt, Kip, and Tim—who tumbled on the front lawn while we chatted with Anderson and Washburn about how an early thaw had hurt the raspberry crop, why a cold snap had helped sweeten the brussels sprouts, and what to do with those tomatillos and kohlrabies. Every box was beautifully arranged with Anderson's artistic eye—tiny yellow pear tomatoes ringed with baby bok choy, garlic scapes nestled beside potatoes the size of my thumb. On our drives home, an uncommon sibling truce reigned in the backseat as the boys munched on carrots and fished for raspberries straight from the box.

On CSA workdays, we'd leave our own garden and housework and head to the country to plant, weed, and harvest. For lunch, Anderson would cook up stir-fries, salads, and bean dishes for us volunteer workers and the fifteen farmhands. Among those farmhands were a law-school applicant, a retired food-company executive, a FedEx office manager changing careers, a young couple hoping to start their own farm, and immigrants from Guatemala and Cambodia. When they'd finished their meal, the crew would lie under the trees, hats covering their eyes after a day that had begun at 4:00 a.m.; all were content. No masks needed to protect them from pesticide fumes, no rubber overalls to guard against fertilizer, no huge tractors in sight. Come sunset, we'd kick back for a potluck and sing folk songs accompanied by the strumming of a beat-up guitar.

One afternoon, standing among Anderson's peonies, looking over the rows of kale, the sprouting carrots, and the sprawling zucchini, I sensed my place in this web. I took it in, all of it—the pond, the green fields, the pale-pink-and-white flowers, the buzzing bees, even the mosquitoes—and wondered, how can you love a place, how can you fight to protect it, if all it means is loss? Must it all give way? Like the farm stands of New Jersey, must everything give way?

In my day job of writing about frozen cut green beans and turkey cutlets, I'd learned to develop recipes and give context to a dish, skills I applied to the newsletter I created for Red Cardinal's members. Here I could share news about how many tons of carrots the farm produced, about the gallons of fertilizers and pesticides *not* sprayed on fields to run off into the Mississippi River, and about the foxes, voles, and eagles that thrived on the land. I wrote about how well-tended, rich soil, full of nutrients, grows the best-tasting, most nutritious food, and passed on Anderson's cooking tips and recipes.

More than anything else, the CSA changed what and how I cooked. Every week the CSA box was a surprise and often a challenge. I had learned to cook by closely adhering to recipes, much as I learned to play piano by following the strict dictates of my teacher's sheet music. But now, faced with the wonderfully eclectic and unpredictable weekly share, I began to improvise. I waited. I responded. I relinquished control of my kitchen to the whims of our moody northern climate. Opening that CSA box felt like turning off the radio and walking into the pulse and swing of a live brassy jazz band. And, just like a dancer adapts her steps to the beat of the music, I adapted my cooking to the rhythms of a land that served up so much variety. Finally, conventionality became the exception, not the rule.

Through the past thirty-seven years, as a cook, mom, and cookbook writer, it's those hours in the kitchen and at our table I cherish most, especially in winter when night presses in and the cold glazes the windows with a lacy sheen. Like so many women who settled in this place of fierce winters and blasting summer, of thrift and bounty, I've learned to "neighbor" over coffee, visit with the farmers at market, and listen to the sacred stories of foraging and gathering wild rice. In this region, local food is nothing new.

Our small, independent farmers, processors, and chefs are not romantic innocents. They understand community and honor relationships, work on trust and shun huge bureaucracies. They've said "no" to the culture of the suburb and lives of needless convenience. They live where they work, make business decisions for the future, not immediate profit, and their success depends on their physical strength, endurance, and nerve. They contribute to the local economy, provide jobs, pay fair wages, and treat animals humanely while providing us all with delicious, nutritious food.

What follows is neither a history nor a cookbook, but a tale of friendships forged while walking the fields and cooking in restaurant kitchens, making cheese and slaughtering chickens, and how these experiences have helped guide me as I've tried to live a more meaningful life. And yes, there are recipes, because I hope when you've devoured the book you'll want to cook. Chopping, simmering, stirring, and tasting engage the head and heart. Thus, I've also shared stories from my own life with Kevin, raising our sons, of friendships and of family gatherings. The book is stitched together by themes of tradition and heritage, adaptability and resilience, independence and identity, friendship and community, loss and grief and reconciliation, all written with gratitude for people I've come to know as well as the gifts of this beautiful earth.

Our Minnesota-born sons will always crave the crisp snap of a Haralson apple and the cold flinty waters of Lake Superior, yet I don't think I can ever leave behind the taste of a Jersey tomato or the briny, roiling Atlantic. Through the years, as they've grown into strong, caring men, we've gathered at the table, to joke and to engage in honest conversation about what in our world is not working and how we may become agents of change. And it's here, with open hearts and honest hungers, we commit with joy and hope, to digging in.

IN
WINTER'S
KITCHEN

APPLES

Each of us has at least one "fairy tree" in our life, whether or not we remember. Mine was the apple tree in my childhood backyard; its U-shaped trunk was a wild place for me to hide with Daisy, our gangly yellow Lab. When the blossoms burst open we'd lounge in their fragrance, waiting for spirits to dust the flowers into ruby fruit. Later, I'd climb the branches to fill a pillowcase and Daisy licked the apples' sticky juice from my hands.

Such a tree greeted me thirty-five years later at the western-Wisconsin farm campus, the Land School, of our sons' Minneapolis Montessori school. Predating World War I, this tree reveals the place's history with a simplicity that would elude even the most gifted storyteller. The sturdy, gnarled survivor was the first thing I saw when I came up the hard-packed dirt drive, its low branches open and welcoming, a ready embrace. It blossoms splendidly and produces lady apples, with yellowish skins, pretty red cheeks, and a faint scent of strawberries and rose. It's the variety of apple tree that grows especially well in this region, needing the long cold winter to go dormant and enough snow to both protect it from overly harsh temperatures and, when the weather warms, melt to provide the tree with moisture. At harvest time, our young sons joyfully wriggled up into the branches for this distinctly sweet-tart, ping pong ball-sized fruit, then dropped with a soft thud and chased each other across the fields.

Picking apples is a quiet and absorbing task. You're centered on a thin limb, stretching on tiptoe into the leaves, seeking balance. It seems the most prized apples are always the hardest to grasp. Cradled amidst the scents of ripe and rotting apples, you gain perspective on the earth's daily spin from a sweet, safe perch. A good apple tastes of September sun, the warm, waning light; of its lineage; of the weather, the soil, and the way it was tended.

All this is to say that a good apple is the taste of balance—a range of natural acids and sugars, with notes so complex and different that they come on in waves of flavor with each bite. When cooked, a good apple may lose some of its subtlety—that hint of raspberries or rose or pepper or sage—while the essential character, the sharp and the sweet, becomes more intense. The variety of fruit and how and where it was grown informs the apple, just as the experiences of the eater have everything to do with how its taste is received. I doubt that I'd love apples so much if I'd never climbed into those trees as a child.

The old apple tree at the Land School is a regal reminder of the variety and diversity of the Upper Midwest's small, independent orchards and fertile backyards. Up until the 1960s our region grew over fifteen thousand apple varieties, but today only about three thousand remain accessible to orchard keepers, gardeners, chefs, and home cooks.

Since the 1960s we've lost an estimated four out of five apple varieties unique to North America, many of which once grew in the Great Lakes region. Forty-five percent of the independently-owned nurseries that carried heirloom apple trees have gone out of business, unable to compete with the garden-and-lawn departments of big-box stores. Along with the orchards and trees went the supply of unique apples, replaced by cheaper and more readily available fruit from the large orchards on the West Coast. Gone, too, are many of the orchardists and their knowledge of trees and traditional practices, such as grafting cuttings of apple branches onto rootstock. Add to this climate change, which has reduced the number of winter chill hours critical to the health of our cold-hardy trees.

Yet despite all this, the future for apples is seeded with hope. Over the past twenty years, several organizations have pioneered efforts to preserve heritage trees as well as their related wisdom and lore, efforts inspired by the burgeoning interest in local foods. Gary Paul Nabhan—a founder of Renewing America's Food Traditions (RAFT), internationally celebrated nature writer, and food and farming activist—is a creative force bringing the "all-American apple" back to our plates. In 2010, RAFT hosted a conference spearheaded by the country's fifteen leading apple authorities. The result, *Forgotten Fruits Manual and Manifesto*, provides a national strategy for saving and restoring heirloom apples. A status report on apple conservation and loss, it makes the case for returning heritage apples to home tables as food and cider. It's having an impact.

Sales of heirloom apples have increased significantly over the past ten years, driven mainly by the remarkable revival of the cider industry. Cider production rose over 200 percent between 2005 and 2012, according to the Beer Institute. Some financial support for these efforts comes from Slow Food, with two hundred thousand members in the US, and the Ceres Trust. Seed Savers Exchange in Decorah, Iowa, whose mission is saving and sharing heirloom seeds, is a leader in this effort.

Seed Savers Exchange's orchard manager and pomologist (apple expert), Dan Bussey, is on a mission to restore vanishing varieties by identifying their unique role in our culinary and ecological conversation. This "James Audubon of apples" is a vigorous man with piercing blue eyes, ruddy cheeks, and weathered, muscled arms that resemble the limbs of the trees he dearly loves. Over the past five years, he's been cataloging over seventeen thousand different varieties for a seven-volume series, nearly three thousand pages titled *The Illustrated History of Apples in North America*. It describes the varieties known to have grown between the years 1623 and 2000.

Raised in the 1950s in rural Edgerton, Wisconsin, Bussey remembers his family's trees and their generous branches where he hid after school to daydream and avoid homework. A prodigious apple picker, he made award-winning pies with his mother; he continues to do so today, using her recipe for a flaky crust. "I've learned which varieties really lend themselves to a good pie," he told me. "You want some that stay firm and keep their slicing, and others that sauce down around it so you've got this wonderful filling of apple sauce with apple slices."

When Bussey purchased his family's land, he began restoring the orchard even before remodeling the old house. "By then, the orchard had been left to disrepair and I was set on reclaiming it," he said. "I remembered my grandfather's stories of his favorite apple, the T. E. Pippin, and was determined to find it. So I put an ad in the local paper offering a twenty-five-dollar reward to anyone willing to share seedlings or cuttings. The guy who replied said, on the phone, 'I don't want your money, I'm just happy to meet someone interested in these apples.'" As we strolled Seed Savers Exchange's heritage apple orchard, Bussey told me, "That first early effort made me realize how deeply connected to this romantic fruit we all are. I've been connecting with apple lovers ever since."

At Seed Savers Exchange, Bussey is charged with reclaiming the older varieties, by sleuthing leads in newspapers and on websites, and foraging through abandoned farms. "The network of apple enthusiasts devoted to this fruit is amazingly wide and passionate," Bussey said. "I've been to big orchards, where the owner will put the most popular varieties out for sale—Honeycrisp, for example—but when that knowledgeable, long-time regular customer shows up, he'll reach under the table and pull up his special heritage apples."

All things apple seem to find Bussey, as well. "When I first began pressing cider on my own farm, people brought me apples from their backyards and shared their childhood memories; everyone seems to have a story. I believe these things come to me for a reason. It's my destiny."

The rolling Historic Orchard is a Grand Central Station of trees—the tall and straight rub shoulders with the gnarled, skinny, and squat—with over eleven hundred different varieties forming one of the largest collections in the country. "I love the names of some of the older apples," Bussey said, pointing them out. "Sheepnose, Chenango Strawberry, Cow's Snout. It's part of what makes them so interesting and worth seeking out." Their names only begin to suggest the wild variety of their flavors and strengths. "Every apple has a purpose," Bussey continued. "Most of the older varieties were bred for baking, sauce, and cider. Storage was the major concern." Many of the very old, wilder varieties have thick skins and a strong acid content to repel harmful critters, so make for poor eating out of hand.

Bussey reached into a big tree's full, wide canopy, so heavy with fruit its branches were weighed low to the ground. "Geneva Crab," he said, plucking off a perfectly round, bright-red apple and cupping it in his outreached palm. "This was developed by Miss Isabella Preston, in the 1930s, who worked for the Department of Agriculture in Canada. It's descended from the Russian crab apple, called *niedzwetskyana*." He spelled it out for me. "Came to South Dakota in the late 1800s with Mr. Niels Hansen, via Virginia . . ." Bussey sliced the apple crosswise to reveal a white star surrounded by shockingly red flesh the color of the peel, and then offered me a slice. It was gently astringent, soft and memorable. "It's not bad for eating," he commented, rolling his piece up to the roof of his mouth like wine. "But it adds spectacular color to cider."

Along with all the culinary benefits from these different varieties comes a healthier, more successful orchard. A diverse orchard is a secure orchard because different trees will respond differently to the pressures of weather, pests, and disease. If one type of apple tree is destroyed, others may still survive. "It's critical to have a variety of apple trees. Diversity is the key to resilience; it's also the key to flavor," Bussey said.

The classes and workshops Bussey offers at Seed Savers Exchange and across the country sell out as soon as they're posted. He teaches the time-tried skills of grafting, pruning, and identifying apple stock. And the economic prospects for heirloom apples are, in many ways, better than they've been in over a century, thanks to the recent resurgence of hard cider, apple wines, and spirits. The astonishing growth in artisanal cideries is helping drive demand for the wilder, more unusual fruit.

Cider apples tend to be small with a large skin-to-flesh ratio. "There's really nothing new about hard cider," Bussey said. Until the late 1800s, it was preferred over beer and folks drank it instead of water, which was often unsafe. Even kids drank cider because milk was reserved for making butter and cheese. Good hard cider relies on mostly tart apples, high in tannin, the throat-catching acid most often associated with wine. Cider apples can be so astringent that they are known as "spitters," but when blended with juice pressed from sweet apples, they help make a nice balance. "And there's cider vinegar and apple spirits," Bussey continued. "I know we can distill a brandy as good as any French calvados.

"The challenge we have in trying to restore these apples is in helping people understand their different uses," Bussey said. "They cover a gamut of flavors and textures and each variety has a purpose. Communicating this information is the hardest part of my work."

RAFT, Seed Savers Exchange, and orchardists like Bussey are making it possible for researchers, commercial orchardists, and amateurs to preserve and share heritage seeds, learn how to graft and raise apple trees without chemicals, press cider for distilling and drinking fresh, and market their fruit, all funded by foundations, individuals, and grants with scant support from the US government.

"Particularly flavorful apples grow on trees that are deeply rooted in particular kinds of soil and in the rich traditions of particular landscapes," Bussey said. Widely heralded apples such as Wolf River present a certain terroir, the taste of a place that is influenced by environmental factors, not just genetics alone. Flavor drives Bussey's work and is becoming the key to reviving the industry.

When your favorite tree gives you too many apples, make sauce. Picking apples is mesmerizing and getting our sons to come down from the Land School's tree to head home was a challenge. The trunkload of fruit filled the car with the sweet scents of damp grass and decay.

Back in our kitchen, our oldest son, Matt, the most cautious one, sliced the apples to reveal the star in the center and passed them to Tim, the youngest, who took this work seriously and removed the skins with a peeler. Then Kip, the least patient and most easily bored, pitched each half into the pot, a few feet from the counter. On the stove the sauce burbled its cinnamon comfort. They'd take turns stirring the pot until the sauce simmered into a fine, caramel mash.

One indigo afternoon, just as we returned from the orchard, my father called to say he'd landed in town and hoped it wouldn't be an imposition to spend the night. Because he was an amateur pilot, it wasn't odd for him to fly cross-country, earning "air miles," but he never arrived unannounced. That night, he entered the kitchen subdued and weary. What had motivated the trip, and why was he so downtrodden? A spat with my mother? A business setback? Distracted by homework, dinner, baths, and applesauce, I didn't ask.

But what I recall now is how, as he sat at the table, he relaxed in the glow of a Scotch in his hand, seemingly soothed by the boys, who scrambled up on his lap and hopped down to stir sauce. The kitchen filled with good smells while he shared stories of his war years on an escort ship in the Pacific and then of "bumming" through Alsace, France, and the orchards and the calvados of our exotic ancestral home.

The other day, our now twenty-five-year-old son, Kip, invited me over for dinner, and as I tripped over the bushel of apples in his doorway, it wasn't hard to discern that he needed my help making applesauce and apple butter. As we peeled and sliced I realized that apples embody the endless qualities of motherhood: of risk, comfort, and promise.

Cooking in my son's kitchen, I was knocked back into the presence of my father and of our boys in the trees, and into the moments of reckless joy balancing on branches myself.

Some say the apple doesn't fall far from the tree, but as our sons mature, I watch myself becoming the child of my children, just as my father sought parental comfort from me. As I witness my sons' journeys into adulthood, I vicariously experience their delights and disappointments, a privilege and a curse. I seem to grow older and younger at once, as the child I was, the mother I used to be, and the grandmother I hope to become collapse together.

In the late 1950s, when small orchards and regional markets began to give way to huge West Coast growers and supermarket chains, the range of apple varieties shrank. By the 1970s the selection of apples in most supermarkets was limited to the McIntosh, Red Delicious, and Golden Delicious. Apple breeders were aiming to create durable, long-lasting, and attractive fruit that grew quickly and was easy to pick. But beautiful-looking apples often taste terrible. Price, not quality, was a determining factor as growers and grocers engaged in a race to see who could produce the largest yields and the lowest prices. In just a few decades, the commercial apple industry had turned this once delicious, portable, healthful snack into a bland product no one wanted. The ubiquitous, insipid Red Delicious gave all apples a bad rap.

In the early 1980s the sudden popularity of Granny Smith (England), Fuji (Japan), and Braeburn (New Zealand) apples proved that shoppers would pay more for a less-than-perfect apple if it tasted good. That's when the apple-breeding program at the University of Minnesota began work on the Honeycrisp apple. Like Apple's Macintosh computer, the U of M's Honeycrisp upset the industry's cart. Growing and selling apples would never be the same.

The U of M's apple-breeding program is the nation's oldest and largest. Funded by the Hatch Act of 1887, which provided research and development money to land-grant universities for the promotion of agriculture, by the early 1970s the program had released twenty-seven new varieties of apples—including Beacon, Haralson, and Prairie Spy—beloved by Minnesotans for their range of flavor and cooking qualities, but unknown in the rest of the country.

On its thirty-acre parcel of rolling hillside—about thirty miles west of Minneapolis, near the Minnesota Landscape Arboretum—the U of M's research orchard is planted with over twenty thousand apple trees. To make apple crosses, pollen from one promising variety is swabbed onto the stamen of another, and then the flowers are bagged to keep out pollen from other trees.

The apple that grows on the branch will be true to the mother tree's DNA, the seeds will contain equal parts of both parents' genes, and every seed is distinct. The idea is to combine the best characteristics of both parents into trees that produce apples with a unique identity. Then the budding trees are grafted onto rootstock the next summer so that in about five years there will be new varieties that may become the next big apple. The successful results are then grown out for several years in a test orchard that replicates commercial conditions.

Dr. David Bedford, a U of M senior research fellow, credits the Honeycrisp's success to its especially sweet flavor and extraordinarily crisp texture; its unusually big cells retain excess moisture and contribute to crunch. Now ranked America's favorite, Honeycrisp appeals to those who previously claimed they didn't like apples at all, preferring sweeter fruit brethren such as peaches or pears.

Honeycrisp, as with all university-bred apples, was a patented apple. Anyone who paid the U of M's royalty fee of about a dollar per tree could plant a Honeycrisp. The problem is that since anyone could, everyone did. The huge orchards in Washington, Oregon, and Michigan grew great quantities of fruit and shipped it back into Minnesota, selling it at prices below what smaller Minnesota orchards could bear. This raised questions over whether the breeding program had strayed from its mission. Why wasn't the U of M breeding more apples suited to this particular region with flavors unique to this particular place? Apples like those Haralsons?

The Honeycrisp earned the University of Minnesota more than $10 million in royalties before the patent expired in 2008. The Association of University Technology Managers named the Honeycrisp one of twenty-five innovations that changed the world, akin to Google and the V-chip. Honeycrisp's biggest grower in Minnesota is Pepin Heights, whose owner, Dennis Courtier, is the apple's biggest advocate and defender. The Honeycrisp is a "persnickety apple," and Courtier claims that because it is not an easy fruit to grow, large orchards, especially those on the West Coast, are producing substandard Honeycrisps that are hurting this variety's image. Courtier contends that the Honeycrisp may become the next Red Delicious.

Bedford shared Courtier's concerns about the fruit's quality as well as the fate of the U of M's research in volatile economic times. When the state cut $4 billion from its budget in 2008, the U of M's apple-breeding program was slashed by two-thirds. So Bedford decided that new apples would be patented, licensed, and released as "managed varieties," a concept introduced by Australia's state-run apple-breeding program with its Pink Lady apples.

The U of M entered an arrangement with a consortium founded by Courtier—named the Next Big Thing—responsible for growing and marketing the U of M's new fruit. Interested growers are required to apply to the consortium for permission to grow the new U of M varieties and, if accepted, follow strict guidelines for cultivating and selling them.

The SweeTango and Zestar!, released as "club apples," are available only to those growers approved by the Next Big Thing for the wholesale market. Forty-five growers, mostly from Washington, Michigan, and Nova Scotia, were admitted to the "club" along with Pepin Heights, the only Minnesota grower. Club members pay royalties on both trees and fruit. Under the plan, Minnesota growers not approved by the Next Big Thing are restricted to planting three thousand trees (at first it was one thousand) and are permitted to sell apples at farmers' markets, farm stands, and local grocery stores, but not via wholesalers.

Angered by exclusion from the "club," a group of Minnesota and Wisconsin growers filed a lawsuit arguing that SweeTango and Zestar! were created with public funds just like the twenty-six varieties of apples before them, and that the University of Minnesota, a land-grant institution, was not fulfilling its mission of passing along agricultural advances to state farmers. The growers claimed the University of Minnesota had become their largest competitor and cited examples of Michigan-grown SweeTango apples, labeled "local" and placed alongside Minnesota fruit. The U of M countered that the "managed-varieties" arrangement ensures quality and maximizes revenue for ongoing research. It reasoned that it could license apples just like any other product created in a university lab.

Subsequently, regional growers created the Midwest Apple Improvement Association. Its mission is to support research and breeding of cold-hardy Minnesota apples and distribute them to a variety of wholesale and retail outlets. MAIA's recently released EverCrisp apple tree is available to any grower willing to pay the association's yearly dues.

Hoch Orchard, Minnesota's largest organic apple grower, wasn't party to the lawsuit against the Next Big Thing, but owner Harry Hoch is vocal about his objections to the "club arrangement." "The university may inadvertently play a role in destroying the Minnesota wholesale apple industry because most of the SweeTango crop will not be grown here, but will be shipped thousands of miles back into our state. This cuts state growers from their own markets. We should be resourcing and growing more fruit that's sold 'near place.'"

Hoch Orchard is located near the Mississippi River Bluffs, not far from Pepin Heights. Harry is an intense, burly man with a full beard, and his wife and business partner, Jackie, is the kind of woman who can drive a tractor all day and then spend hours in the kitchen, chatting and rolling pie dough. Though their farm had been in the family since the early 1950s, it wasn't until the late 1990s that Jackie, Harry, and their two daughters moved back on the land and began to work in the orchard full time. They left behind off-farm work in the city, Jackie in medical technology and Harry in the University of Minnesota's Horticultural Research Center.

In our region, growing organic apples for market is extraordinarily difficult because of fungus and pests. Harry's educational background and research work has proven instrumental in Hoch Orchards' success. In fact, Harry wrote the book (literally) on Integrated Pest Management (IPM) for Upper Midwest orchard keepers. Thanks to his laborious IPM practices, Hoch Orchard uses no chemicals on its fruit. And he and Jackie are helping like-minded orchardists to do the same.

Hoch grows some Honeycrisp and SweeTango, but the rest of his orchard is devoted to over fifty different varieties, a mix of older and newer apples that naturally resist pests, disease, and fungus. Take the Duchess apple, planted by early pioneer farmers, which makes a fabulous pie, or the Viking, an older summer variety, especially sweet-tart and mild. The new generation of apples bred by the University of Minnesota all flourish without fungicides and pesticides: Pristine, a tangy, incredibly crisp dessert apple with a texture so delicate that it's graded and polished by hand; William's Pride, a resilient apple with a spicy edge. Hoch Orchard is proving that the newest apples, bred to grow organically, are economically viable, environmentally responsible, and delicious.

The orchard benefits from the Mississippi's convection breezes, which rise to warm the fruit on cold nights and cool them on hot summer days. In August, the cycle of temperatures, coupled with the natural ethylene released from so much fruit, helps them sweeten and turn red. Hoch's nine thousand trees, on more than twenty-five acres of land, flourish without dangerous pesticides, fertilizers, or fungicides. Hoch ripens the apples naturally, without plant growth regulators or ripening agents. The apples are cleaned and packed on the farm, without application of wax, food-grade shellac, or any post-harvest pesticides. Eagles soar above the trees, carried on the big river's winds. Hoch, thousands of miles away from the West Coast's commercial orchards, has redefined this iconic fruit.

West Coast growers in Oregon and California manage up to one thousand trees per acre on as many as thirty thousand acres of land. This provides efficiencies in pruning, spraying, and harvesting, but it creates huge challenges as well. As with humans, diseases, pests, and fungus spread rapidly among close neighbors, especially when they are genetically identical. As a result, farmers rely on fertilizers, pesticides, and fungicides that employ such toxins as AZM and Phosmet. The Environmental Working Group (EWG), a public health advocacy group, recently named conventional, commercially grown apples as one of the most contaminated fruits grown in the US. To reduce the use of these toxins, plant geneticists created GMO Red Delicious apples using transgenic technologies to code in genetic resistance to diseases, fungus, and pests. The first field trials of GMO apples were conducted in 1992 in the US, Great Britain, and New Zealand. But there's no proof that these trees are any better than those nature has provided, and the encoded resistance is beginning to break down so that even more chemicals must be applied to resist disease and blight.

Last year, the Next Big Thing growers produced more than half a billion SweeTango apples. Recently, the NBT joined with twelve fruit marketers from eleven countries and five continents in a global consortium called IFORED. Currently SweeTango apples are sold in all fifty states and in Canada, and perhaps soon they'll be grown and sold throughout the world.

What do we forfeit when we rely on other regions to provide us with food we could grow ourselves? We gain reliability and consistent supply, of course, but we also lose the flavor of a diverse life, and its savor—the knowledge that this flavor is only a season long, or only found with some searching. By growing a diverse food system in the Heartland, organizations like Seed Savers Exchange and small, independent orchards like Hoch are ensuring that there is yet magic in the world to attract our children to the outdoors and the richness that can imbue their lives with the memories of a vibrant past.

The apples we find at the Land School are a product of its isolated history. The school is in a remote area half an hour from supermarkets and shopping malls. The neighboring farmers who remain here eke out a meager livelihood raising dairy cattle, goats, sheep, and CSA vegetables, as well as some hay, corn, and soy. This farm's isolation has allowed my old tree to thrive through four generations of families who picked the fruit, made sauce and pies, and stored the apples, wrapped in newspaper, in baskets in the root cellar.

The school's apples are unique to this farm, to its soil, rain, and sun. I've never eaten anything like them. Will our kids recall their flavor? It's the taste of fall family work weekends with wheelbarrow races, basketball in the hayloft, flashlight tag; of the day our big sloppy black Lab was ambushed by the bossy rooster. It's the hours our youngest son, Tim, spent on the creek's shore building "troll" houses with sticks and leaves; it's the scent of the campfire's wood smoke as parents and kids talked late into the night after dinner; and it's that sticky, apple-rich scent that filled the packing shed when we sorted apples into the CSA boxes for the weekly share.

The new varieties from the U of M, SweeTango, Zestar!, and their forerunner, Honeycrisp, were not created in nature and are not the happy accident of wind or bees. Yet they've become the industry standard, exploding with juices and a crackling crunch, bloated and thin-skinned. That first snap of sweetness quickly turns cloying because they are a one-note fruit—big, and often hard to finish. The Land School's neighboring farmer Dale told me that even his pigs seem to have tired of them. "If I put Honeycrisp or SweeTango in their trough they'll tip it over. They've just gotten used to more complex flavors," he jokes. "They're interested at first, but then, you know, I can tell that they're looking for something else."

That saying—"The apple never falls far from the tree"—is often used as a catchall for the inevitable strengths and weaknesses that the older generation passes on to the young. Among farmers, the wisdom being passed can only be seen as a positive. The work being done to preserve heirloom apples is making it possible for those eager to learn the old ways to carry them forward, melding modern technologies and ecological wisdom. Our nineteenth century's apple diversity reflected different purposes and different needs, but reflected an appetite for differences. When I taste a good apple, I taste the biodiversity it represents. If we succumb to a world of the generic apple, we are in danger of our taste buds becoming generic as well. Cultivating ourselves is the first step toward diversifying our orchards.

Dan Bussey's orchard grows apples in fascinating shapes, colors, and flavors that can delight and nurture us all. As such, the apple is a "democratic" fruit, as varied and interesting and diverse as our country itself. An affordable luxury, apples are within the means of every person. Their enjoyment requires nothing more than our attention to the variety of trees and the stories they tell. Simple and straightforward, this fruit has a special meaning among people who know what they are eating. In many ways, the apple may lead us to a greater understanding and appreciation of our food and our land, in the same way the original apple, in the Garden of Eden, provided another kind of wisdom that carried us forward.

WHEAT

After that first Thanksgiving in Minneapolis, the farmers' market stalls were given over to Christmas trees, and I felt little of the holiday merriment. Afternoons were long and gray, my job hunting proved fruitless, and I was envious of my husband's work and long hours. One night, after gazing through the kitchen window onto patches of crusty snow, I turned my attention to the table my brother had built and a wooden bread trencher filled with unopened mail. "Get the flour from the pantry, the yeast, and the salt," I could hear my late grandmother's voice intone beneath the sweeping tick of our kitchen clock. "Set out the measuring cups, tie back your hair, and for pity's sake, wash those hands with the brown soap over the sink."

As the cold laced my windowpanes with crystalline ice,

I mixed and kneaded, warmed by the thump-whacking rhythm of making bread. I drifted back to my grandmother's kitchen, where as a child I would stand on a step stool to reach her speckled Formica countertop and help roll out a thin slab of her holiday bread dough. We'd cut it into small circles with a juice glass to make the "elf rolls" that we baked to a golden brown and slathered with sticky white icing.

That night, as flour dusted my counter, table, and chairs, I made my first loaf of bread in our new kitchen and so laid claim to our home. Since then, on dark, weary, wintry evenings, I seek refuge in this work, conjuring images of my grandmother: her long, knobby fingers and faded purple-flower apron; her yellow kitchen on Claremont Avenue in Maplewood, New Jersey. All of this links me to the generations of women who have baked bread through the ages and I come face to face with the moment when bread meant life.

For many of our region's early settlers, bread was salvation, sometimes the only food on the table after the root cellar had been emptied and spring was months away. Back then, amber waves of wheat shimmering with prosperity drew immigrants to our fertile plains. Even our currency's bright pennies were minted with the image of sheaves of wheat until 1959.

This iconic crop is a strange little grass. "One of the most complex plants in existence," said Dr. Abdullah Jaradat, a research agronomist with the US Department of Agriculture (USDA) at University of Minnesota–Morris. Both scientist and wheat historian, Jaradat is on a mission to revive the early varieties of wheat that made the Upper Midwest the "breadbasket of the world."

This slight, well-tailored scholar in his late fifties moved to Minnesota from Jordan nearly thirty years ago to research sustainable grain crops so they might grow again across our plains. He's a passionate cook and accomplished baker, and he told me he has a personal interest in heritage wheat because he has trouble digesting food made with commercial flours. On a tour of the research facility, Jaradat relayed the story of how wheat evolved nearly twelve thousand years ago into the industrially farmed commodity crop, bred for easy harvesting and storage, that's traded on the grain exchanges of Kansas City, Chicago, and Minneapolis today.

Wheat, derived from wild species, consists of three different subgenomes joined in two events of natural hybridization. Emmer, the progenitor of our modern grain, was first grown in the Fertile Crescent on the southeastern coast of the Caspian Sea, in what is now Iran. Around the same time, einkorn wheat grew near the mountainous area of southeastern Turkey.

Amid the expansive fields of commodity corn and soy, Jaradat is growing out trials of the earliest strains of wheat—einkorn, farro, and emmer. He's also propagating Turkey red and red fife wheat, the varieties first grown here in the 1800s. "I can enjoy baked goods made from heritage grains," he told me.

"I come from the birthplace of wheat. Ever since wheat's domestication ten thousand years ago, farmers have developed and improved wheat's genetic diversity as a 'landrace,' the term we use to describe plants that have adapted through natural selection to a region's particular environment. Wheat does this especially well. It's a very smart, highly versatile plant," he said, and continued with the story.

Through harvesting and sowing, farmers helped guide the natural breeding process to produce wheat crops with desirable traits. These early strains of wheat grew in the Karadag Mountains of Turkey around 9600 BC and spread through Greece, Cyprus, India, Egypt, and eventually into Germany and Spain by 5000 BC, finally reaching England and Scandinavia by 3000 BC.

"The best farmers always planted several varieties of wheat so as not to rely on one particular crop should it fail and leave the family without sustenance. It's something we need to remember and to practice," Jaradat said. "Relying on one variety of any plant is dangerous. It leaves the farmer vulnerable if the crop is struck with a blight, or pests, or foul weather." He related how, in the US, a few early colonists tried to grow wheat on the East Coast. But it wasn't until the mid-1800s that European settlers really planted wheat crops. The German Mennonites brought the best variety, Turkey red, to Kansas. It's a high-gluten grain that makes beautiful flour and wonderful bread.

These German Mennonites were conscientious objectors, and they'd sought refuge from serving in their country's army. Russia's Catherine the Great had offered them asylum in return for growing wheat for her own soldiers. She provided them with large tracts of fertile land. But by the mid-1800s, the Russian government had begun meddling in the Mennonites' affairs and pressuring them to turn their fertile parcels over to the rebellious, landless peasants.

A close-knit society, the Mennonites decided collectively to leave Russia to create a settlement in America. They were enticed by homesteading opportunities in the Midwest and encouraged by railroad companies seeking farmers to grow wheat for transport to the markets back east. To avoid having their precious wheat seeds confiscated at the Russian border, the women sewed them into their undergarments and planted them as soon as the immigrants had settled.

Within the next fifty years, Turkey red displaced corn as the Midwest's primary crop, changing the region's farm economy and landscape. Turkey red was well suited to its new home. Planted in the fall, it became dormant through the harsh winters and so was resistant to disease and fungus. When the weather warmed in the spring the wheat sprouted and grew into lush crops to harvest before the freeze.

Farm journals of that era detail the beauty of Turkey red's burnished brown stalks, shimmering in the sun, rippling in the winds, and growing so tall a man could hide deep in the wheat fields. But the wheat's majestic height, as well as its bounty, presented a challenge at harvest. Until the

1840s, crews of men used long-handled sickles to cut down the wheat, and with their neighbors, bundled and brought in the harvest. Then the mechanical combine or harvester, invented in Scotland, made its way across the ocean to Midwest farms. Though clunky and slow-moving, this machine helped to ease physical labor and expedite the harvest. These machines were expensive to buy and difficult to maintain, so neighboring farmers shared the combines and worked together to bring in everyone's harvest as a yearly community event.

"Bringing in the sheaves" was sweaty, backbreaking work. Harvesters toiled in the hot, dusty fields as their combine's loud, grinding gears screeched in their ears. To incent workers through their arduous, twelve- to fifteen-hour shifts, women cooked and presented the men with huge, bountiful meals and snacks.

"We often competed to serve the best spreads," wrote prairie-life authors Carrie and Felicia Adele Young of their childhoods in North Dakota. The sisters cooked all day for three or four dozen men—breakfast, forenoon or mid-morning lunch, dinner at noon, afternoon lunch, and supper at the end of the workday. Roasts, stews, breads, pies, cookies, cakes: the list of food seemed endless. Girls stayed home from school to help. Usually it took a week to complete. "We knew that a well-fed worker was a hard worker, and the better the food, the more quickly the crew would finish the job."

Feeding so many helpful neighbors and hired hands

was the cost of bringing in the crops. Soon as every farm's crop was in, the whole community danced. "Not a simple, Saturday-night dance, but a big hoedown where the whole community joined in and danced to the fiddlers late into the night under the huge harvest moon."

It took those crews several days to cover about 160 acres of wheat, which yielded fifty bushels. As they went from farm to farm, the men worked together and reaped, threshed, and winnowed the grain. By the 1920s, as the fields expanded and demand for wheat continued to grow, migrant workers traveled by train from Oklahoma, through the Dakotas, Minnesota, Wisconsin, and Canada. Newspapers from that era reported boxcars packed so tightly men stood shoulder to shoulder en route to the wheat fields. By the early 1930s, American radicalism, in the form of the Industrial Workers of the World (IWW), spread rapidly so that it became unsafe to ride the freights without a "red card." Soon laborers began striking for better wages and living conditions. But the farmers responded with vigilante mobs that drove the agitators from the fields at gunpoint. Class warfare broke out in the most "American" regions of rural America.

Following World War II machines became increasingly efficient and eventually evolved to replace human labor. Today, one person, driving an enormous combine that cuts and processes the grain at once, covers fifteen hundred acres in two to three days. Older farmers remember the hoedown dances and community celebrations with fondness, but very few of them miss the much harder, grueling fieldwork.

Bread brings us together—to break bread is to commune— and ties us to centuries of ritual. One summer, when our boys were toddlers, a neighbor and intrepid baker stopped by with a jar of five-year-old sourdough starter. While I'd been reading about how to make sourdough for years, I'd been too chicken-livered to try it on my own. After all, I just squeaked by with a C– in high-school chemistry.

I packed the starter in the coolest spot in our car the afternoon we headed to a rental cottage on Madeline Island for a week's vacation. The broad expanse of Lake Superior, with its dunes and grass, was the closest thing in Minnesota to the Atlantic beaches where both Kevin and I had spent childhood summers. I wanted a place within driving distance where our children could build sandy memories of their own.

In the cottage's narrow, dim galley kitchen, while the boys napped, I followed our neighbor's copious instructions, typed out double spaced. I patiently fed the starter for three days and then created the dough. The loaf it yielded was not the most perfect, with one side heavy and a little too moist, but it was good enough to slice and toast, with a distinct sour tang and toothy tug. And I saved a little of the starter, feeding it at the same time every morning through the week, in a ritual that followed breakfast. Indeed the starter seemed alive, and I named it Maddy. On the kitchen's cracked linoleum counters I kneaded dough, as the late-afternoon sun glanced off the lake and waves lapped the dock in rhythm with the boys' easy breathing, and realized moments of stunning grace.

The word focaccia, the Italian flatbread, is derived from the Latin word *focus*, meaning hearth or fireside, the focus of the family and home. That summer my bread-making brought a focus to our week, during which I also breathed, and rose, and felt myself come more alive. A simple mixture of water and flour fed the bacteria, which became the agent for leavening bread, which then tasted better every time I baked. I reveled in the ancient practice, and was humbled by the realization that we need so little to eat well. Even when fields lie fallow and the snow knee deep, with the larder plundered and just flour and water left, anyone can still make good bread.

That summer, our oldest son, Matt, learned to jump off the dock into Kevin's arms and relax into a dead man's float. We caught enough fireflies to light a full mason jar, and dug to China on the beach. But once we'd come back home, in a mad flurry of reentry, I neglected to feed the starter. Within two days it flattened out, and I grieved the end of the season and another of our boys' summers crossed off the calendar.

My generous neighbor shared another batch of her

starter, and so I tried to make bread once more. But those loaves were not nearly as successful, missing the summer sourdough's distinctly tart taste and chewy crust. Perhaps they needed the sun-kissed magic of the cottage kitchen, the cold and flinty lake, those pink streaks of sunset, the music of the loons, and the nearby sailboat's clanging halyards that sent us to sleep each starry night.

In our region's first cookbook, *Buckeye Cookery and Practical Housekeeping*, published in Minneapolis in 1877, author Estelle Woods Wilcox advised her readers to be choosy when selecting flour. "The quality of the flour will determine the quality of your bread," she wrote. Back then flour was sold in bulk or directly from the mill in large sacks. Wilcox instructed home cooks to beware of weevils and "be sure it has a fresh 'wheaten scent,' before purchasing."

In those days, flour was ground with enormous grindstones in the town's community mill. These heavy stones shattered the "middlings," the tough part of the kernel's coverings, leaving the flour full of bran and hard bits. It took the baker a great deal of hand sifting to create the treasured white flour. The world's best flour came from Hungary and was produced with a steel roller that cracked open the wheat kernel without crushing the middlings so they were easier to remove. Because the roller process was slow and inefficient, the flour was limited to small batches, extremely expensive, and enjoyed only by European royalty. Back then, a family's status was judged by the color of its bread.

In the US, the flour-milling industry was founded by Cadwallader Washburn, the son of a lumber baron in Maine, who recognized the power of the Mississippi River's falls on a visit following his service in the Civil War. He built his first mill on St. Anthony Falls in present-day Minneapolis, for the Minneapolis Milling Company. It sported the new "Middlings Purifier"—a vibrating sieve that processed whiter flour at record speed and produced a wildly popular product. But success came at a cost; the purifier created hazardous amounts of combustible flour dust that would explode when ignited by a spark from machinery. On May 2, 1878, a thunderous detonation leveled Washburn's building as well as six neighboring mills, which covered a total of five city blocks.

It turned out the disaster was only a minor setback. The ruins provided Washburn with a blank slate to build a new roller mill using state-of-the-art Hungarian technology. To this end, he dispatched his engineer, an Austrian immigrant, to Budapest. William de la Barre secured a job on the night shift of the city's newest mill and secretly sketched its machinery. On his return to Minneapolis, he designed the nation's first roller mill for Washburn-Crosby, which later became General Mills. Washburn's chief rival, Charles Pillsbury, quickly followed suit with his own roller mills and Minneapolis became home to "The World's Best Flour—Gold Medal."

Not everyone was eager to embrace this new "pure" white flour, however. Just as Washburn was building his "monster mill," Sylvester Graham, a Presbyterian minister from Philadelphia, was denouncing the roller millers for "putting asunder what God has joined together." Graham hit his soapbox lecturing against the practice of removing the wheat germ from the flour. To him, wheat was "a natural food that the Creator has designed for man in such a condition as is best adapted to the anatomical structure and physiological powers of the human system." Graham's legacy, a small legion of supporters who promoted whole-grain "Graham flour," gave voice to the idea that traditional American food, homemade and eaten on farms, was the "natural," best choice.

The minister created the Graham cracker as a health food, fundamental to his Graham diet. The original cracker was a mix of unbleached wheat flour and coarsely ground wheat bran and germ, mildly sweetened with a touch of honey. No doubt Graham would have been appalled by today's commercial crackers, made of refined, bleached white flour and plenty of refined white sugar.

By the late 1930s scientists had confirmed whole-grain flour's benefits, supporting Graham's claims. In response, consumers pressured companies to refortify white flour with niacin, iron, and vitamins B1 and B2. When wheat is milled by grindstone, the vitamins contained in the hard wheat germ along with the fiber remain intact. Whole-wheat flour, unlike white flour, is not bleached or aged with chemicals that also affect vitamin content. And yet, until this point the greatest technological advances made were in the milling and processing of commercial flour. The biggest change in bread was still to come—through a fundamental change in the wheat itself.

Shortly after World War II, Orville Vogel, a USDA scientist at Washington State University, created hybrid wheat by crossing American kernels from Turkey red and other tall varieties of wheat with low, shrubby Japanese wheat kernels provided to him by a US serviceman stationed in that country. This work inspired Dr. Norman Borlaug, a University of Minnesota geneticist with the International Maize and Wheat Improvement Center (IMWIC) near Mexico City, to develop a new wheat plant. Charged with ending world hunger by increasing the yields of agricultural staples, Borlaug created a new variety of wheat that produced huge quantities of large kernels when heavily fertilized. Because this wheat variety grows low to the ground, it does not topple under its seed head's increased weight and is far easier to harvest by machine.

Borlaug, known as the Father of the Green Revolution, was awarded the President's Medal of Freedom, the Congressional Gold Medal, and the 1970 Nobel Peace Prize. The extraordinarily productive wheat he developed now comprises more than 90 percent of the wheat grown worldwide and has essentially replaced most other strains of wheat in the US. According to Dr. Allan Fritz of Kansas State University, 98 percent of US flour is ground from this wheat.

But no safety tests were ever conducted on the new food. Scientists simply assumed that any variations in gluten content and structure or changes in the wheat's enzymes and proteins would not affect humans. Yet analyses of the proteins in the new wheat hybrid show that 5 percent of the new wheat's proteins are not present in either parent. It is a different plant altogether. It is a plant that is far needier than its ancestors.

The hybridized strains of modern wheat are sterile and unable to pollinate naturally, and so require chemical agents to reproduce. In addition, they need excessive amounts of petrochemical fertilizers, pesticides (such as the extremely toxic sodium azide), and fungicides. Farmers apply hormone-like substances or "plant growth regulators" to control time of germination and strength of stalk.

The harvested wheat is sprayed with chemical "protectants" and its storage bins are doused with insecticides. The grain is then dried at very high temperatures, which diminish its protein, nutritional properties, and baking qualities. Next it is ground at high speeds that destroy vitamin E content and treated with conditioners and preservatives to prevent sticking. Wheat and flour were the first foods the Food and Drug Administration approved for irradiation, using high-speed electron beams to eradicate pests, in 1963. Studies show, however, that irradiated foods may disrupt lymph cells in humans.

Whether whole wheat is healthier than white flour is irrelevant: both are ground from the same strain of hybrid wheat. The changes in this wheat's gluten structure are now being blamed for the digestive problems of over eighteen million Americans. Wheat is the only grain that contains glutenin and gliadin, the essential molecules that form gluten, an elastic material that gives bread dough its viscosity, thickness, and extensibility—in short, its muscular strength. The word means "glue" in Latin, and in China, gluten is referred to as the "muscle of flour." When professional bakers talk about the dough's "strength" they mean the amount of gluten it contains. To help dough rise, the flour's gluten traps the carbon-dioxide bubbles created through the yeast's activity. High-gluten dough will yield a lofty loaf with a crispy crust.

This new form of gluten is being blamed for wheat allergies as well as celiac disease. According to Dr. William Davis, a Milwaukee internist, the hybridization efforts to confer baking and aesthetic characteristics on flour have generated numerous changes in wheat's gluten-coding genes. "These genetically transformed glutens are thought responsible for triggering celiac disease and many of the odd health phenomena humans suffer," Davis has said. After putting himself on a wheat-free diet, Davis lost weight and claims to feel energized. His patients make the same claims. Yet this new wheat may not be the only villain in today's flour. Chemicals—fungicides, leavening agents, whiteners, texture-enhancing products and the soy they contain—are probably harmful, as well.

It is difficult to separate the dangers of modern wheat from those of commercial bread. The most recent studies suggest that "vital wheat gluten," or wheat protein added to commercial bread dough to create a loftier and more tender loaf, may also be responsible for the spike in wheat allergies. Nearly twenty million people in the US contend that they experience distress after eating products containing wheat and one-third of American adults say they are trying to eliminate it from their diets.

I am one of those Americans, though stepping away from bread wasn't easy for me. As a child, while my sister begged for lollipops and my brother stashed potato chips in his room, I tore the insides out of Wonder Bread to eat slathered with butter and sugar. I learned to bake bread from *Betty Crocker's Cookbook* and discovered how to braid together rye and wheat dough into fancy loaves to sell to the local gourmet shop. Several years after we arrived in Minneapolis, Gelpe's Old World Bakery on Hennepin Avenue began selling hand-shaped loaves of artisan bread, better than anything I'd tasted in New York City or San Francisco. Shortly after, I stopped making my own bread and relied on Gelpe's for my loaves.

The only problem with Gelpe's was that it was simply *too* good. I ate more of it than was right for me. After our second son was born, I found myself suffering from chronic fatigue and sought help from a chiropractor. She tested me for food sensitivities. Wheat was the number-one food she suggested I eliminate from my diet.

That night, as I sat in my kitchen, hoping that some steamed sweet potatoes might subdue my craving for a slice of Gelpe's dense whole-wheat miche, I felt pretty sorry for myself. Bread was more than part of my diet—too many nights, it *was* my diet. On busy, rushed evenings, racing to sports practices and parents' meetings or staying up late to make a deadline, I'd relied too often on a bagel or a heel of good rye, slathered with sweet butter and sprinkled with coarse salt. Like a friend who keeps you up late watching bad TV reruns, this habit was one I needed to give up.

Going wheat free opened up a range of good food I already knew I should be eating. I sought and introduced to my children more sweet potatoes, roasted and drizzled with balsamic vinegar; Yukon gold oven fries with aioli; and chili-spiked black beans. I became slightly thinner, but I also became a more interested and interesting cook, with a shelf full of vinegars and delicious oils. When we entertain, we'll still fill a basket with delicious slices—but the focus of the meal won't be the bread.

With the creation of our modern wheat, scientists avoided one disaster—they fed the world and made a product that could continue to do so for decades to come—but they did it by tricking nature. According to Jaradat, the work was unnecessary and harmful. He explains, "Wheat can evolve without the use of chemicals; it can adjust naturally to the soil conditions, withstand pests and diseases, and thrive in a variety of locations in countries throughout the world. Before modernization, farmers left the stalk on the ground after harvest. The plant's roots helped stem erosion and as the plant decomposed it enriched the soil. Today's fields are stripped and replanted with each new crop. The constant tilling and planting is responsible for the tremendous soil erosion and runoff.

"Today's wheat is lazy. It's spoiled, we feed it everything it needs," he continued. "By tampering with its genetics, we've created a food that provides farmers and manufacturers with maximum yield at the lowest cost." Besides bread, crackers, pasta, etc., this new modified wheat is also processed into a cheap stabilizer used in luncheon meat, hot dogs, salad dressings, and even self-basting turkey.

"But more dangerous than anything else, modern wheat is unsustainable," Jaradat contends. "We are witnessing the near elimination of diverse strains of wheat, vital to human and environmental health and food security. It requires tremendous amounts of toxic chemicals to grow and process this crop." Arguing the need to reintroduce heritage strains, Jaradat added, "The recent genetic management of this crop has shifted to the hands of industrial breeders, but with hidden costs. Modern wheat has evolved through a genetic bottleneck of breeding for uniformity and high yield; it's dwarfed and designed for ease of harvest with goliath combines and dependent on chemical protectants to survive. In contrast, the landrace wheat evolved in low-input fields. These strains are genetically diverse, are better adapted to organic systems, are the robust survivors of adversity, and have greater adaptability to weather extremes. Research suggests that landrace wheat strains are more digestible for gluten sensitivities, too.

"Diversity is essential to our food security, especially as the climate becomes unstable and as pests and weeds evolve to withstand the chemicals used to control them," Jaradat said. Because commercial wheat dominates the market, it's difficult for farmers to find heritage grains. Jaradat encourages farmers to save the seeds of their grains to share with the Heritage Grain Conservancy community seed bank.

"We are continuing on-farm seed saving for evolutionary conservation of these wheat landraces," Jaradat said. "This research has direct application to farmers. We don't want to work in isolated labs. We need the cooperation of farmers to increase the genetic diversity for stable crops."

"Seed saving is my most radical activity to date," Bryce Stephens, of Jennings, Kansas, said over the grinding gears of machinery when he answered the phone. Working with the Heritage Grain Conservancy, Stephens plants the same varieties of wheat that the Mennonite women carried to Kansas in the hems of their skirts, Turkey red. It's bronze, whiskered, and grows a majestic six feet tall across Stephens's one thousand acres of the high plains the Cheyenne call *toxto*, "place of freedom."

Stephens's passion for this wheat pulsates through the receiver, which he was cradling against his shoulder the day I called, while installing a part under his tractor. A self-described two hundred and fifty pounds and six feet tall, this Vietnam vet turned antiwar protester is booming and loquacious. He was involved in the American Indian Movement's armed conflict at Wounded Knee in 1973, and is quietly proud of the FBI's prolonged interest in him.

A participant in a class-action lawsuit against Monsanto's GMO patent-infringement claims moving through the

courts in Washington, DC, Stephens is working to keep
Monsanto from creating genetically modified wheat. So far,
resistance among Canadian and US growers, plant scientists, and activists has been high enough to stave the development off. That is, until the spring of 2013, when, on an
unnamed farm in Oregon, a farmer discovered an unrecog-
nizable plant in his wheat field. The USDA labs confirmed
this was a strain of wheat created by Monsanto in early
2000, tested in authorized fields. No one could say where
this GMO wheat had come from. At stake is the $8 billion
wheat export business; over sixty countries refuse to purchase GMO products.

If it is approved by our government and introduced
in our fields, GMO wheat will enter rotations with corn,
canola, and soybeans, which all require massive amounts of
fertilizers, herbicides, and pesticides. US government studies have documented that GMO crops require 30 percent
more chemicals than non-GMO crops. While by weight,
the world's farmers produce more corn than wheat, most of
that crop ends up feeding animals or in the gas tanks of cars
as ethanol. As a food, wheat remains the biggest crop. The
Plains states produce about 10 percent of the world's wheat.

"Wheat kernels have been saved by farmers to plant
and trade since the beginning of civilization. Why should
a corporation own what farmers have been relying on and
sharing for centuries?" Stephens asked. "I'm interested in
maintaining the integrity of these seeds so that all organic

farmers have access." His daughter, Demetria, grabbed the phone and added, "It just seems natural to me that we would save our seed year after year. We've never felt the need to purchase seed."

Turkey red wheat, planted by a handful of growers like Stephens, is in an "identity-preserved" program critical to the wheat-revival effort supported by researchers and conservationists like Jaradat. During a recent drought, Turkey red outperformed modern varieties thanks to its strong, deep root structure. Its tall height helps it compete with weeds, making fertilizers and herbicides unnecessary. In growing this grain where it has not been grown in living memory, farmers like Bryce Stephens and Father Mark Stang, of Long Prairie, Minnesota, are propagating landraces, the focus of Jaradat's research, plants that develop and adapt to their environment naturally. In contrast to agribusiness-bred plants, landraces draw on a rich gene pool to become resilient despite the threats of drastic weather events, unstable climate, diseases, and pests.

Father Mark often weaves lessons from his fields into his Sunday sermons at St. Mary of Mt. Carmel Church. Easygoing and in his mid-forties, he is as comfortable in jeans and flannel as he is in his clerical collar. Father Mark grew up farming with his father on land that supported a family of nine kids. "My granddad planted it in the 1940s, but by the time I was a boy, my dad grew only the shrubby kind. But Turkey red goes without chemicals, and plants that can fend for themselves naturally fascinate me. Why not celebrate what God has provided us?"

Several years ago, Matt, then in his late twenties, moved to Durango, Colorado, seeking mountains, sun, crisp air, and fresh snow. After going to college on the East Coast, our oldest son had traveled through Europe and worked in Boston. But whenever he came back to Minneapolis, he'd proclaim his love for this place, biking along the Mississippi, canoeing in the Boundary Waters, and camping on Lake Superior's shores. He's found some of those pleasures, and more, in Colorado: he has planted a garden, has found love, likes his work teaching high school, and volunteers as a medic and firefighter.

The other day, Matt called, requesting a family recipe for gingersnaps. When my father was diagnosed with lung disease, he'd brighten and proclaim, "You are the best medicine," every time I made the trip east to visit. In the afternoon hours when he napped, my mother and I, not wanting to leave the house, baked gingersnaps to keep busy, fill the house with the smells of ginger and spice, and temporarily reconnect with Minnesota.

In researching a magazine story about Christmas cookies, I interviewed Hilda Kringstad, a Norwegian immigrant living in Minneapolis, whose *pepperkaker* were always the first to sell out in the local church bake sale. "I always grind my own cardamom and nutmeg," she said. "I learned to bake with my mother and grandmother, and though they spoke an older dialect which I didn't understand, there was for me an air of mystery and excitement in this work that included me, and that I could immediately comprehend."

The question of commercial viability is the biggest argument corporations use to discredit the work on heritage grains by plant researchers, medical doctors, and small, independent organic farmers. Corporate farmers are heavily invested in the equipment required to grow vast crops of short, productive commercial wheat. Is it unrealistic to expect them to change their practices overnight to plant more sustainable, healthier crops?

"Yes," argues Dr. Don Wyse, a plant geneticist at the University of Minnesota. "The responsibility of a land-grant institution is to address the key issues of our time. We should be working to solve the environmental crisis caused by conventional farming practices," he told me when we met for coffee near the U of M's research plots on the St. Paul campus.

"If we really expect conventional farmers to grow food that does not destroy the planet *and* that is good for us on a large scale, we have to provide them with a profitable alternative to these unhealthy and environmentally damaging crops," he continued. "Farmers are running a business. They are concerned with profit and loss; they need to make a living." The afternoon we met, Wyse was easy to spot—he entered the shop carrying a round, squat loaf of dark bread. It was warm and freshly baked with flour he'd ground from the wheat grown in the U's trial plot. The slice he cut for me was dense, chewy, a bit dry, but very flavorful. Wyse's long gray hair was pulled back from his receding forehead into a tight ponytail and his broad shoulders stretched his neoprene U of M training shirt. He spends his days in the test plots or hiking through the world's most remote regions, seeking wild plants that might become sustainable crops.

"We must put our intellectual and financial resources into figuring ways to grow real food on a commercial scale," he said. For the past twenty-five years, Wyse has been working with Wes Jackson of the Land Institute, in Salina, Kansas, to develop perennial commercial crops of wheat, sunflowers, and flax. He calls the initiative "High-Efficiency Agriculture." Once planted, these crops will return naturally year after year. "Wheat is a grass, after all, and grass is perennial," Wyse reminded me. These crops do not require tilling and planting, the major causes of soil erosion. They grow prolifically without doses of harmful chemicals. "Perennial wheat is a sustainable crop," Wyse said. "Its root system becomes more robust through the years so that it can withstand floods and drought. These plants hold a lot of promise as real food, animal fodder, and biofuel."

Is the flour from heritage and perennial wheat significantly better than that from commercial wheat, which at first seems far easier to plant, grow, harvest, and mill? Are the efficiencies created by our industrial system worth what it will take to change them? What is the price of plant diversity and food security; what is the price of our health? Most important, what is the price of flavor?

I sought an answer from Jeff Ford, founder of Cress Spring Bakery in Blue Mounds, Wisconsin, near Madison. Ford has been profiled in the *New York Times* for his award-winning breads, made from the heritage grains he buys from neighboring farmers and grinds himself—einkorn, emmer and Turkey red. They are leavened naturally, not with industrial yeast, and baked in an enormous wood-burning oven built by the legendary mason Alan Scott.

Cress Spring is located off narrow County Road F, which winds through the piney hills in south central Wisconsin. It's not easy to find. The location eluded Google Maps, and after several wrong turns, I pulled into the long and bumpy driveway, scattering geese and chickens away from the car and drawing out a few curious piglets that trotted to the edge of their pen. As I stepped out of my car, I was hit full on with the glorious, toasty, slightly sour scent of freshly baked bread.

I pushed open the door to a sunlit room lined with wire shelves of wicker baskets cuddling rising dough. On others, rows of dark oblong loaves and fat raisin-studded rolls, just out of the oven, were cooling.

Ford is tall and slender. His wispy gray curls, secured with a ponytail, were sprung around a yellow bandanna. Wire-rimmed glasses perched on the bridge of his nose. Serene and soft-spoken, he got his professional start in a Madison bakery as an accountant and then left nearly thirty-five years ago to build Cress Spring on communal farmland, constructing his bakery around the wall-sized oven. Wendell Berry-inspired and Rumi-quoting, Ford chops his own wood for the oven and buys all the ingredients for his breads and pastries from his neighbors and fellow farmer's-market vendors.

Twice a week, on baking days, Ford grinds the grains to maximize nutrition and ensure freshness. The natural fermentation method he uses to create the starter that leavens the loaves makes them especially easy to digest. In comparison to yeasted dough that puffs up quickly and flavorlessly, Ford's bread requires nearly twenty-four hours for its slow rise. The process imparts a sweet, complex acidity and changes the grain to make its nutrients more accessible to our bodies. Because the bread is made of such simple ingredients, it tends to last longer, too. The kamut-raisin and mixed-grain loaves I brought back to Minneapolis stayed fresh in a brown paper bag for about a week. Ford said that plastic traps in moisture and turns the bread moldy. "Bread needs to breathe," he said.

Many of Cress Spring's most devout customers come with wheat allergies and have found they can digest the kamut, spelt, and rye breads. Ford agrees with Jaradat and others that America's wheat issues start on the farm. "The varieties of wheat are bred by industrial production to stand up to machines are all monoculture, chemicalized, and lack any nutritional value," he said. "We feed people this stuff that their bodies are not designed or adapted to eat. Of course they're sensitive to it, and it's not good for them and causes problems."

Over the years, Ford has intentionally reduced Cress Spring's business to a more manageable scale, dropping wholesale sales to make more profitable home deliveries in his muddy blue truck. At the Madison Farmers' Market, he always sells out of four hundred loaves. "Saturdays at the market, people tell me they love what we do and hand me money all day. At this point, it's not work; it's my social life," he quips. Sure, these whole-grain, organic, locally sourced, naturally fermented, and gluten-sensitive loaves are nutritious, environmentally responsible, and supportive of the local economy. But the reason they sell out each week? Spring Cress loaves are burnished gold, their edges slightly burned; they are wheaten and fragrant, tooth tugging and tender, indescribably good.

Turkey red wheat is ground by Sunrise Flour Mill, in North Branch, Minnesota, and sold at the Mill City Farmers' Market in Minneapolis. Darrold Glanville, Sunrise's founder, opened a sack and spilled a few Turkey red kernels into my palm. Shiny, rich mahogany brown, they squirmed through my fingers and skittered to the floor as though alive. "When wheat is ground fresh, there's a different quality to the flour," he said. "It has distinct flavor and makes a very responsive dough. You'll see when you make bread, how evenly the dough rises then springs up in the oven. Bakers call that 'bounce' and the loaves develop beautiful, firm crusts."

"Fresh" is not a quality I associate with the five-pound bags of all-purpose white flour on grocery-store shelves. Darrold, a retired corporate executive, became interested in heritage grains when he realized that commercial bread was causing him digestive troubles. "I found a source for Turkey red wheat and began milling my own flour, giving it to friends, and eventually selling it in small batches. Pretty soon, the demand was so great, it grew into a business." He opened a bag of his all-purpose flour. A pale golden color, it released an aroma of warm toast. "Not many farmers are willing to grow this wheat, so it's hard for me to source and it's expensive," he said.

"Wheat is a seasonal food, like blueberries. The region,

the variety, and the growing conditions, as well as freshness, all affect flavor and performance," Glanville continued. "I can hardly keep up with the orders from home bakers, commercial bakeries and cafés, and restaurants." Amazing—just like my favorite apples, or spring's first peas, the taste of wheat will vary through the year. I've always thought of flour as a staple, a cheap commodity, and though I'd made bread for years, it wasn't until I met Glanville and kneaded Sunrise flour into a springy dough that bounced to life in the oven that I understood the difference. Jeff Ford's award-winning loaves are fashioned from the most humble ingredients—water, flour, and salt. Yet their true worth extends well beyond his remote bakery in rural Wisconsin.

Wheat is grown on more acreage than any other commercial crop in the world and continues to be the most important grain source for humans. Its production leads all crops, including rice, maize, and potatoes. Given its role in our diets and its place in our history, isn't wheat worth our attention, time, technology, and resources to grow it well? We have the intelligence, if not the wisdom, to grow beautiful, bountiful wheat. How do we teach people the value of this reality?

Make them good bread.

POTATOES

There was nothing ordinary about my mother-in-law's mashed potatoes. Betty Dooley whipped russet or Idaho bakers into fluffy mounds, turning them golden with plenty of butter and cream. Come summer, she steamed golf-ball-sized red potatoes to toss in a tangy mustard-dill dressing. Betty was a tiny woman with boundless energy who took potatoes seriously. A generation before, her "people" had fled Ireland for New Jersey to escape the potato blight.

The story of the potato famine provides one of the strongest arguments for preserving genetic diversity. In the eighteenth and early nineteenth centuries, all potatoes were descended from a small handful of varieties that were closely related. Through constant inbreeding new potatoes were created, yet genetically they were nearly identical. When the blight struck, no potatoes of this variety were resistant, so the disease spread quickly and lethally.

By the early 1900s growers understood the key to resilience, and crossed wild potato varieties from Mexico and South America with cultivated varieties. The resulting offspring were the especially tasty potatoes—Colorado rose, Yukon gold, and yellow Finn—that I find in my farmers' market today.

As a young mom, I told those family stories of the potato famine to my children as we planted potatoes at the Land School. In the late spring, those potatoes burst into pale-purple, pure-white, and candy-pink blossoms. Anchored in low mounds, their flowers nodded and bobbed in the breeze. At duskfall they'd close, and they'd droop at the faintest hint of rain.

Delicate and ethereal, potato buds belie the sturdy tubers they become. To this day, digging potatoes always fills me with a surprising tenderness. Gently brushing the soil from a freshly harvested potato's paper-thin skin feels like wiping dirt from a child's tender cheek. Potatoes are such an important food, a culinary staple and nutritional powerhouse; I'm grateful to have good fresh potatoes in all their splendid variety—delicate Colorado rose, buttery Yukon gold, nutty-tasting fingerlings.

Potatoes are loaded with protein, minerals, and vitamins. Since their development in the mountains of Peru, potatoes have broadened into more than five thousand different varieties that grow throughout the world. And while beetles, fungus, and mold make potato growing somewhat harder in our region than in others, our organic farmers grow tons of potatoes by saving some of the last year's crop to plant for the future. Unlike lettuce or peas, potatoes can be stored for several months when properly handled, and unlike other vegetables, they are both food and seed. Year after year, crop after crop, good farmers are paid back in plentiful yields.

The potato's essence relies on how and where it's grown; the vitality of the soil will determine a potato's texture and taste. When I lived in New Hampshire as a graduate student, I craved those tiny "salt potatoes," with a briny savor, that thrive in the low-lying New England coastline. In contrast, our region's potatoes taste of the sweet prairie and flinty limestone bluffs along the Mississippi River. Freshness determines quality, too. I once ordered a box of "gourmet" potatoes from New England, but when we served them alongside the potatoes from our farmers' market, their flavor was flat and indistinct. Those Maine potatoes had been stored too long and flown too far to retain their character. You just can't separate the quality, flavor, and general goodness of a potato from how and where it's grown.

Is it any surprise, then, that the potatoes sold in five-pound plastic bags at the bottom of the produce bin have no flavor? They are grown with fertilizers, herbicides, pesticides, fungicides, and sprouting retardants. The plastic bags they're stored in trap moisture and encourage mold. Potatoes sold fresh make up 40 percent of the commercial market. The remaining 60 percent are processed into fries and chips.

These commercial spuds are bred to size, weight, and starch specifications. To grow, they're heavily sprayed with toxic chemicals that dull their leaves with a white bloom. Just recently, J. R. Simplot, the Idaho-based and long-established power in the potato business, was granted USDA approval for its new genetically modified potato. Engineered to stay white when cut, resist bruising, and fry especially well, the potato's DNA has also been altered so that less of the chemical suspected of causing cancer is produced when the potato is deep fried in fast-food restaurants or processed into chips. This is the first GMO food to boast health benefits to the consumer. The Center for Food Safety, an advocacy group, responded to Simplot's data with a statement calling the USDA's approval premature and the technology used to create the potato not adequately regulated.

Potatoes are especially porous and absorb everything in the soil as they grow. Thus when we eat potatoes sprayed with toxins we're ingesting compounds the Environmental Protection Agency has deemed dangerous. The Food and Drug Administration does not have jurisdiction over pesticides.

In June 2014 the *British Journal of Nutrition* found that potatoes treated with fungicides early in the season, herbicides before harvest, and sprouting retardants contained high levels of dangerous chemicals and metals. Organic potatoes, chemical free, were far higher in antioxidants, minerals, calcium, potassium, and zinc.

While organic potatoes constitute a tiny portion of the market at present, organic cultivation on a large scale is very possible. In collaboration with the World Wildlife Fund, Wisconsin potato growers have voluntarily cut the use of high-risk pesticides and switched to Integrated Pest Management (IPM) systems, reducing toxic chemical pesticides by 60 percent.

The first year in our new city, I landed a job as an account executive in a large marketing firm and was assigned to the Pacific Gamble Robinson account. PGR was once the region's largest produce distributor, the first in the nation to brand apples. At my first meeting with PGR, Jim Kwitchak, the vice president of marketing, sat behind a bare metal desk in his dim office above the company's warehouse while I nervously and earnestly presented the promotion plan and budget, employing every marketing cliché I knew. But before I could finish, he stifled a yawn, winked, and pulled a crimpled paper bag from his creaky desk drawer. "Do you like venison sausage?" he asked, flipping open a pocketknife to cut me a thick slice.

Kwitchak was a tall drink of a man with big ears and a lanky gait. "Folks call me the Norwegian bachelor farmer who married Ann," he joked. He'd worked his way up the corporate food chain by sweeping floors and stacking produce for the old Red Owl grocery stores. "I grew up on a farm and couldn't wait to get away from it. Long hot hours, nothing to do in the country. I wanted to live in the city, especially after the war," he said. Despite his genius for selling potatoes from Idaho, Kwitchak's pantry was stocked with the food he grew, caught, trapped, and foraged, as well as the fish, duck, and venison he smoked in an old refrigerator he'd converted and fired with applewood. He threaded wild mushrooms to hang and dry on attic rafters, and he put up pickles on an old stove in his garage while watching the Minnesota Vikings on Sundays.

We met every Friday for a "business lunch" of pasties at Milda's Café in the North neighborhood of Minneapolis. A specialty of Minnesota's Iron Range, these sturdy meat-and-potato pies were originally developed to stay intact if accidentally dropped from a miner's pocket down a shaft. At Milda's, they're slathered in gravy—a point of contention for those from Upper Michigan, who douse them in ketchup. One afternoon after lunch, Kwitchak presented me with a loaf of traditional Polish potato bread. "It's beautiful," I said, admiring the light, airy round. He laughed while trying to get me to pronounce its name, *okragly chleb kartoflany.* I asked, "How did you learn to make it? When did you serve it?"

He seemed taken aback, shy. "My mother made bread and we ate it. Not a big deal," he replied. More than anything, Kwitchak disliked talking about himself or being the center of attention.

This corporate lieutenant, though loyal, had no interest in the tomatoes shipped to his own company's warehouse, picked while hard and green to save them from bruising and rot and ripened with ethanol gas, or the apples held in "controlled-atmosphere storage." Kwitchak made his own food, his own life, and enjoyed every bit of it with the blissful ignorance of a native Minnesotan. I knew that East Coast gourmet shops were selling the kinds of products Kwitchak made himself for fifty dollars per pound.

I admired this quiet, unassuming man. While I didn't hunt, forage, or grow my own ingredients, I could learn a great deal from him. Kwitchak was earning a living selling corporate food, yet lived as his own man; I could hold my marketing position as long as I needed to without losing sight of my ideals or goals. This is what it takes to create a life—the belief that no matter one's day job, the real work is at home and with yourself.

Fiercely independent even in close proximity to corporate agriculture: independent farmers are leading us toward widespread organic farming. One such grower is Jack Hedin of Featherstone Farm in Rushford, Minnesota. Hedin grows terrific-tasting varieties of organic potatoes, a lot of them, enough to supply his nine hundred CSA members, plus thirteen natural food co-ops and restaurants in the Twin Cities. Featherstone's vegetables are proof that consumers will pay more for good-tasting food.

Hedin is a rangy man with wild, graying hair, and in his thirty years of farming, he's been a fierce advocate for organic practices. "As someone who cares about healthy food and careful land management, I'm interested in seeing a diversity of crops return to the Corn Belt," he told me as we toured his farm one foggy afternoon in October. "It's the monocrop culture that's doing us all in."

Hedin's jeans hung loose and his faded, frayed T-shirt draped his lean, leathery limbs. He strode gracefully and purposefully, with such long steps that I had to jog alongside him to keep up. Featherstone's fields, bordered by deep woods, stretch over flatland and rolling hills where the morning fog hugs the valley and softens early light. It's quiet and lush. Who knew there could be so many shades of green—emerald kale, lacy carrot tops, assorted cabbages? Fifty different organic vegetables, grains, and legumes grow on 250 acres, sculpted into the hillside in curves that capture the heavy rains and help prevent topsoil runoff. These graceful patterns waver with vibrant life.

Well into the harvest, Hedin was a gracious host to me and didn't miss a beat, shouting rapid-fire instructions to field workers in Spanish and answering cell phone calls and texts. He seemed to know exactly what was happening on every inch of his farm at every minute.

Featherstone Farm's name is taken from the township in Goodhue County where Hedin's great-grandfather A. P. Anderson homesteaded in the nineteenth century. By the early 1920s, A. P. had expanded his family's farm to five hundred acres and practiced some of the conservation tillage methods employed by many organic and conventional farmers today. A. P., trained as a botanist at the University of Minnesota, was a visionary who grew a variety of vegetables, fruits, and grains. He generated all of the farm's energy, fertility, and feed on-site.

"A. P. saw the destructiveness of pre-dust bowl agriculture in the area as well," Hedin said. "He was keenly sensitive to the richness and diversity of the high grasses and woodlands that he had helped to plow up, chop down, and grub out in his youth. So to help restore the landscape, he planted tens of thousands of trees and shrubs on his farm, replacing what he'd destroyed." Featherstone's practices are inspired by A. P.'s wisdom, relayed in his self-published memoir, *The Seventh Reader*.

Hedin and his wife, Jenny Hughes, a midwife, are Ivy League-educated and relentlessly engaged in national and local farm-policy initiatives. Hedin travels to lecture and attend conferences, and contributes regularly to the *New York Times* as well as local publications. "There isn't a day that I don't refer to A. P.'s memoir as I work and care for this land. I discovered his book during my idealistic college days," he said. "It is full of musings on nature and agriculture and on our role in the environment."

In this farming community, many of Hedin's neighbors grow conventional corn and soy or are employed by corporate seed companies using practices directly opposed to the organic systems responsible for Featherstone's success. When I met Hedin's neighbor, Paul, a seed salesman, he showed me neon-pink seed corn. "Don't touch," he warned. "The color indicates the high levels of toxins." Paul and his family don't eat the corn grown from these seeds; instead they have an organic garden and raise heritage pigs. "There are very few jobs in this region. I'm lucky to be able to support my family, and have a house and enough land to grow the kind of food that's good for us. We all do what we can," he said.

Each year, demand for Featherstone's produce outstrips supply. Throughout the country sales of organic produce have increased at the rate of 21 percent annually, farmers markets have multiplied by 15 percent, and the number of CSA farms has tripled—all in less than ten years.

Yet while the statistics are optimistic, Hedin is not. Small farmers supply less than 1 percent of the total amount of our country's food, and an even smaller percent is organic. The rest of our agriculture is devoted to the industrial production of animal feed, ingredients for processed food, and ethanol. "The farm bill does not support growing real food," Hedin said.

The term "farm bill" is shorthand for legislation that comes up for review every five years. In 2002, it was called the Farm Security and Rural Investment Act; in 2008, it was known as the Food, Conservation, and Energy Act. The latest version is the Agriculture Reform, Food, and Jobs Act of 2013. The legislation dates back to the Great Depression and the New Deal in the 1930s. US farmers had mechanized and stepped up production during World War I to feed troops and a war-weary Europe, and had thus created huge surpluses that led to falling prices for basic crops. To reduce the excess quantities and support prices, the Agricultural Adjustment Act paid farmers not to grow crops, and the provision has remained through subsequent bills. The AAA also created the Supplemental Nutrition Assistance Program (SNAP), initially known as the Food Stamp Program. This was meant to fund the government's purchase of excess grain and corn from farmers who'd lost money due to the surpluses and low prices. The food was given to unemployed and homeless citizens and the government also provided food vouchers for the purchase of dairy products, eggs, and staples.

Today, the farm bill doles out subsidies only to farmers who grow commodity crops—corn, soy, rice, cotton, and wheat—and it underwrites crop insurance. This guarantees a price for commodity crops, protecting them from market swings, and reimburses farmers for crop losses due to weather. SNAP underwrites school meals (many of which rely on commodity foods), food shelves, and food vouchers. Weighing in at $1 trillion, the bill is widely disparaged for its handouts to wealthy farmers and its misdirected incentives. It would be hard to find a more contentious piece of legislation.

"So much money goes toward commodities, no one wants to grow vegetables or can even afford to," said Hedin. He recalled his experience renting a parcel of land from his corn-growing neighbor several years ago to expand his vegetable crop. But midseason the landowners discovered that the commodity program forbade them from growing noncommodity crops. The penalty was withholding payments for the farm's entire corn acreage. Rather than fight, Hedin simply forked over nearly nine thousand dollars to his corn-growing landlord. "If we as a nation want good fresh produce, we need to devote more land to growing vegetables, not corn and cotton. It's something this legislation makes nearly impossible."

We hiked over to a field where Featherstone's cabbage was coming on strong. The crew swiped the heads from the ground with long-bladed knives and then heaved them up. Like dark-green soccer balls, they arced against the slate-gray sky into the hands of the men in the pickup. In their dirt- and sweat-stained T-shirts, foreheads bound in bright bandannas, they were laughing and jostling like high-school kids, occasionally breaking into song. The truck filled quickly with a money-colored harvest as it rolled along the rows.

"This is some of the most fertile agricultural land in the country—in fact, in the world—but we are doing nothing as a nation to protect it. In its twenty years of existence, my farm has not received a single dollar of federal support of any kind," Hedin said. And he is not quiet about it. For all the serenity and peace Featherstone has to offer, it also remains deeply connected to the wider world. Hedin's articles in newspapers and magazines relay how national farm policies impact his land and the food in our kitchens. "The large corn and soybean producers that I know in my area love the farm bill," he said. "Insurance programs and federal subsidization levels have made it almost impossible for a big corn producer to lose money in a given season."

Who is the biggest winner in the most recent farm bill? The insurance industry. The federally subsidized crop-insurance program was not cut, while commodity subsidies took a small hit. The insurance program is administered by eighteen private-sector companies that are paid $1.4 billion annually by the government to sell policies to farmers, and pays for 62 percent of farmers' premiums (included in the bill is a provision that forbids the disclosure of recipients of crop-loss insurance). The best thing about this latest farm bill is the attention it drew to the USDA from all corners of the country. The debates shone light on how disconnected agriculture policy is from growing real food.

The latest farm bill also restored a little long-overdue support for organic-agriculture research and programs that help farmers transition from conventional to organic practices. It also includes increased funding for the Farmers' Market and Local Food Promotion Program as well as beginning-farmers initiatives. These measures will generally help support the growth of organic practices.

To become certified organic takes three years. The time allows the soil to reclaim its microbial activity and become naturally fertile. But during this time, the crops are not as productive and the farmer can't charge organic's higher price. So as the land transitions, the farmer's income drops. Farmers go out of pocket to pay fees for the required inspections and must also keep meticulous records in order to earn and maintain organic certification. By contrast, European governments provide enormous tax incentives for farmers to become certified organic.

Organic farming is complex farming, reliant on natural systems. It demands long and complex crop rotations to prevent the buildup of crop-specific pests. Hedin plants flowering crops, peas or alfalfa, on the margins of his potato fields to attract beneficial insects that eat the potato-beetle larvae and aphids. He'll introduce ladybugs as well. By growing ten different varieties of potatoes, Hedin creates biodiversity in the field. These complex fields, diverse with species, are more productive than those sprayed year after year with chemicals.

Lacking the political heft of corporate agriculture, organic farmers have little sway in crafting legislation. The agricultural-services and crop-production-industry lobbying groups spent $111.5 million protecting crop insurance and commodity price supports in the final 2014 bill, more than even the defense industry and labor unions. There's no compost or ladybug lobby; there just isn't that kind of money.

Organic farmers don't rely on seeds engineered in a lab or the chemical "regimes" specified to grow them. The industrial method of monocropping ropes conventional farmers into relying on corporations like Monsanto and Simplot. By contrast, organic farmers draw on the wisdom of generations and shared information from like-minded farmers who understand their land, its wildlife, and its natural cycles.

There's no doubt that conventional farming practices that rely on petroleum to fuel tractors and transport food are contributing to climate change and the volatile weather patterns that make production even harder for all farmers, conventional and organic. In 2007, raging storms swept through the Midwest's Driftless area, flooding homes and fields and destroying crops. Photos show butternut squash in treetops five miles down the road from their gardens. Featherstone Farm moved to higher, better ground, but through the past several years, summer's torrential rainfalls have wiped out crops and the wet fields have encouraged moisture-fueled diseases. Not always apparent is the soil erosion and nutrient loss.

"As climate change accelerates these trends, losses will likely mount proportionately, and across the board. How long can we continue to borrow from the 'topsoil bank,' as torrential rains force us to make ever more frequent 'withdrawals'?" Hedin wrote in a *New York Times* op-ed piece. Jack continued to tell me that the jump in the cost of rented land means that there's an intense push for greater yield and less attention paid to sound soil conservation.

Using the simple conservation measures that are central to organic practices could prevent 97 percent of our topsoil loss. "I see fewer acres in our area planted with erosion-preventing techniques that are pretty simple. Buffer zones between rivers and fields, and contour strips on sloping fields; planting regimes that keep cover crops on soil by rotating three and four crops, not just corn and soy. The current agriculture policy rewards the quantity of acres planted, not the quality of practices employed."

Smaller operations such as Featherstone just can't charge enough in good years to cover losses in the more frequent bad ones. Small farmers are running out of options as the weather becomes increasingly harsh; no new field-drainage scheme or hardware or technologies can provide a fix.

"If global climate change is a product of human use of fossil fuels—and I believe it is—then our farm is a big part of the problem. We burn thousands of gallons of diesel fuel a year in our ten tractors, undermining the very foundation of our subsistence every time we cultivate a field or put up a bale of hay," Hedin wrote in the op-ed. "I accept responsibility for my complicity in this, but I also stand ready to accept the challenge of the future, to make serious changes in how I conduct business to produce less carbon." As we concluded our visit, Hedin walked me through Featherstone's new warehouse, which features solar panels to control temperatures and powers two of the tractors I saw out in the cabbage fields with the crew. Nearby a geothermal greenhouse sheltered a tangle of tomato plants.

Why do we continue to commit our tax money to systems that seem hardwired for failure, but we don't incent farmers to take responsibility for the problems they help to create? And why isn't more money dedicated to transitioning farms to organic practices that restore and protect our soil, water, and wildlife? The farm bill is written so that home cooks like me will give up on its obtuse language and convoluted payment schemes. But I do understand that these policies undermine the farms I rely on for our good, real food.

"I don't see that I have a choice, if I am to hope that the farm will be around for my own great-grandchildren. Featherstone's vision won't be realized in my lifetime," Hedin said. And that's the point. If more businessmen, farmers, and cooks made decisions based on a future we cannot see, we might all be better able to hold our government accountable for policies that are short sighted and destructive.

There is a bright side to Congressional intransigence. Resistance to the farm bill has provided a surprising juncture for those on the far left and the far right. Liberals concerned about healthy food, the environment, food access, the rural economy, and social-justice issues have allied with conservatives focused on cutting government spending and reducing national debt. Both sides are wary of concentrated wealth and centralized policy-making power. There is hope for compromise and for change. Our legislation is only as good as our ability to comprehend its effects. After the latest's bill's passage, Republican senator John McCain said, "How are we supposed to restore people's confidence with this monstrosity? . . . The only policy that gets bipartisan traction in Congress is Washington's desire to hand out taxpayer money like it's candy."

Jim Kwitchak taught me that life's turns are unpredictable—that you might find yourself living somewhere and doing something that you could not have foreseen. But the road of life is long; you don't have to let its twists define you.

Growing potatoes, like living, is all about trust. It requires attention and knowledge, of course, but also the wisdom to allow nature to do its work. Hedin's focus is on process, not products; he grows diverse plants in small amounts, not single crops with big yields. In rejecting the

economies of scale embedded in monoculture, he's rejecting simplification. He's embracing the way nature works.
That requires skill and experience, but also letting go.
When planted in well-tended soil, potatoes mature in their
own time, nurtured by the sun, the rain, and remarkable
microbes, all held together in the world's gentle spin.
Organic farmers like Jack Hedin are custodians of our precious threshold—the land, the sky, the water, and the air—
which they hold in the rhythm of the seasons and the beat
of nature, its sublime pulse and patience.

BEANS AND CARROTS

At 8:00 a.m. one bright, humid July morning, I met Tameka at the Youth Farm stand in St. Paul's West Side Farmers' Market. Youth Farm, the nationally acclaimed year-round program for urban youth ages nine to thirteen, grows food throughout the Twin Cities to sell in neighborhood farmers markets and to restaurants. Tameka had arranged baskets of tiny yellow and red cherry tomatoes near piles of plump snap peas. In her thick-soled wedge sandals and a tight pink-striped T-shirt, her hair braided into sleek rows, this preteen looked like she was ready for a day of shopping summer sales. But Tameka and her crew had been up since 6:00 a.m. to harvest—green beans, carrots, collards, salad mix, tomatoes, and these sweet peas—in a nearby city plot.

"Two dollars a pound," she told me, scooping several handfuls of peapods into a plastic bag and setting it on the hanging produce scale. "You should get more. They're so crunchy—super sweet, like candy. I ate a ton for breakfast already." West Side is tucked into an old Dairy Queen parking lot not far from the enormous and bustling St. Paul Farmers' Market. But even at this early hour, West Side was busy: young parents with strollers, a bike team stopping in for fresh strawberries, an older woman with a walker sipping coffee at one of the picnic tables, a conga and a guitar player setting up to play. The sandwich board near the entrance listed a schedule of gardening classes, live music, and the beloved kids' character "Silly Miss Tilly" (who decks herself out with bright orange hair, feathers, outrageous tights, and huge clogs to dance and sing songs). This was Tameka's third summer growing vegetables and flowers for markets in housing complexes, urban neighborhood farmers' markets, and restaurants in exchange for a small weekly stipend.

But to call the Youth Farm simply a kids' program is like saying farming is a food business. "Growing and marketing food to a community teaches valuable lessons in the natural sciences, mathematics, communication, and commerce," said Gunnar Linden, executive director. A sturdy, bearded, youthful man in his early forties, Linden was helping unload cartons of tomatoes from a van when he spoke. He began as a Youth Farm program director and has helped grow the program into one of the biggest and best in the country.

Over his fifteen-year tenure, he's become an efficient admin-
istrator and effective fund-raiser. Self-confident and direct,
he moves easily from gardens and greenhouses to corporate
boardrooms, changing his T-shirt for a button-down and tie
on the fly. While he may occasionally pick a tomato or help
make deliveries, he insists the kids run the show. "They
own this work, that's why the program is so successful," he
said. "It's not the kind of summer program intended to fill
time. These kids know what they're doing is important." He
wiped his sweaty forehead with a bandanna.

"We have gardens and farmers' markets in low-income
housing projects where the only option for fresh food is the
convenience store. But we do more than just sell vegetables.
Youth Farm is about community involvement, pride, men-
torship, and empowerment," he added.

Youth farmers have captured the attention of the Twin
Cities' best chefs, too. Nearly fifteen years ago, a farmer like
Tameka knocked on the delivery door of Lucia's Restaurant holding a big, clear, garbage bag-sized sack of freshly
washed salad greens. The owner, Lucia Watson, was prep-
ping lunch. She invited the young farmer in and has been a
steady customer ever since, even serving on the Youth Farm
board of directors and hosting fund-raising events. Likewise,
the James Beard Award-winning Restaurant Alma relies on
Youth Farm for cherry tomatoes and kale. In managing their
restaurant accounts, the youth learn how to take advance
orders, draft invoices, collect payments, and stay on schedule.

Youth farmers are paid from the farmers' market and restaurant sales, and any leftover income goes back into the farms. "The stipend recognizes their time and labor in an adult way and acknowledges these children's capabilities," Linden said. "I'm always amazed at how hard they work and how responsible and committed they are. I trust these kids completely. They show up on time, do what they say they will do."

It's not the money alone that brings the young farmers back year after year. "They love this work and are involved in all the key decisions right from the start. They decide what to plant and organize the schedule of weeding, watering, harvesting, setting up the stands, and pricing and selling. They really like market day—talking with customers, figuring out change, and being treated like adults," Linden added.

Youth Farm was seeded over twenty years ago as a tiny neighborhood after-school program. It now engages over eight hundred Twin Cities youth annually in food- and farming-based leadership work, partnering with twenty schools and 150 neighborhood organizations. Over five thousand youths have helped grow and distribute over one hundred thousand pounds of produce and have prepared over forty thousand healthy lunches and meals. Project LEAD, the program for older youth, has employed over one hundred teens, and many have returned after college to join the staff.

By providing fresh produce to residents in "food deserts," these youth connect with a diverse population, especially underserved seniors and immigrants, in significant ways. "An elderly Chinese woman would buy her braising mix from one of our burlier, tougher-looking guys every week," Linden told me. "And every week, she'd hold out her purse so he could take out the money and put in the change. He'd always count it out slowly so she could see he was being fair." Seniors who live in housing complexes near the gardens make terrific volunteers, sharing their wisdom and expertise. A retired carpenter from Liberia helps the kids make signs and flower boxes in the program's woodshop to sell in the markets. A Hmong elder helped find seeds for strong Thai basil, then plant and harvest it for sale.

During the summer, the farmers break for lunches prepared by the kitchen crew. As an occasional volunteer, I've helped roll pasta dough for ravioli, make eggplant parmesan, and toss fresh green salads. I've helped put up their carrots and beans, using one of my grandmother's recipes, to sell in their market stands. The meals are cooked and served in nearby church and community centers at long tables set with tablecloths, plates, and cutlery. "For some, it's the only square meal they get all day," Linden said. These lunches last a good thirty minutes or longer since staff, youth, and occasional guests linger to chat after the meal.

After lunch, the day includes a variety of activities. The graphic-design group makes T-shirts; woodworkers build flower boxes, garden whirligigs, toys, and plant stakes. In collaboration with a neighborhood paper, the journalism group publishes a newsletter. The sewing group makes lavender sachets. Lucia Watson helped the group collect recipes from local celebrity chefs for the Youth Farm Cookbook. All items are then sold at the markets.

Youth Farm generates nearly a quarter of its income from produce sales; the balance of its support comes from private foundations and individuals. Imagine the individual and collective benefits we'd experience if we redirected even a small percentage of the farm bill's commodity price supports and crop-loss insurance dollars to programs like these, which teach kids to grow real food and learn life skills along the way. The victory gardens of World Wars I and II illuminate how we might do so, today.

"A Garden for Every Child. Every Child in a Garden" was the rallying cry of World War I's gardening initiative. At the start of the war, the Bureau of Education created the United States School Garden Army, funded by the War Department. Politicians and government officials declared growing food to be vitally important to national security and an act of civic responsibility and patriotism. The Garden Army's aim was to make communities self-sufficient so that trains and trucks would be free to transport farm crops for processing and shipment to troops and allies overseas. But it was also designed to address health concerns expressed by military officials who found too many young men unfit for service. By the 1930s, 40 percent of the rural population had migrated to America's burgeoning cities. People had moved off farms and though their lifestyles had become more sedentary their dining habits hadn't changed. Most were still eating heavy meals, but laboring at a desk, not in the fields. Gardening provided fresh air, exercise, and healthy food.

Inspired by posters hung in schools, government buildings, and post offices—"Join the Harvest War Crops—The Women's Land Army," "SOS Boys to the Farm: Bring Your Chum and Do Your Bit. We Eat Because We Work," "Wanted! Soldiers of the Soil!"—people got together and planted gardens in schools, backyards, and city parks. Woodrow Wilson planted a liberty garden on the White House grounds and kept sheep to mow grass and provide fertilizer.

Twelve days after the bombing of Pearl Harbor and the beginning of our country's direct involvement in World War II, the government held a National War Garden Defense Conference and launched the victory garden campaign, calling upon Americans of all ages to garden for the nation and the world. The victory garden program became one of the most iconic wartime mobilization efforts in either world war. This time, our food supply was secure, so Americans were encouraged to garden more for unity and service to the nation and as a morale booster for troops and those at home.

The effort was also directed at improving Americans' health and reconnecting them to the land.

Eleanor Roosevelt led the nation's home-gardening effort, planting an enormous and productive vegetable patch, prominently visible to tourists, on the White House grounds. The USDA as well as large agriculture companies, such as International Harvester and Beech-Nut, printed pamphlets with basic information on seeds, planting, harvesting, cooking, and preserving. In those days, my grandmother would put up enough produce—tomato sauce, canned tomatoes, dilly beans, picnic carrots—to last the winter. In addition, advertisements in magazines—*Better Homes and Gardens* and *Life*—promoted gardening fashions for women: Katharine Hepburn-style pleated trousers and button-down blouses.

By 1943, these local victory gardens produced nearly 40 percent of an American household's food. By comparison, in 2014, a mere 8 percent of our produce comes from local sources, even during the growing season. Before the end of the war, an estimated 35 percent of the American population was actively gardening, compared with 15 percent today.

The program was an unprecedented government effort to make growing food a formal part of the public-school curriculum. The vegetables cultivated on school grounds were used in school lunches as well as families' homes. By today's standards, the lessons were progressive, focused on experiential learning that empowered students to engage in meaningful work beyond the classroom walls.

Today's farm-to-school initiatives are taking a page from the victory gardens' success. In the Hopkins Public Schools cafeterias, near Minneapolis, lunch ladies (and guys) are winning the war on Lunchables one meal at a time. Six of Hopkins's elementary schools, two junior highs, and one high school, totaling about eight thousand students, are enjoying fresh local food and learning healthy habits.

Hopkins Public Schools' director of student nutrition services, Barb Mechura, reached out to Greg Reynolds of Riverbend Farm to develop a plan to improve the quality of the school system's lunches. She was a fan of his tomatoes and peppers, which she'd been buying for her family at her local co-op.

Mechura, with her cropped gray hair and flowing skirts and scarves, is soft spoken and welcoming, but when she talks about school lunches, Excel spreadsheets and calculator in hand, she sits up straight, sharpens her voice, and sounds fierce. "We were seeing all kinds of issues in our lunchrooms that I was sure had to do with the quality of the food," she said. "Behavioral things like pushing, shoving, inability to just sit still. The kids were hungry and just eating the wrong things. They weren't touching the vegetables we served in the cafeteria and they were throwing a lot of food away. Couldn't blame them, the quality wasn't very good. I wanted them to have the same good food I serve my family."

Reynolds, a former software executive who traded his desk for a tractor thirty years ago, is a tall, solid man with a gentle smile and lively blue eyes. He carries a scent of fresh-cut hay and damp soil into any room. He's easy to recognize by the striped engineer's cap he wears while making deliveries, and seems able to remember everyone's name. A vocal advocate for organic farming and fresh local food, Reynolds was game to work with Hopkins Public Schools to not just sell his food, but help students understand where it comes from and how it's grown.

Mechura drew her cafeteria supervisors and cooks into meetings with Reynolds to address purchasing arrangements in line with menu cycles and budgets. Together they beat down barriers of regulation and price, the bugaboos of institutional food. "Everyone was committed to success," Reynolds said. "It wasn't easy; it took some flexibility and creativity to get it done." Hopkins tapped into their commodity entitlement dollars and the little money left in the Victory Garden Defense fund—though yes, it's still available—to spend on Reynold's produce.

"We worried that our costs would increase when we dropped prepared food-service products because making meals from scratch requires more labor," Mechura said. "But those costs were offset by the lower price of raw ingredients. The food tasted better. Guess what? There was far less waste." When cooks saw that students were actually eating Riverbend's potatoes from the potato bar, unlike those weary spuds from a food-service giant, they were elated.

Mechura's team instituted other changes, too: scheduling recess before (not after) lunch so students enter the meal relaxed and hungry; dropping unhealthy snacks—cupcakes, cookies, ice cream—from birthday celebrations, opting instead for cards, songs, and fruit; eliminating junk food and sweetened beverages from school meals and vending machines. Concession offerings were upgraded to fresh-made deli sandwiches, salads, yogurt, and baked potatoes; baked goods such as muffins, breads, buns, pizza crusts, rice, pasta, tortillas, pancakes, cereal, and pita breads contain whole grains.

The elementary schools initiated a food-coaching program that engages parent volunteers in the cafeteria. Food coaches help younger students identify and understand different menu items. Last year, Riverbend's multicolored carrots—purple, red, white—became the "must-have" choices. The school cooks offered samples to entice students into trying unfamiliar dishes and bestowed silly names—"X-Ray-Vision Carrots," "Clever Corn."

Reynolds came to classrooms to talk about the science of growing food and joined the students at lunch. He provided starter plants for the school garden and helped teachers and parents prepare the beds and sow. Posters of Reynolds on his tractor, in his striped cap, decorate cafeteria walls.

Last year, Hopkins Public Schools served up twenty-two thousand pounds of carrots, tomatoes, peppers, radishes, squash, potatoes, zucchini, cucumbers, melons, cornmeal, eggplants, and onion, all from farms like Riverbend—Thousand Hills Cattle Company grass-fed hotdogs and burgers, Homestead Orchard apples, cheese curds from Castle Rock Organic Farms, and wild rice and black barley from Indian Harvest—food that was ten thousand miles fresher, from places and people with names.

Cafeteria cooks were happy to be *cooking* once again, not simply reheating prepared foods. "We all get excited when those beautiful eggplants of Greg's come in," Mechura said. "Our cooks like serving real food. They consider preparing these meals from scratch the best part of their job because they know they're making a difference in the experience the kids are having in school. They see themselves as teachers, too."

"Educating the whole child means more than three R's," Mechura said. Parents want this; the community needs this. "We had one dad who chose our first-grade program because of the food we serve. He thought a good lunch was an important part of his daughter's education; he's right."

Youth Farm and Hopkins Public Schools apply the values of my grandmother's generation to addressing today's biggest issues—health, access to good food, and food security. Three-fourths of America's youth ages seventeen to twenty-four are considered unfit for military service because they are medically obese and/or diabetic. No wonder. Forty percent of the vegetables eaten by our teenagers are in the form of French fries and potato chips, washed down with two full cans (twenty-four ounces) of caffeinated, sugared soft drinks per day, the equivalent of a full cup of sugar. Continued unchecked, "Generation Wired" will live shorter lives than their parents, and the toll of their poor health is expected to bring spending on medical care for health-related issues to nearly $240 billion by 2020.

If a foreign power were to inflict the same kind of damage to our nation's health, land, water, and air as our industrial food system presently is, we'd expect our leaders to create a plan to combat it. The call to action is as urgent now as it was in the victory garden days.

Victory gardens provided valuable life lessons in personal nutrition, food waste, conservation, sustainability, and the environment, lessons embedded in today's Youth Farm work. Learning to grow, prepare, and cook healthy food is the most direct path to self-care and personal independence. A recent National Institutes of Health paper confirmed that even with modest exposure to these activities, kids chose to eat more fruits and vegetables. The experience of cooking changes the eater's relationship with food from that of a passive consumer to that of a participant in the creation of a meal. It's the simple difference between heating frozen spaghetti marinara in the microwave and simmering sun-split ripe tomatoes into a thick, lush pulp redolent of garlic, basil, and oregano, so tangy and full of summer that it stirs genuine hunger and draws people to the stove to taste.

When kids garden and cook, they understand, in a deep and personal way, what it takes to grow food and are less inclined to take it for granted. In choosing the tomatoes for that sauce, they may recall how easily the heavy ripe fruit dropped from its stem and what the earth smelled like after a hard rain. Anticipating a good dinner and delaying satisfaction while sizzling garlic, slicing, dicing, and simmering adds to the savor of a dish.

Our food is too cheap as well as too convenient and too unhealthy. Americans spend less on food than people in any other country. We spend about 6 percent of our incomes on food purchases. The average French household spends about 15 percent of its income on food. When it comes to health care, however, the numbers are reversed. Americans spend an average of 17 percent on health care, more than any other industrial country; the French spend 7 percent on it. These numbers make the correlation between food and health indisputably clear. Too much of our food is making too many of us sick.

Before we had children, I had endless time to wander the market and spend long afternoons curled up in an armchair with the latest issue of *Gourmet*, dreaming of tarte tatin with a crackly crust and lush raspberry mousse. The morning of a dinner party I'd truss a chicken and rub it with a pomade of butter, garlic, and fresh thyme.

Young boys put a crimp in those elaborate, time-consuming preparations, but I continued to grow—sometimes in small ways—in the kitchen. For one thing, I had to create meals using the healthy ingredients from our CSA share. This gave a focus to my freelance assignments for newspapers and magazines, and I had modest success with several cookbooks for Garden Way Publishing. Still I yearned for bigger projects that would help me grow as a writer and cook.

At an annual St. Patrick's Day party, a friend introduced us to his date, Lucia, a strikingly handsome woman with chiseled features and honey-blonde hair. It took me a few seconds to realize that this Lucia was Lucia Watson—the same woman who became so involved with Youth Farm, and owner of Lucia's Restaurant, the first farm-to-table establishment in the Twin Cities, celebrated locally and lauded by national media, including *Gourmet*.

Chance meetings with Lucia have magical outcomes, it seems. That first encounter seeded a very dear friendship as well as a turning point in my career. Along with our interest in food, we shared a love of dogs and long walks. Hiking through the woods behind Cedar Lake, we talked about recipes and industry gossip while our sloppy, playful, and naughty mutts raced off leash, galloping, giddy, and defiant.

Lucia had won awards and developed a national following for her hyperseasonal menu. Her cooking draws on her professional experiences working with America's greatest chefs—the late Charlie Trotter, Madeleine Kamman—and her early lessons at a wood-burning stove in her family's cabin on a Canadian island in Rainy Lake. There she cleaned the fish she caught and the game she shot, and with her grandmother, Lulu, mastered the art of real "nose-to-tail" cooking.

On a walk and a whim, we decided to work on a project together and sought the help of a friend and literary agent, Bonnie Blodgett. A writer herself, Bonnie connected us with Knopf's Judith Jones, Julia Child's editor and a legend in the cookbook world.

We set out to define Northern Heartland cuisine for the series *Knopf Cooks American*. In those days, before e-mail and computers, Judith typed her own notes on an old Olympia with a sticky *e* key, corrected pages by hand in red pencil, and still was ahead of her time. She saw the need to celebrate the local, heritage, artisan, and farmstead foods we embrace today.

Judith, with her husband, Evan, a cookbook writer and historian, had lived in Northfield, Minnesota, the year the two ran his family's newspaper. She brought to our project a fondness for the generous cooks and farm-fresh ingredients she'd experienced while here. "Northern Midwest food needs to be celebrated," she told us. "Just like California or New England, this region has its own distinct culture, quite separate from the southern Midwest. People lump them together, but Duluth and Cincinnati have nothing in common. There's no wild rice in Kansas and persimmons don't grow along the North Shore."

Lucia and I researched, developed recipes, and wrote together, weaving practical kitchen information with stories of lumberjacks, miners, and farmwomen who "neighbored" over coffee. We came to understand and appreciate how rich our tradition of home cooking with local ingredients has always been.

All the best qualities of a happy, resilient friendship played out as we created the book, telling jokes no one else could understand, indulging in just enough competition to keep us sharp, and knowing exactly what the other needed when she needed it. Our collaboration was all-consuming, hard, tedious, and joyous. When we met to share notes, test a recipe, or review pages, we basked in the unbroken delight of the other. And when *Savoring the Seasons of the Northern Heartland* was finally published and nominated for a James Beard Award in 1997, I felt a postpartum loss. Lucia is a godmother to our three sons (their "goddess mother"), present at every graduation, privy to many of their secrets, a cherished member of our family, and a reason to call this place home.

Sometimes it takes the smallest encouragement—the sunshine of friendship, a mentor's guiding touch, the passion of an advocate—for someone, or something, to grow. Gardening programs, left dormant for a generation, are now spreading across the country, thanks to grassroots efforts such as Youth Farm and national leadership. When Michelle Obama dug up part of the beautifully manicured South Lawn to plant over fifty different kinds of vegetables—broccoli, collars, kale, carrots, beans, a range of lettuces, and assorted heirloom edibles, providing a playground for honeybees—she sparked our collective dinner conversation. Likewise, the USDA's impressive People's Garden shows how much food can be grown in a limited urban space. The garden is the primary donor of fresh food to DC Central Kitchen, a nonprofit that provides about forty-five hundred meals per day to those in shelters, halfway houses, and transitional homes. And it serves as a culinary training center and helps with job placements for those they serve.

Policy changes are being lobbied for by organizations like the National Farm to School Network, which recently introduced the Farm to School Act in Congress to expand the amount of support provided by the Healthy, Hunger-Free Kids Act of 2010. This legislation provides $5 million annually for a farm-to-school competitive grant and technical-assistance program. The USDA Farm to School Grant Program helps schools connect with local farmers to purchase produce, support the local economy, and provide opportunities for field trips and lessons in science, cooking, and health. The demand for this program is more than five times higher than the available funds.

In my grandmother's garden, sitting on the soft earth in the sun, I shelled innumerable peas, zipping them from their tight green pods to plink into the metal bowl I held in my lap. So sweet that I ate them by the handful, like M&M's, and often ate so many that I wasn't hungry for dinner. Science supports what we intuit in a garden—that health and flavor are inseparable. In August, we'd put up quart-sized jars of dilly beans and picnic carrots, the kettle rattling and the kitchen blazing. I'd help my grandmother stock the shelves in the basement, where the gleaming jars stood like sentries against hunger and want.

When kids grow, harvest, and cook good food, they savor it. "There's real excitement and anticipation when we head out of the garden to lunch," Gunnar Linden commented. I overheard a Youth Farmer saying hopefully, "Maybe we'll have that pizza with tomatoes and kale again today." When kids learn to preserve food, opening the jar of homemade tomato sauce or dilly beans conjures summer memories and links them back to the garden, to light and hope and warmth yet to come.

What if our country declared war on diabetes, obesity, and other devastating illnesses? What if gardening was the most patriotic duty? What if we joined ranks to save our land and protect our children? What if victory-garden posters hung in our post offices? I'd want my sons drafted as "soldiers of the soil."

Youth Farm and the Hopkins Public Schools are serving change, one vegetable, one meal at a time. Such programs will go a long way in countering the food industry's public-relations and lobbying push. By helping to create a better and more equitable food system, these efforts are the best expression of a democracy in action, and that itself is a victory.

SWEET POTATOES

P reparing for our first Thanksgiving in Minneapolis, I set out to find the best sweet potatoes for my father's favorite dish. Strolling through the St. Paul Farmers' Market, I was drawn to the vast assortment of roots at the Vang family's stall. Mai Vang, a slender teen whose long, glossy black hair shone indigo in the sun, translated my questions to her mother who described each sweet potato—Hannah, with golden skin, pale flesh, and a nutty taste; kobobuka, deeper gold, smaller, and mild; and Diana, with dark-purple skin and deep-orange flesh, and brown-sugar sweet. About the width of bratwursts, coming long and twisted or round and stubby, none of these resembled my Jersey sweets, golden, plump, and thin skinned.

Vang told me the Hmong use sweet potatoes in soups and

stews and stir-fry the spinach-like leaves and vines, wasting nothing. These salty, fiery, sour flavors were a far cry from my family's Thanksgiving concoction of brown sugar, butter, maple syrup, and bourbon. But over the years, Vang has become a source for ideas and recipes for my articles and cookbooks, and I've helped her understand our traditional American foods.

The Jersey sweets for my family's table came sometimes from small farms in Cape May and sometimes from Dave's Market, down the street from our home. Sweet potatoes prefer the mild, even temperatures of the mid-Atlantic and southern regions and are tricky to grow in the Upper Midwest. Until the advent of the local food movement in the mid-1970s and of Hmong growers at farmers' markets, our region's sweet potatoes were shipped up the Mississippi from Louisiana farms. They were considered a delicacy, reserved for Thanksgiving. How the marshmallow-topped sweet-potato casserole became an iconic Midwest Thanksgiving dish dates back to the booklet "How Famous Chefs Use Campfire Marshmallows," published in the 1930s by the Angelus-Campfire Company. The recipe, reprinted in *Ladies' Home Journal*, was distributed throughout the Midwest. The butt of jokes about Midwest food, it's since figured, along with Jell-O salads and tuna hot dishes, in Garrison Keillor's monologues of Lutheran Church suppers on *A Prairie Home Companion*.

Yet marshmallows aside, sweet potatoes are the world's

most nutritious vegetable. Their low glycemic index (with a neutral effect on blood sugar) makes them a great choice for diabetics. This "smart carb" is loaded with vitamins C and B, calcium, protein, and iron, as well as beta-carotene and antioxidant and anti-inflammatory agents. It may be the ideal crop for ending world hunger and disease. And it may also be the oldest vegetable to be cultivated, dating back to 8000 BC, its history as interesting and tangled as its vine. A staple in Asian, African, and South and Central American diets, sweet potatoes store well and can be dried and ground into flour and meal. During times of war, they have been the one crop that endures, hidden underground, to feed survivors when fields are destroyed.

But this ancient food is ill suited to modern industrial farming methods. Sweet potatoes bruise easily and are unable to withstand the rough handling of machine digging and sorting. The substantial labor involved in producing them at a commercial level is reflected in their price. Given the higher cost of production, there's less incentive to process sweet potatoes into cheap chips, fries, and ingredients for junk foods. It's no surprise, then, that the Hmong, one of the oldest, most resilient societies, are growing the best-tasting, most interesting sweet potatoes, using age-old methods.

Cultivating sweet potatoes was already familiar to the Hmong, who settled in the Upper Midwest shortly after the Vietnam War ended, some forty years ago. They were granted political asylum by the US State Department in return for their service fighting the communist Pathet Lao in Cambodia and Laos. Fearless pilots and airmen, they knew the jungles and mountains in which they rescued downed American soldiers and brought them to safety. Following the war, they made the dangerous and difficult escape across the Mekong River to refugee camps in Thailand.

Sponsored by Catholic Charities, Lutheran Social Service, Church World Service, and other nonprofits, the Hmong were drawn to the University of Minnesota's extensive language retraining and interpretative programs. Hmong is an oral language and knowledge is passed through spoken instruction and stories. Learning to communicate in English and adapt to our way of life and the extreme weather was, at first, exceedingly tough. But after the first wave of immigrants settled in Minnesota, their extended family members came to join them, and now the Hmong make up 10 percent of St. Paul's population, second to California in numbers.

In their former mountainous homeland in Laos, Hmong communities often numbered ten or more per household, with three generations under one roof. Men hunted and women and children tended the vegetables, rice, corn, and soy. Pigs, goats, chickens, and turkeys were raised for meat, eggs, and compost. Opium was the only cash crop, traded for silver when the French were in power.

All farmers juggle risks—extreme weather, rising production costs, uncertain market prices. Hmong farmers have the additional hurdles of language and cultural differences. The first generation of Hmong had come from lives of farming as the only means of providing food for a family, not as a commercial endeavor intended to generate an income. But in the US, the Hmong couldn't afford to own land to farm and live on, yet they lacked other workforce skills. So they worked for farmers or rented pieces of land to grow their vegetables on. Or they farmed on abandoned city lots and vacant parcels near light industry, seemingly able to cultivate small crops in the most unlikely places.

"Farming is in our DNA," said Pakou Hang, founder of the Hmong American Farmers Association (HAFA), the first and largest of its kind, serving five hundred members. "We've learned how to farm and to cook from our elders. They are a valuable asset in our community," she added. Hang is the sort of woman you might expect to be opening the screen door of a farmhouse kitchen, welcoming you in for coffee. She is small and compact, her hair pulled into a no-nonsense bun. As we chatted, she nearly bounced in her chair with enthusiasm, stabbing her finger at the conference table to make a point and punctuating the conversation with spurts of good-natured laughter. If you had to pick one word to describe her, "avid" would work.

Hang is a wonderful cook who celebrates the birth of a niece or nephew by delivering Hmong chicken soup and brings sweet rice for a funeral feast. "We grow beautiful vegetables, and many of our farmers are the best in the region. We know how to keep the soil fertile and healthy using the traditional methods. We've never used chemicals, we couldn't afford them. My mom is proud to grow things that please her customers at the farmers' market. She thinks doing so is a gift to the people of her adopted home in this new country."

You could say Hang earned her position as a leader in the local-food movement from the ground up. As a young girl, she helped grow vegetables and sell them from her family's farmers' market stand, and now has over twenty years of experience with farming and vegetable production. With undergraduate and graduate degrees from the University of Minnesota and Yale, she's devoted her career to Hmong farming issues. She's served on the board of directors of the St. Paul Farmers' Market, worked with the University of Minnesota to examine the role of traditional Hmong medicinal plants in integrated health, and spearheaded studies into the challenges and opportunities facing immigrant farmers in Minnesota. Along with her Ivy League-educated siblings, Hang continues to work at her family's market stand each season, no matter what.

"Just like many immigrants in this country, I grew up very poor," Hang told me. "We moved from Laos when I was fifteen days old and settled here because my parents wanted a better life for their seven kids. They believed that a good education would open many doors for us. They wanted to send us to Catholic schools, but that was expensive. So in the summers my family and I picked cucumbers for Gedney Pickles and grew and sold vegetables at the farmers' market to pay for our education," she said. "Farming is humbling, but out of those experiences I learned perseverance, hard work, and how I could always count on my family. I also saw the importance of community and social justice, and that has profoundly shaped how I view the world and my role in it."

Hmong growers represent about 70 percent of the vendors in the Twin Cities suburban markets and more than half of all growers in the Minneapolis and St. Paul markets, said Jack Gerten, St. Paul Farmers' Market manager. "Hmong farmers in particular have contributed so much to the Twin Cities food economy, but they've been at a real disadvantage," Hang said. In 2013, determined to work on issues of disparity in her community, Hang organized a panel of Hmong farmers to discuss what social investors could do to support immigrants in creating sustainable businesses. "We worked to identify and prioritize the areas we needed to concentrate on. Afterwards, the farmers said, 'Hey, we should stop waiting for someone to save us, we can do it ourselves.' That's when I decided to file documents at the Minnesota secretary of state's office to incorporate HAFA," she said.

Using a report from the University of Minnesota's Department of Applied Economics, Hang created a plan for success that focused on five areas: land, capital and credit, new markets, trainings, and research. "I quickly realized that if you were only helping the farmers look for land, or just land and new markets, you were creating conditions that were necessary, but not sufficient for long-term success or true prosperity. That's when the tenets of the whole-food model began to emerge for me. I realized you have to work on all five important spokes at the same time to truly move the wheels forward toward intergenerational wealth. The whole-food model is really our theory of change."

Hang explained, "Our culture recognizes the elders and it values their perspective, their wisdom. We embrace the family structure and we work collaboratively within the community. HAFA's mission is grounded in strong communitarian principles." To give an example, in 2014 HAFA worked with a benefactor to purchase a 155-acre farm in Dakota County. Having access to land long term changed everything for the farmers. "Suddenly they were planting perennials and cover crops, taking soil samples, composting, and charting out crop maps." But it wasn't just the land; HAFA raised funds for an area where the farmers could aggregate the produce to sell to institutions—schools, hospitals, corporate cafeterias. They began analyzing sales records to determine which crops made the most money. They launched a business-development program to help farmers create business plans, balance sheets, and financial records needed for microloans to purchase assets. "Suddenly the farmers were buying tractors and high tunnels, and discussing how they could collaborate to save money on seeds and packaging. By emphasizing the interconnected-ness of all these programs, everyone shares in the success."

Success, defined by the whole-food model, transcends money and individual accomplishment. "It means that Hmong parents and grandparents feel financially secure and able to offer their children new and better economic, social, and political opportunities. The children and grand-children can then build on those to spur even greater com-munities. What makes us unique is the way we engage our older, experienced Hmong farmers. We're dealing with a lot of complex issues—poverty and social exclusion—so we aim to involve everyone at all levels in place-based renewal."

Accessible, affordable land close to the Twin Cities mar-kets continues to be the biggest barrier for all small farm-ers. "What once rented for three hundred dollars per acre is now going for fifteen hundred dollars per acre," said Bon-nie Dehn of Dehn's Garden, an anchor farmer at the Min-neapolis Farmers' Market and president of the Central Val-ley Growers Association. Dehn, a third-generation farmer, recalls riding to the market at 3:00 a.m., asleep on a sack of potatoes in the back of her father's pickup. "I don't think I could be a farmer today without our family's land," she said. "We never could have afforded to farm at the scale we do today without this acreage." Consider this: in the city of Woodbury, a suburb perfectly situated less than thirty miles from the Twin Cities, the price of land has increased by nearly 125 percent over the past thirteen years.

Small organic farmers like those in HAFA need but a mere two to five acres for their plentiful crops. The average organic farm in this region is capable of producing about eleven thousand pounds of vegetables on just one acre of land each season. The Minnesota Department of Agriculture estimates there are over two hundred immigrant and minority farmers on a waiting list to secure a few acres for growing organic produce. To be successful, they need to lease long term or purchase the parcel. "If small farmers don't have land, they're not going to be selling produce at the farmers' markets or to the local schools and institutions who seem to want more of it each year. What does that do to our larger food system and our local economy?" Hang asked.

"No one wants us to lose good farmland to development," Hang said. Along with the Dakota County parcel, HAFA is connecting growers with longtime Minnesota farmers reaching retirement age. Through leases and purchase arrangements, farmers are converting their acreage into land trusts with conservation easements. The older farmers find this a more rewarding alternative than selling outright. "They love what the Hmong are doing to care for their land," Hang said. "Using our sustainable, 'old-fashioned' methods, Hmong are building soil health, or tilth. They shun pesticides and use friendly pests, they plow crop remains back under the soil to add nutrients to the next year's crop, and they compost. They're keeping the property lively and beautiful." But Hang told me that the Hmong learn as much through playing music and games together as they do working hard side by side in the fields. Take the traditional game of *sepak takraw*, a thrilling mix of kickball and volleyball, which requires timing, athleticism, balance, and skill. The Hmong are experts at bringing together education and delight.

Winter flourished during the years our sons played hockey on Lake of the Isles. We'd drag bundles of sticks and skates in a sled down the snow-covered street and across the lake to the warming house. How tenderly Kevin took each boy's small ankle in his broad hands to carefully lace each skate, just firmly enough to be snug but not too tight. Once on the ice, he'd reach around one of our sons from the back, cover the tiny hands with his, and adjust the boy's fingers to properly grip the stick. In that backward bear hug they'd push off and glide, left and right, and nudge the puck forward until the fledgling could stick handle to a rhythm of his own. Kevin wanted our sons to have, in the parlance of hockey, "good hands."

Thanksgiving weekend was the home opener for Lake of the Isles pond hockey. The boys skated faster and faster, and through the seasons, it became hard to tell who led the pack as they raced in hooded sweatshirts and baggy pants, wool hats in Golden Gopher colors pulled low over their brows. With grace, speed, and precision, they circled the rink, circled the calendar, passed and received, challenged themselves and each other in the magic and beauty of this game.

Those years, it seemed, winter itself was a major character in our lives. We'd leave the rink as the setting sun lit the snowbanks neon pink and indigo blue, the temperature so cold that our footsteps squeaked on the snow. There is something to be said about extreme cold, a cold that holds the breath for several moments, a cold so sharp that too deep a breath can feel like a punch in the lungs. But it's this cold that stirs hungers like no other force, a cold that startles the senses and makes one feel so very alive. Returning from an afternoon of skating, the batch of cocoa tasted richer and sweeter, and leftover maple-sugar sweet potatoes were devoured before I could warm them up, along with Thanksgiving's leftover apple pie.

Hmong farmers have contributed more than $13 million per year to the state's economy through the farmers' markets. But I've benefited from their priceless contributions to our culture and my life. They've introduced over twenty-three new varieties of fruits and vegetables to our markets along with vibrant herbs and spices, according to Jack Genten, St. Paul Farmers' Market manager. Just as the Italians introduced us to Roma tomatoes, garlic, and basil, and the Mexicans to chilies and cilantro, the Hmong have brought tiny hot peppers, lemongrass, long beans, and bitter melon to our kitchens. What's more, their joy and generosity are contagious. When I talk with Mai Vang and Pakou Hang, I want to cook.

Ever since that first time I met Mai Vang in my sweet-potato search, her family's market stall has been my source for lemongrass, leghorn peppers, and those deep-purple sweet potatoes. One Saturday morning, she invited me to a "small" birthday celebration, to participate in a traditional feast. She assured me that when Hmong cook for a party, they cook a lot. Later, as I approached her home on the outskirts of an outer-ring suburb and tucked at the end of a cul-de-sac, I could hear the din of Hmong, English, and laughter long before I parked on the car-lined street. As soon as I entered the open front door, I tossed my flip-flops onto a pile of tennis sneakers, pumps, oxfords, and running shoes and headed straight for the steamy kitchen. There women were elbow to elbow, chatting, stirring, tasting, smiling, and gesturing for me to come in.

Vang handed me a knife and pointed to a pile of cilantro and I happily began to chop, chop, chop, then helped carry bowls and platters to a long table, covered in a bright-blue-and-orange cloth, that stretched the length of the living and dining rooms. It groaned under bowls of fragrant jasmine rice, sticky purple rice, garlicky long beans, lemon-scented pork, a stew of sweet potato and sweet potato leaf, beef and eggplant soup, chicken with sour bamboo in cilantro pesto and a huge platter of laarb, the traditional lettuce-wrapped mix of chopped beef, mint, basil, and bean sprouts seasoned with ginger, fish sauce, chilies, and lime. Dessert, at the end of the table, featured bowls of berries, mangoes, and creamy coconut rice, and an off-putting but classic neon-orange, green, and red tapioca treat. Here was presented a broad spectrum of Hmong cooking—earthy and fiery, tangy and salty, healthy and wholesome.

Kids raced in and out of the rooms; a muscled teen in a tank top and sweatpants, baseball cap turned sideways, leaned against a doorframe near a wrinkled, elderly woman, a brown knit cap on her head and sleeping infant on her lap. Once everyone's plate was filled, the men and women bowed their heads and an older, bald, bespectacled gentleman rose to offer a blessing. He honored the ancestors and thanked the spirits of the trees, the birds, and the flowers near the house. The men raised glasses of beer in a toast; the women who sat together tried to rein in the rambunctious children, rising often to refill platters and pick up empty plates. I helped scrape, stack, rinse, and pack leftovers into containers and ziplock bags for cooks to take home.

It's the women who convey Hmong food traditions through food. Each holiday and special event is marked with a special meal—"Calling In the Soul of a New Baby"; "Bestowing an Adult Name on a Man after His First Son Is Born"; "Honoring and Protecting the Family Spirit"; "Tying Strings on Wrists to Protect Loved Ones." Because recipes have not been recorded, each family has its own spin on the different ritual dishes. No two families sweet pork, papaya salad, laarb, or chicken soup for new mothers will taste the same. Everyone who gathers is expected to participate in the feast. Not to do so is considered rude. A cup of tea or plate of food should never be refused. "Whether you eat or not, at least hold a spoon; whether you laugh or not, at least force a smile" is an old Hmong proverb.

Parents teach their children through stories passed down through generations. Mhonpaj Lee, who, with her mother May, created Mhonpaj's Garden, the Twin Cities' first certified-organic Hmong farm, told me, "Most of what I learned from my family, I learn out working in the field or cooking. We are a culture of land, not place. It's an old proverb that means we rely on the wisdom of nature and can apply it wherever we live. Our traditions and beliefs, passed down from one generation to the next, will thrive anywhere in the world."

May Lee, born in Laos, began farming when she turned eight years old. By the time she'd escaped to a Thai refugee camp, she was married, with two children. She and her husband, Chue, fled to St. Paul in 1981. The family began growing pickles for processors and expanded their operation to include a variety of Hmong vegetables and herbs for the farmers' markets.

"Farming has always been a way of life for me," Mhonpaj said. "But when I was a teenager, I couldn't wait to get away from it. I wanted to be like all my other friends, hanging out in an air-conditioned mall on a Saturday, not out in the blazing sun, sweating. In college, all that changed. I began to miss it, was homesick for my family. I realized that if I lost farming I would no longer be Hmong."

Through her interest in health, fitness, and nutrition, Mhonpaj decided to return to her place on the land, but this time as an organic farmer. "For us, the term 'organic' has broader implications," she said. "It's really a holistic approach. You can't just eat greens and say you're OK, that's all you need to do to be healthy. The role of food is to help support a healthy, whole person, a positive person who contributes to the community. When you eat good food, you feel good, and you're motivated to do good things and so everyone benefits."

Before launching their business, Mhonpaj and May enrolled in the Minnesota Food Association's farmer training program, a public-private collaboration operated on the Amherst H. Wilder Foundation's Big River Farms, ten miles from St. Paul. "We needed a business plan and also knew that we had to learn how to meet the government's standards for safety and quality so we could sell to schools, colleges, and cafeterias," Mhonpaj said.

May Lee is a tiny woman whose bright eyes, quick, shy smile, and cropped jet-black hair belie her age. She is efficient and, in her rapid, halting English, doesn't mince words. In 2009, their first year of operation, Mhonpaj's Garden was awarded "Farm Family of the Year" by the University of Minnesota. But despite the honor, May said, "This is a way of life. How we grew up. We don't think our lifestyle should get recognition. We are still waiting to buy land we can farm on that has a house so we can sustain our lifestyle. That will be our recognition."

Since that time, Mhonpaj's Garden has purchased land and a home, and the business has expanded to supply organic produce and herbs to seven colleges, CSA members, and three farmers' markets. It also donates about ten thousand dollars of excess food to area food shelves each season.

While she would love to be farming full time, during the week Mhonpaj works as an interpreter at the Hennepin County Medical Center, a job that requires she wear business clothes with her hair cut in a sensible bob. "Monday through Friday I look like a stereotypical East Asian, straight-A student," she said. The off-farm income provides a dependable salary, so that on evenings and weekends she can get her hands in the dirt. "Farming makes you appreciate things. It's a form of meditation and a great stress reliever. It provides time for our family to work together," she said. "This is where I can pass along the stories I know."

Mhonpaj learned the power of medicinal herbs from

her grandmother, a Hmong medicine woman. When the beloved elder passed away, Mhonpaj decided to focus on documenting the Hmong culinary and medicinal herbs that can be grown here. Through a grant from North Central Region Sustainable Agriculture Research and Education, she named those herbs and described their uses in a curriculum packet.

Mhonpaj and May offer classes and workshops through community centers, in hospitals, and at several arboretums. "There is so much interest in our herbs and it's important we share this information now so that it can benefit everyone. We are losing so many of those who hold this valuable knowledge. Our medicines relieve pain, treat cramps, and heal wounds, and are just as effective as those you'd find in a pharmacy," Mhonpaj said.

Mhonpaj convinced the Hennepin County Medical Center to plant a garden of culinary and medicinal herbs and peppers on the rooftop of the Level One Adult and Pediatric Trauma Center for patients and staff. It provides the postpartum herbs Hmong women rely on to recover from childbirth. "The hospital had tried to accommodate this need by offering new moms chicken soup and white rice, but without the traditional herbs, the efforts fell short," she said.

The program has been so successful, North Memorial Medical Center is following suit. "It just makes sense," Mhonpaj commented. "Before the hospital used vegetables from the garden and farmers' markets, the shelf life of the peppers they used was two weeks. They were lifeless and tasteless. My peppers last only three to four days. Food is a key to health and fresh vegetables and herbs are key. In Hmong, our healing herbs translate to 'green medicine.'"

Mhonpaj is working on a book about Hmong herbs and dreaming of a restaurant that will serve her culture's traditional meals. "So many of my friends were told by their parents not to go into farming. They wanted more for their children, and urged them to become lawyers and doctors, to live the American Dream. But if we don't pay attention to our stories, and our foodways, if we don't pass these on to our children, so much will be lost," she said.

"I just keep doing this work out of passion, and it all seems to come back to growing and cooking food. It always comes full circle. There's a lot of interest in small farms and in being sustainable. For Hmong, the word 'sustainable' means continuing to grow our traditional foods and herbs. We must use this knowledge in the present. This is how we will sustain ourselves and pass all that we love and believe in, the very best of ourselves, on to future generations."

How could I have known that a simple desire to please my father, to replicate my family's Thanksgiving dish in my new home, would lead me to Mai Vang, Pakou Hang, or Mhonpaj Lee? In spontaneous, casual conversations, they've shared cooking tips, history, and insights into their lives, so richly different from my own. But my quest was for more than the flavors in that sweet-potato dish—it was guided by memories of cooking with my father. Those nights before Thanksgiving when I was a teenager, we'd whip up the maple glaze, wipe down counters, and talk. He'd share stories of his workdays, of the people he met, lunched with, drank a beer with, and of the people he would never see again, yet whose stories he remembered and recounted to me. Ever curious, always hungry, he asked questions and he listened well.

When I cook with my sons, I hope to create such memories and share stories of my encounters with the generous Hmong families. I want my boys to cook; to know how to hold a knife, chop, simmer, and sauté; and to be invited into other people's kitchens and cultures, and share those intimate and significant moments of others' lives. Cooking is a universal language. Preparing food for and with others helps us become citizens of this vast and delicious world.

At the Vang family celebration, I asked an aunt why there are no Hmong cookbooks, why the Hmong do not record the recipes for their favorite foods and ritual dishes. Using her hands and her eyes, she smiled and said in broken English, "When you cook Hmong, you don't cook with your head; you must cook from the heart." The language of cooking is a language of plenty; it is the language of love.

CRANBERRIES

The arrival of cranberries at Dave's Market threw my grandmother into full throttle each Thanksgiving week. Up from the basement came the cast-iron meat grinder, cleaned with Clorox and clamped to the counter. While I cranked its wooden handle, she fed those brilliant, bouncing berries and slices of orange into the maw. Though I grew up not far from New Jersey's cranberry country, in the Pine Barrens, it wasn't until I moved to Minnesota that I experienced a harvest. And it was certainly worth the two-hour drive from Minneapolis over to central Wisconsin's cranberry land.

The crimson fields, ringed with emerald pine, shimmered and pulsed under a severe, blue October sky. Along the bog shores, sandhill cranes dipped graceful necks and ducks paddled by. Wisconsin is the fresh-cranberry capital of the world, with over 60 percent of the market; most of the cranberries grown in New Jersey and Massachusetts are processed into dried fruit, jelly, and juice. The cranberry's flavor is intense, yet balanced; the signature holiday dish, it tastes, too, of the conflict inherent in farming, of weighing benefits against risk. How fitting that the nature of this beautiful food is bittersweet; cranberries are the final fruit of the season, earth's bonny farewell until spring.

The cranberry is especially well suited to Wisconsin's wetlands, water-soaked areas that create transition points between dry land and open water. The plants don't grow directly in the water but lay their roots at the edge, thriving in the alternating layers of peat, sand, clay, and rock. Add this region's cold winters and mild summers and the growing conditions are perfect. Along with blueberries and Concord grapes, cranberries are the only fruit native to North America that are commercially cultivated. Appropriately nicknamed "bounce-berries," cranberries hop and skip when they roll from the counter onto the floor.

Long before the white settlers arrived here, Native Americans relied on cranberries to preserve animals, dye fabrics, and treat wounds in poultices; they pounded the berries with meat to make pemmican, which nourished them through the harsh winters. On the East Coast, European settlers first cultivated cranberries for savory meat dishes, sweet jellies, and juice for wine and vinegar. The cranberry's high vitamin C content was a sure defense against scurvy.

In the early 1800s, East Coast growers seeking new bogs heard reports of wild cranberries in the underbrush of Wisconsin timber lots, and so founded an industry here. Today, the Wetherby Cranberry Company and the Habelman Bros. Company are the only two independent, family-owned cranberry businesses that remain. Many of their tended marshes date back to those early founders. Massachusetts-based Ocean Spray, a seven hundred-member co-op and the world's largest processor, contracts with nearly half of the 250 Wisconsin cranberry growers who farm 60 percent of Wisconsin's cranberry acreage.

Every July, this woody perennial with long runners and small, dark-green, oval leaves bursts into blossom, creating a carpet of vibrant pink. The plant's horizontal stems extend up to six feet long and sport vertical branches that can grow about eight inches high; such uprights can produce as many as seven blossoms. During the critical four-week growing period, flowers must be pollinated to produce fruit, and bees do most of the work. Honeybee keepers place crate like hives around the bogs and release swarms of bees that feast on the cranberry-flower nectar, pollinate the crops, and produce a honey prized for its delicate flavor.

But these last five years, cranberry growers are having a hard time finding enough bees to do the work. Our honeybees are suffering from Colony Collapse Disorder (CCD), a condition that causes colonies to die or disappear. The USDA estimates that since the 1940s, the number of managed honeybee colonies has dropped from five million to about 2.5 million, enough to qualify honeybees for the endangered-species list. CCD is attributed to farm chemicals, pathogens, and poor nutrition (due to habitat loss). A toxic mix of pesticides, fungicides, and miticides used on about 140 farm crops, including cranberries, are to blame. While cranberry growers only apply pesticides before and after pollination, the bees still pick up residue and bring it back to their hives. Since 2009, when Italy, France, and Germany banned "neonics," those countries' incidents of CCD have dropped dramatically. Recently researchers proved that fungicides are making bees more vulnerable to the pathogens linked to CCD. These findings are notable because this class of chemicals had been considered fairly safe.

Renting hives has become increasingly pricey; it's now the highest cost growers face (ranging up to $600 per acre last season). Growers have begun deploying bumblebees, efficient pollinators that can venture off to feast on wild flowers as well as cranberries before flying back to the hives. But the same farm chemicals have reduced the number of wildflowers whose varied nutrients are necessary for bee health. Dining on cranberry flowers (especially those covered in residue) alone just isn't enough.

Working with researchers at University of Wisconsin–

Madison, growers are trying to attract wild bees to their marshes. These natives aren't as susceptible to pesticides and are efficient pollinators, though their behavior is less predictable. To help increase the bees' population, farmers are planting a range of native wildflowers. A new pollinator provision in the farm bill directs financial assistance to farmers for conservation efforts that support bees. The region's Natural Resources Conservation Service provides guidelines and cost-sharing information. Because over 98 percent of cranberry operations are family owned and span, on average, three generations, growers are working with university researchers to support bee health and the future of their farms.

Cranberries evolved to contain a tiny pocket of air that allows seeds to float and be dispersed through the marshes. The fruit's bobbing ability is a boon to farmers, who flood their fields to make the berries easier to pull from their vines. Mechanical "beaters" help detach the berries, and workers wade into the marshes and use booms and rakes to vacuum or scoop the fruit into trucks bound for the sorting, packing, and distributing facility.

Growing cranberries is tough, risky business. The season is short and the wet, marshy environment supports all manner of lethal bugs—black-headed fireworm and fruit-worm—noxious weeds, ruinous plant diseases, and fungus.

To help manage these challenges, growers flood their marshes prebloom to drown pests and again before a freeze, to form a protective shell of ice through the winter. The local, state, and federal authorities regulate wetlands, so growers need permits from the US Army Corps of Engineers and the Wisconsin Department of Natural Resources. In the past ten years, as growers have expanded their bogs, about 50 percent of the region's wetlands have been converted to cranberry marshes, reservoirs, ditches, and dikes to hold and circulate water for the cranberry fields.

The chemicals discharged into our waterways and cycled into our underground drinking water are known carcinogens and hormone disrupters. While we may not be eating a lot of cranberries compared to other fruit, we're still consuming the quantities of toxins required to grow it. Growers concerned about the chemicals and the loss of natural wetlands formed the Cranberry Clean Water Coalition, which merged with the Wisconsin Wetlands Association to craft stricter legislation.

Wisconsin's cranberry industry is a significant political presence. It contributes over $400 million annually to the state's economy and provides nearly eight thousand jobs. Cranberry growers receive preferential treatment when it comes to chemical abatement and use of water. Under the "Old Cranberry Law" of 1867, growers may convert wetlands, alter trout streams and lakes, and avoid state dam-safety inspections.

November brings consistent hard frosts. Cold-hardy perennials simply die back and wait out winter under frozen ground; other plants survive within the snowpack, having acclimated to the subfreezing temperatures through "hardening," a poorly understood and complex phenomenon. It's because of hardening that cranberries survive under a layer of protective ice and the sand that growers use to stimulate growth after thaw and to thwart damaging pests. The most dangerous time in the cycle of growing cranberries is not winter, but spring, when the vulnerable flowers can be easily damaged before producing fruit.

Like these vines, I've relied on a principle of hardening to make it to spring each year. My life has known its share of challenges—leaving family and friends in New Jersey at a tender age; rejections from publishers, and too many teaching assignments; my mother's cancer, my sister's cancer and the summer her son and daughter stayed with us so she could recover, my father's untimely death, my husband's heart attack, my brother's divorce and the years he chose to live with us; the exhaustion of love and the anguish of work, the smell of our children and the taste of loneliness—but for me, none of these temporal setbacks compare with the crushing, ever-present weight of our region's winters. Caught in the grip of its iron bough, the months of bone-chilling cold and the absence of light, I am a prisoner to my bleakest thoughts and grimmest doubts. Like the cranberries, I move inward as the season changes—retreating to the darkest corners of my soul, where there's room for ordinary losses and grief. I can then make peace with dashed hopes, diminished friendships, and hasty decisions.

No liturgical practice or family tradition, fed by my fancy and dreams, can save me from myself during in the gloomy winter months. But I survive. I've learned to soften as the days lengthen with the new season's gentle light, and trust, in the worst moments of winter, in the earth's next turn.

Time marches on. The older growers remember when the work of the harvest was backbreaking and so very hard. This was a time before the advent of chemicals and mechanization. Back then men, women, and children in straw hats and canvas aprons moved across the bogs on their hands and knees, gathering berries in long-tined scoops. Until the 1950s, immigrant workers and Native Americans filled the bunkhouses in Tomah and Wisconsin Rapids. Pay for picking was about seventy-five cents per bushel, and a good picker could bring in about two bushels per day.

"It was hard, cold, wet, slow work," said Nodji Van Wychen, co-owner with her husband of the Wetherby Cranberry Company. A third-generation grower, Van Wychen, at sixty-six, is the matriarch of the region's industry. She is short and strong, dressed in cranberry red, her gray hair sensibly cropped, a boundless source of enthusiasm and knowledge. Her son and son-in-law grow cranberries on their own marshes. "I always keep on saying that if I have anything to do with it there's going to be a fifth generation on this marsh. I'm just hoping and praying that will happen." Van Wychen's home shares a driveway with her son's family, and the grandchildren's toys scatter the edges. Her living room overlooks the cranberry marshes, bordered by deep forests. "When I was a girl, the harvest days were incredibly dreary and cold, even snowy," she said. "My mother-in-law likes to tell stories about the dances after the crops were all in, the music and singing, of the festivals and the big parades. People came from miles around and camped out for the weekend."

An indefatigable promoter, Van Wychen helped found the world's largest cranberry festival in the tiny city of Warrens, a stone's throw from Tomah. Every year over three hundred thousand visitors overwhelm this town of three thousand. The weekend is packed with festivities—cranberry bake-offs, juggling contests—and cran-novelties, bordering on the absurd—cranberry coffee, cranberry corn dogs. The Cranberry Museum displays the season's largest specimen, usually about the size of a red grape.

During the harvest, Van Wychen leads over sixty bus tours of her farm, handing out bags of dried cranberries to schoolchildren and urging them to get their parents to buy more. Weekends, she's at the Dane County Farmers' Market, selling pound bags of fresh berries, chatting, and passing out recipes. Several years ago, the floating American flag she designed in her marsh drew media from all fifty states and several foreign countries. Just recently, she climbed into a cranberry bog with the advertising icon Ronald McDonald to promote the fast-food chain's oatmeal with cranberries.

Wetherby can pack about ten thousand pounds of cranberries per hour with admirable efficiency. Yet Van Wychen retains two women who have been working for the company for over forty years to inspect the berries after the computerized machine sorts them, looking for discolored berries and rolling test samples in their palms to feel for soft spots. "It's probably not necessary," Van Wychen said. "But we've had hand sorting for as long as I can remember. They're such dedicated employees, they can sort for as long as they wish. When they retire, we will not replace them."

"Everyone has gotten better at growing big crops," Van Wychen said of the cranberry glut that had caused prices to drop precipitously in the past several years. A mere fifth of the country's cranberry supply is eaten between Thanksgiving and Christmas, so the industry has been promoting use beyond the holiday season and across the world. Outside the US, Germany is the biggest market; there the fruit's tangy flavor is prized in condiments for wild game and sausage.

This past season, Wisconsin growers hosted Chinese buyers during the harvest. They donned waders, tromped into the flooded fields, tasted the tart raw berries, and sipped cranberry wine. Interested in the cranberry's prodigious health-promoting properties, the Chinese bought nearly 3 million tons of cranberries that year. Cranberries are a superfood, chock-full of vitamins C, E, and K and antioxidants that can protect cells. And the berry's antibacterial agents help prevent urinary tract infections.

Thanks to the industry's work, the USDA has agreed to buy excess cranberries to distribute to food banks and nutrition programs as juice, sauce, and dried berries. The USDA also just added cranberry juice and sauce to the list of commodity foods available to public-school cafeterias.

In an effort to decrease supply and thus boost prices in 2014, growers in the US and Canada requested permission to destroy part of the collective crop. The process, called volume control, would have reduced each grower's annual sales by 15 percent. But the government denied the request, concerned that such cooperation between Canadian and American farmers might violate antitrust laws.

"All of us who live here and do this work here are, in our hearts, conservationists," said Van Wychen. Wetherby and Habelman Bros. are using updated methods for recirculating water, harnessing solar and wind energy, and planting more wildflowers for pollinators. In the past ten years, about 165 growers (1 percent of the US fresh-cranberry industry)

have become certified organic using alternative methods, and a few are experiencing success.

Three hours north of cranberry central, the growing marshes in north-central Wisconsin are less sandy and contain more peat. "The soil is naturally richer here," says John Stauner of James Lake Farms, near the small town of Three Lakes. With sixty-five acres in production, he's one of the largest organic growers in the country. Square-jawed and ruggedly handsome, Stauner completed the work of transitioning the land from conventional to organic methods in 2006. Before the shift, he'd wait to hug his wife until the "spacesuit" he wore while spraying came off and he had showered. "Usually after two weeks of spraying, things went quiet," he said. The sounds of singing birds, croaking frogs, and buzzing, whirring insects just stopped, the eerie quiet conjuring Rachel Carson's *Silent Spring*. "I wanted the diversity as well as the challenge of bowing to Mother Nature," Stauner said. "We love this land and its wildlife, and we're passionate about growing good food. Each year, the habitat continues to improve. There's a pair of loons that have returned every year since 2010. Our biodiversity is inspiring—toads, frogs, tadpoles, freshwater sponges."

Stauner, with his son Ben—just returned from several tours in Iraq—has helped expand the farm's acreage. They employ friendly pests to control the fireworm and hand-pull the weeds. Today, the organic marshes are blooming with health, alive with pollinating insects and fish. "It's always interesting, and tough as it can be, it's always rewarding," Ben said. As an advocate for organic practices, Stauner has helped other cranberry farmers to try alternative methods on their conventional farms. Respected for his experience and success, Stauner, who is treasurer of the Wisconsin State Cranberry Growers Association, was recently recognized for his service to the industry with the Cranberry Growers President's Award.

Of all the challenges cranberry growers face—severe weather, low prices, fungus, and rot—bugs are the worst. To combat pests, organic farmers use Integrated Pest Management (IPM) practices in lieu of toxic chemicals and flood the marshes in the late spring and again prebloom, as I've mentioned. Flood too late and the blooms are damaged; flood too soon and the insect populations may not be killed off. Timing is everything.

In 2003, Dan Wandler of Sandhill Cranberry, in Vesper, transitioned his farm to organic. Like John Stauner, he, too, was weary of contract growing for Ocean Spray and, as a young dad, was suspicious of chemicals. Within three years, business was booming. Wandler is strapping, lean, open, and friendly; his deep, resonant voice conveys a self-effacing confidence and his handshake is firm. Entrepreneurial, mechanical, practical, and tough, he became the only grower in the country to own and manage a certified-organic on-site processing, packaging, and distribution facility. From start to finish, this investment in the entire line of work saved money, reduced waste, and produced the best-quality berries on the market. Retailers loved his product and he loved the work. "I was so grateful for what happened to the farm when we converted to organic. The wildlife is astounding; it felt good to take care of this land; it was more than a job."

In the good years, Wandler's harvest of organic fruit was equal to the average amount of his chemical neighbors. And even when he fell a little short, he was able to make up the difference in volume on price. He'd gotten so skilled at IPM that he became a consultant to other growers, guiding them in reducing their dependence on chemicals and advising them on using flooding to control pests.

But just last year, Sandhill Cranberry closed. "There were a number of reasons," Wandler told me. "The market tanked, we lost an entire crop two years running, and I was undercapitalized. I just couldn't ride it out. But boy do I miss it," he said. "These days, I'm playing the stock market; it's a lot less risky."

It takes three years for a farm to be certified organic and the transition time can be difficult. As the soil recovers its biodiversity and natural fertility, the crops are less productive, yet the farmer cannot charge the higher price organic produce commands. For Randy Jonjak of Jonjak Cranberry

Farm, in Hayward, Wisconsin, the decision to convert some of his organic marshes back to conventional methods was a setback. "Insects and weeds," he said. "It's that simple. We were losing the battle." This third-generation farmer, a sturdy, fiftyish, plainspoken man, looked out over his crimson field and said, "I just couldn't sleep at night knowing the crop was being eaten and destroyed and there was nothing I could do. Hated watching all of our hard work go down the drain. We couldn't keep up with the weeds by hand-pulling; didn't have enough hands. No one wants to do this exhausting, tedious work anymore."

Success in cranberry land may be a matter of scale. One of the smallest organic farms, Ruesch Century Farm, grows three acres of organic cranberries on the eighty acres of Brian Ruesch's family property. "My father, a retired conventional grower, knew everything about cranberries. When he put in a quarter-acre cranberry bed, he just never bothered with chemicals, so when the bushes started producing, he realized he could become certified and sell organically," Ruesch told me. But cranberries are not the family's main source of income. Ruesch, soft-spoken and friendly, relies on his job as director of development and alumni relations at Assumption High School in Wisconsin Rapids for financial stability, though he'd rather farm full time.

Unlike the larger operations, Ruesch does not flood fields for harvest because the ripe fruit absorbs too much water. Using old-fashioned methods, he "dry rakes" the berries to bring them in. "It's best if the berries grow in the same direction by training the vines," he said. "This makes the raking easier and helps us from tearing out the vines when we harvest." To harvest, Ruesch stands on the thick mass of vines, leaves, and berries that prevent him from sinking into the muck below. He drags a wooden rake, crafted by Amish farmers, through the greenery to lightly tug off the berries and deposits them into a wooden bin.

This "dry method" is gentler on the berries, keeping them from swelling and then shrinking or becoming too soft during storage. They'll stay fresh longer. "When you look at the history of cranberries being shipped to Europe in the early 1900s, the growers made sure the cranberries were dry before sending them off on a three-month sea voyage under the worst conditions," Ruesch said. "I know that when you dry rake cranberries, they stay in good condition for a longer time and maintain their integrity. Drying and cooling berries right as they are harvested ensures a longer shelf life."

The berries are then put into a shallow wooden crate to dry over the next few days. If the weather is wet, the crates are stored in barns, where fans finish the process. "It's kind of a one- or two-man show. Last year, it took a couple of weeks and we literally hand-raked the entire acre," he said. Ruesch and his wife, Mary, rely on volunteers for labor. "We send them home with plenty of fruit," he said. "They are neighbors and friends, really more like family." The berries are then sorted and packaged on a neighbor's farm. To finish the rest of the harvest quickly, Ruesch floods the bogs and sells the berries to a broker for organic juice.

Ruesch's yield often dips to about 50 percent below the commercial average. "We do continue to get more money per pound, but that doesn't really offset the effort, time, and hard work we devote to this small operation. Still I have to say it's worth it," he said. "My biggest concern for the future of the organic industry is scale. I wonder if a small organic grower can be of any consequence? Because we are small, we can be more innovative and responsive. We care deeply about this land. It provides far more than a paycheck."

After putting the cranberries through the grinder, my grandmother served the ruby relish in a cut-glass bowl, where the light refracted the condiment's splendid colors onto the white tablecloth. The brilliant flavors lifted a simple menu of turkey, mashed potatoes, and gravy into the special Thanksgiving meal. Every year, the tart and sweet essence of this relish sparks memories of holidays past.

All cranberries taste the same, unlike tomatoes or apples, no matter the variety or how they're grown. It's difficult to discern organic cranberries from convention by looks or flavor alone. But understanding how this fruit comes to our tables gives it even more savor.

Perhaps it's too much to ask that a seasonal food be available throughout the year. Why not simply enjoy cranberries in their prime? Why not rein in our expectations? Encoded in the tart-sweet essence of this iconic dish is the message of thanks and of giving: of being present and paying attention.

CHESTNUTS

f cranberries represent the conundrum of commercially cultivating an indigenous food, then the Upper Midwest chestnut is a curious counterpoint. This Native American tree, once nearly extinct, is now a key player in restoration agriculture.

Until the mid-1900s, American chestnut trees filled our forests from Georgia to Canada, stretching west through Ohio to southern Wisconsin, Minnesota, and Iowa; one out of every four hardwood trees in America was a chestnut. Parks and town commons featured chestnut trees that widened to eight to ten feet in diameter. In the forests, where trees compete mightily for sunlight and nutrients, some chestnuts grew larger across than a dining-room table and rose as high as a seven-story building. They came into flower just before the Fourth of July, making the rolling hills they favor seem buried in snow.

Nicknamed the "bread tree," the chestnut provided a staple that could be boiled and mashed like potatoes or dried and ground into flour to make bread. Chestnuts were eaten out of hand, raw, or roasted as a satisfying and nutritious snack. Native Americans and pioneers even employed chestnut leaves to treat whooping cough. Every fall, for generations, the vast stands provided a limitless supply of food, dropping nuts that glistened like gems and fed people, turkeys, pigs (whose hams made Virginia famous), and wild game. Chestnuts, easy to dry and preserve, provided early farmers an income that could be tapped over time and a way to survive the winter.

All of this ended sometime around the turn of the twentieth century, however, when exotic and unusual species became the fashion in the formal gardens of mansions across the East Coast. Plant hobbyists introduced Asian chestnut trees and inadvertently imported a fungus. By 1904, scientists had discovered that this same fungus was causing cankers on New York City's American chestnuts. The Asian trees are resistant to the fungus, but on the American species, the cankers cut off the tree's ability to transport water and nutrients and quickly "strangle" the tree to death. The fungus that causes the blight lives in the bark of other trees, such as oak and ash, without killing them. Carried by the wind, birds, and animals, the fungus spread swiftly and the blight raced through the forests at up to fifty miles a year. Lumber companies assumed that the chestnut tree's end was inevitable and clear-cut forests for the valuable timber. Chestnut wood is easy to work with, light, and rot resistant. It makes handsome paneling and furniture—many of the fences built along the Appalachian Trail by the Works Progress Administration are made of chestnut trees.

In La Crosse County, Wisconsin, twenty-five hundred descendants of the trees planted by Martin Hicks, a settler from the late 1800s, are the last surviving true American chestnut trees in the country. Thanks to their geographical distance from the East Coast, they escaped the fungus's initial onslaught. But the blight arrived in 1987, and since then researchers have been scrambling to stave off the infection with a vaccine. But "the jury is out," said Dr. Albert H. Ellingboe, professor emeritus in plant pathology and genetics at University of Wisconsin–Madison. "The DNR has been inoculating trees against the virus. At first, these trees will appear healthy, then suddenly they suffer the full effects of the disease. I have tried to replant several seedlings from that chestnut grove in my backyard." His voice sounded resigned over the phone. "Oh, they did well for a while, they leafed out and seemed strong. But now I have just one left, but it's not looking good. So I'm afraid it too was struck with blight and won't make it. We tried very hard, were hopeful, but I have to admit that there is no future for the indigenous American chestnut."

The revival of the American chestnut has been *the* challenge for American botanists and plant pathologists. Those who know anything about these magnificent trees call the blight "the most devastating ecological event of the generation." Up until the 1960s, all efforts at creating a blight-resistant tree through traditional methods of crossing Asian with American chestnut trees had failed. The work was terribly slow, because it takes at least five years to prove that a cross is blight resistant, and results were frustrating, as the crosses resembled the short, bushy Asian variety. The intensive efforts begun in the 1920s petered out in the 1960s as funding dwindled.

But a different method, called backcrossing, inspired hope in the late 1970s. Charles Burnham, a plant geneticist, collaborated with Philip Rutter, a Minnesota biologist and ecologist, to winnow out the undesirable Chinese characteristics, retaining the disease resistance along with the statuesque American height. Seized by the chestnut dream, Burnham, Rutter, and other researchers founded the American Chestnut Foundation in 1983. While these new trees don't yield nuts as big or attractive as those of the Asian and European species that grow in California, they do benefit wildlife and help reforest barren areas devastated by weather-related events and man-made calamities. Americanoid chestnut trees grow 30 percent faster than oaks and offer hope for restoring forests in strip-mined regions.

Adapting to our adopted home has allowed me to cross-pollinate my interests and groups of friends. As a young bride, I arrived in this land of tight-knit families and high-school allegiances free to create an identity of my own. My friendships defy social standing and cut across demographic lines in ways I doubt I might have managed in the more cultivated grounds of my East Coast suburban home.

Shared enthusiasms for running, talking about books, cooking, and dining are the warp and woof of these friendships. Who could have known that I'd be invited to help shear lambs, pull carrots, pack apples, or make cheese? Some of my happiest memories are of roasting a pig one steamy August for a farm-to-table dinner for fifty; of frying whitefish on a Lake Superior beach while a Native American storyteller relayed tales of wild rice; and of picking blueberries on a friend's farm to help make vats of jam.

Diversity creates a vibrant and resilient community among people just as it does in a forest's ecosystem. "The person who is least like you is the one you have the most to learn from," Eugene Kroger, from the Minneapolis Farmers' Market, once commented. Along with formal black-tie dinners, cocktail parties on rooftop gardens, theater openings, jazz performances, poetry readings, and university lectures—some of the myriad joys of Minnesota life—I've been able to experience early mornings at the farmers' markets, with the scents of frying peppers and grilling sausages, and the music of the Hmong, Somali, and Spanish languages. I've lived here most of my life, yet it's a place I'm still getting to know, full of charms and delights.

Chestnuts are key to my family's Thanksgiving stuffing, my grandmother's signature dish. Their creamy texture and mild, sweet flavor made this simple combination of stale bread, sautéed onions, stock, sage, and cream a distinguished holiday item. As a girl, I helped my grandmother in the kitchen, chopping celery and sizzling onions, and she'd tell me about the "real chestnuts" she once gathered from her backyard tree. But lacking the real American chestnut, she turned to the Italian varieties, bigger and tougher to crack—and the same as those we bought in New York City at Christmas, sold in paper bags by street vendors whose big tin carts emitted wonderful roasted scents.

Roasting chestnuts is a tricky, finger-singeing task that requires scoring the hard shells so that they'll curl open in the oven, allowing the nuts to be eased out and the dark, sticky pith scraped off. The painful, tedious work itself is the Thanksgiving dish's most vital ingredient; this process, requiring the fierce energy I inherited from my grandmother, gives the dish character.

But recently, I noticed the chestnuts I was buying in our co-op were smaller than both the Italian and the Chinese varieties, and far easier to work with in the kitchen. These Americanoid chestnuts are being cultivated in southern Minnesota and northern Iowa and they're easy to peel, creamy, with a wonderfully, delicately sweet flavor. Eaten raw, the taste and texture resemble that of water chestnuts, but the two are not related. Because of its high ratio of surface area to volume, this chestnut converts starch to sugar much faster than its European and Asian cousins, which tend to be soft and bland. The first time I roasted and tasted these chestnuts, I had to know how this ghost of the forest had been brought back to such delectable life.

To find the heart of chestnut restoration, I headed down to Canton, a small town in a remote corner of southeastern Minnesota. Just off a highway traveled by Amish horse-drawn buggies, I found the Badgersett Research Corporation, founded by Rutter, the cofounder of the American Chestnut Foundation. For the past forty-five years, Rutter and his son Brandon have been slowly and patiently reviving the American chestnut. The good news is that several of these Americanoid chestnut trees are thriving across the Midwest on farms and college campuses such as Oberlin, in Ohio. Growers in this region are forming co-ops to market chestnuts, such as the Prairie Grove Chestnut Growers, representing farmers in Iowa, Minnesota, Illinois, Ohio, and Missouri. The nuts are appearing on menus, like that of New York City's famous Daniel as well as James Beard awardees Heartland, in St. Paul, and Restaurant Alma, in Minneapolis.

Rutter is a wiry, energetic man with steely blue eyes and an electric presence. As we toured his grove one blustery October day, he expounded on the potential for "woody agriculture" in a sustainable farming system. The term refers to the intensive production of agricultural staples by woody perennial plants that do not require toxic farm chemicals or tillage, the primary cause of erosion and topsoil loss. To this end, Badgersett is also cultivating hazelnut trees and a pecan-hickory cross.

The chestnut tree's deep, permanent root system helps farmland withstand drought and the flooding that destroys annual crops, and provides a wind barrier to keep precious topsoil from blowing away on windy days. Through erosion and runoff, we're losing topsoil at ten to thirty times the rate it's forming, even on well-maintained farms.

There's more. Chestnut leaves contain more nitrogen, phosphorus, potassium, and magnesium than leaves from other species, and the soil in which they grow contains high levels of carbon, nitrogen, and moisture. Chestnuts return more nutrients and life-building molecules to the earth to make them available to numerous other plants, animals, and microorganisms. They both protect and improve the quality of the farm's land.

The chestnut is also a charmingly generous tree. Once

every five or ten years, chestnut wood can be harvested for biomass by coppicing, cutting the tree down to the roots in a way that allows it to regenerate and produce nuts the following year. Simply put, American chestnut trees are eager to give, easy to please, and ask only that we give them a second shot.

"Just think," Rutter expounded, "these chestnuts are delicious in all sorts of dishes, soups, stews, desserts—and they can be dried and ground into the kind of flour that the French cherish in delicate cakes." While the smaller nuts of Americanoid trees might not be quite as desirable as the huge chestnuts cultivated commercially in California and Europe, the benefits to farmers, cooks, and wildlife are incalculable. The oaks that replaced chestnuts after the blight produce acorns irregularly, while easy-to-eat chestnuts are dropped every year. A mature tree is known to drop six thousand nuts in just one season. Chestnut trees never stop growing because they produce sugar from sunlight all winter, staying bright green beneath their thin bark year round. And the chestnut is gorgeous.

Phil sliced open a chestnut's spiky green jacket to release a mahogany marble, and quickly peeled back the soft skin to offer me a taste. This very fresh nut was sweeter and creamier than an almond, as close to the real American chestnut as we'll ever get, the nearest thing to the nuts my grandmother gathered in her backyard. Its taste brought back those hours we'd spent at her counter peeling chestnuts for stuffing, the shared effort that made this dish a tradition. Memory-rich, this particular American food has sustained Thanksgivings for generations—and now offered me a sacred ingredient in the dappled light of its glorious, green cathedral.

We walked the rolling, wind-wracked hillside through rustling verdant arches until Rutter stopped to expound on more wonders of chestnuts. Standing as though he too was rooted, his voice rose to compete with the strengthening wind. While the damp and cold crept up through the soles of my sneakers and turned my fingertips numb, Rutter shared stories of his lifelong effort to restore these trees—for their food, wood, biodiesel potential, oil, and majesty. "It took a long, long time," he said. "People thought I was, well, nuts—and perhaps I am. We've always done all of the harvest by hand, but this year we brought in two horses. Yes, we have to water and manage them, and they sure eat a lot, but they take less time than machines. Think about it: horses reproduce, and tractors do not. I love working with animals, things that live and breathe and snort," he laughed. My teeth had started chattering, but Rutter continued on. "We're so far off the grid the weather can do us in. Last year, it was impossible to plow out to get to the highway, and it was so cold, we couldn't ship our tree stock until the end of May." The trees seemed to bow their laden branches in salute to his efforts.

I followed Rutter to the shelling and packing shed, where a machine weighs and grades hazelnuts. There were stacks of boxes, full of spiky green chestnuts that needed to be shucked by hand. Every part of this operation bears Rutter's inventor's stamp: he showed me the low-riding, lawn-mower-like tractor he designed to comb hazelnuts from their low limbs. "The first of its kind," he said, proudly patting its protruding rakes. "We had a few false starts trying to get the levels of the pickers right. The brakes needed adjusting and we nearly lost it on steep hillside, ran like crazy, shouting after it. Course, it wouldn't listen." He chuckled.

Among his many projects, Rutter is working on a hazel-nut-cracking machine and another that will extract hazelnut oil. This dark, thick, rich oil has a wonderful nutty flavor, prized by cooks around the world. "Best thing is that it has a high smoke point, unlike olive oil, which burns when it's too hot. It's loaded with Omega 3s." As we entered the walk-in cooler where the shucked chestnuts are stored before being boxed, he said, "It's important to sort every one by hand. We're careful to box them by size." But I suspect Rutter likes keeping his hand on every bit of this operation. Empty boxes lay helter-skelter and papers browning with age were strewn about. "It's hard to keep up with demand," Rutter confessed. Badgersett's website reflects the dynamic, ingenious, and often chaotic nature of this farm. He confessed, "You can try calling us, but don't expect we'll answer, especially when the harvest is on. We're out in the field where we're supposed to be."

Yet the farm hosts an ambitious schedule of events for farmers, orchardists, and cooks—field days, planting days, and seminars on woody agriculture with other experts in the field. Badgersett also sells its seedlings and starter trees by mail order to enthusiasts around the country.

I had been stamping my feet on the damp ground to keep my toes from going numb and jiggling my arms up and down to get some blood into my fingers when Rutter finally concluded his lesson and invited me to lunch. I gratefully accepted. I confess, though, at that moment I worried about the wisdom of following this strangely intense man to his living quarters. But there was no restaurant or coffee shop within miles.

I trailed Rutter down a narrow dirt path to a small log house with a plume of woodsmoke swirling from the chimney. As we neared, he told me he'd built it with wood from the bordering forest and help from his Amish neighbors. Together they had felled and split trees for the timber, to haul in with horses. He and Brandon had installed solar panels for light and the electricity required to run Badgersett's computers.

Nearby a flock of prairie chickens was raising a racket; most of them perched in the trees, while a few turkeys strutted around some snorting hogs. A huge vegetable garden had been gleaned except for several plump green tomatoes dangling on the vines. Right outside the cottage door were two huge rain barrels for the family's water. For drinking and cooking, Rutter told me, they also take turns pumping from the well right outside the kitchen door.

Rutter's wife, Meg, a cheery woman in her late thirties, greeted us as we entered; their six-year-old daughter had just changed into a party dress for me, a special guest. Meg fed the wood-burning stove she cooks on and it crackled merrily, kicking out dry warmth. She manages the garden, cooks, cans, creates recipes for chestnuts and hazelnuts, and homeschools their child. At a cramped table not far from the stove, we shared steeping bowls of Meg's creamy, mild chestnut soup, chestnut-stuffed acorn squash, chestnut flatbread, and delicate sugar cookies made from chestnut flour. As we finished lunch, Rutter leaned back in his chair and shared the vision he and Brandon were working hard to make real.

In the "off season," father and son travel to symposia and conferences, and speak to groups of farmers, foresters, and university researchers throughout the country and around the world about their progress. The chestnut tree's revival could catalyze the first large-scale success in restoration ecology, where the goal is to return ecosystems to their original working health. Restoration ecologists value the permaculture approach to agriculture, which looks to the patterns of plants in a forest when a farm is being designed; in fact, it mimics the forest's natural system. "Our only hope as a species going into climate change is to maintain diversity in every possible way, and very specifically and emphatically in the genetic diversity of our crops," Rutter said.

Rutter explained how trees and farm crops complement each other in regard to nutrient cycling. The deep roots of chestnuts can act as "nutrient pumps," bringing up minerals from the subsoil. And the minerals released by the decomposition of annual crops provide nutrients for the trees. By growing a vast mix of crops, the total biomass increases, and thus so does the amount of organic matter that can be returned to the soil.

That's not all. Introducing chestnuts to the forests would add a much-needed layer of diversity to help wildlife populations rebound, by providing shelter and nutritious food. Because chestnuts grow so rapidly, they are virtual vacuums of greenhouse gases, pulling carbon dioxide out of the atmosphere and sequestering it in their wood. Chestnuts planted in river bottoms may improve the health of streams, as their root systems appear to be capable of filtering pollutants from the water. The tree is so adaptable that it may be better than any other to weather the extreme changes in our climate. It's a great source for clean biomass fuel. And because it's rot resistant, it doesn't need to be treated with toxic chemicals when used as a building material.

In their materials and lectures, the two men relay stories of patience and perseverance in breeding new varieties of trees. "You don't know where your breeding is going to go when you start doing this work," Rutter told me. "The plants know things we haven't imagined, and if you've got your eyes open and watch them they will show you and they will change what you're doing."

Restoration ecologists work with the Rutters to help

reclaim ruined ecosystems such as strip-mined land and watersheds wrecked by logging or mining. Fast-growing chestnut trees and hazelnut bushes quickly help the land return to its once-forested state, enriching the soil for layers of plant growth and attracting wildlife back into the woods.

"Agriculture as it is today is killing us," Rutter said. "There is just no question we have to do something about that. Woody agriculture presents real possibilities. Perennials, once planted, need no other care until harvest. Chestnuts, hazelnuts, hickory-pecan crosses should be integrated into every farming system." Rutter and Brandon would also like to see chestnut trees in family backyards, where children might hide behind the trees' trunks and climb their limbs. With such trees, we cooks could easily gather nuts for stuffing by simply stepping outside our kitchen doors.

Through the lens of restorative agriculture, we can see what the earth is willing to give us and develop economic models around those gifts for our families, our towns, and our lands.

As Rutter settled in for an afternoon snooze, his daughter sprawled out on the floor with dolls and books, and Meg fed the stove with discarded chestnut shells that crackled and popped. Their scent mingled with that of brown soap and baking bread, all scents pleasantly familiar from my own childhood.

The Rutters' home is so far off the grid that Google Maps couldn't direct me to their driveway, at the top of a hill where those chestnut trees guard this enclave's timeless calm. But with support from cooks, customers, and farmers, these ancient trees may once again stand tall in more public spaces—in town squares, on college campuses, on farms, and in yards. "There is no better brace for our collective will than a big win: something to demonstrate that we can, really can, make a difference," Rutter said. Renewing this industry, still in its infancy, is a labor of love. Resonant with tradition and collective memory, it, like the shimmering chestnut tree, shines with promise.

CORN

The first time I picked corn was on an August weekend, camping at the Land School with our sons and friends. It was eighty degrees that morning and the boys made a game of running deep into the tall waves of shining green. We spent hours snapping off ears to fill the sacks we'd slung over our shoulders while the kids shouted and bobbed in and out of the deep rippling sea. I'd never before tasted raw corn, just shucked, or slugged icy-cold water from a tin cup dipped into a well. That night, as I drifted off to sleep in our tent, I swear I could hear the corn whisper to the pole beans and squash, "Don't worry, the rain is on its way."

That weekend awakened the farmer in all of us. We could taste the real difference in the corn we picked—it was so much sweeter, crisper, just more *corny*—and we understood that the flavor had to do with its freshness as well as how it was grown. Its quality confirmed a truth ignored in the discussion of food and agriculture policy: soil is the fundamental issue that deserves attention. What's happening to the growing of real food is earthshaking, and what's really needed is an information revolution. The best way to understand what's happening is through experience at all levels through smell and taste, and by seeing the difference between organic and chemically treated food.

The way we grow food determines our societal structure, shapes our cities, and makes us who we are. To review the history of the nation's most important crop, corn, is to appreciate the changes within our national psyche.

The Land School grows two different kinds of corn: flour corn, to dry and grind, and sweet corn. Industrial farms additionally grow field corn to make ethanol, plastics, and the ingredients in processed food. Flour corn has huge ears and its kernels are starchy and tough. Prior to the 1940s, most families planted and ate both flour and sweet corn, and cookbooks of the era suggested adding sugar to the water when boiling cobs to guarantee both varieties would taste sweet. By the 1950s, though, corn-seed breeders had developed distinctly different corn plants, one for eating and the other for cornmeal and animal feed.

The weekend we picked corn, our sons' science teacher, Doug, explained this fascinating plant's botany while we shucked cobs for the harvest meal. Doug is a no-nonsense man with huge hands, who can settle a rowdy student with a fierce glance and arched eyebrow. But he earns his students' affections when he dons an apron, as he did the next morning to flip corn pancakes for breakfast.

Corn is a monoecious plant, meaning that to produce seeds, the male and female must cross-pollinate in the fields via the wind or insects. Until the 1930s, all US corn was grown this way, and although the plants looked alike, each had a unique mix of genes adapted to the specific growing conditions on different farms. At the end of the harvest, farmers would keep the ears of the most vigorous plants and save their seeds for the next year.

Corn breeders discovered that if they developed two inbred lines of corn and then crossed them, the resulting "hybridized" seeds would produce plants that were more robust than either of the two parent plants, a phenomenon known as hybrid vigor. The seeds from this plant would produce crops that grew at the same rate and to the same height, and mature at the same time, making them ideal for machine harvesting. The downside was that the hybrid seeds do not reproduce their parents' traits, so new seed has to be purchased each year. The discovery of hybrid seeds changed everything about growing corn.

When I think of any issue related to our food system, I think of Martin and Atina Diffley—and I think of them often. Atina is the kind of woman anyone interested in organic food, cooking, and gardening really wants to meet. She's in her sixties, still naturally blonde, her corn-silk hair streaming from a baseball cap and her piercing blue eyes lively and generous. The husband and wife founded Gardens of Eagan, the largest organic vegetable producer in the state, some forty years ago. Atina's memoir, *Turn Here Sweet Corn*, reveals much about organic systems, but more, it calls us to reclaim our land, our food, and power over our lives.

Ask Atina, now retired, about organic farming and she'll fire off answers with the thorough detail of a PhD in plant genetics and ecology, but the truth is that she dropped out of a music conservatory at age nineteen to grow food. These days she travels the country consulting with organic growers on best practices, speaking at farming conferences, and testifying in DC. Yet she also makes time to pickle vegetables from her prodigious garden and gather friends for dinner on the deck overlooking her fields in the summer. Often guests linger at the table, discussing farm and food policy, well into the night.

"Hybrid seeds are vigorous, predictable, and high yielding," she explained one spring afternoon as we strolled near a field of emerald vetch, or buckwheat, planted to return nitrogen to the soil. "They're crucial for harvest management. But hybrids moved farmers away from the historic practice of saving seed from their own crop—seeds that adapted naturally to a farm's specific climate, soil, and growing conditions—and prevented farmers from trading seed with each other. As corporations began to assume seed production, the farmers began to lose their bred lines. Companies now own the mother lines and have complete control of these hybrids.

"The central issue of hybrids is ownership and control. When Monsanto bought Seminis, a major seed source for fresh-vegetable growers like us, it discontinued many of the best varieties, perhaps because fresh vegetables are a minor market and the sales of these seeds were low. Commercial seed breeders focus their efforts on seeds that are best suited to vegetables for processing, not eating fresh.

"Having purchased most of our small and midsized vegetable seed companies, Monsanto now controls 80 percent of the market," she continued. "It has closed several of the breeding facilities and operates others under the original company's name to avoid the association with Monsanto. Vegetable growers who depended on specific varieties have lost the cultivars that are well suited to the soil and growing conditions, cultivars they've counted on for generations. Through ownership of our seeds, Monsanto controls much of our food supply."

Open-pollinated seeds are not reliable for large-scale farming, she said. "But they are crucial to diversity and plant survival. The climate has become so unsteady and growing conditions are changing much faster than seed technology. Farmers need open-pollinated seeds so they can select and breed seeds based on their unique conditions and needs of their bioregion."

One summer evening, over dinner on Atina's deck, Roger Blobaum explained the rapid changes in farming that followed corn's hybridization. Blobaum is the elder statesman of the organic movement. As a young policy aide to Wisconsin senator Gaylord Nelson, he wrote the legislative ban on DDT in 1972. Now, as a consultant in the organic industry, Blobaum advises Rodale, several international NGOs, and global nonprofits; he knows everyone in the field. His demeanor of a successful bank executive, nattily dressed in coat and tie, belies his fierce advocacy for organic farming methods. He is currently archiving the history of organic farming in this country for the University of Wisconsin–Madison, with funding from the Ceres Trust.

"Hybridized corn has a voracious appetite for nitrogen and water," he explained. After World War II, when chemists discovered that the excess ammonium nitrate used to make bombs was an effective fertilizer for corn, farmers began growing it fencerow to fencerow. It replaced wheat, oats, and barley, growing in regions once thought impossible, and by the 1940s corn was America's dominant crop.

But not all farmers were convinced that chemicals were the silver bullet, and many continued their integrated practices: raising cattle and poultry; fertilizing their fields with composted manure; rotating in cover crops of alfalfa, hay, clover, and grasses to restore nitrogen to depleted fields. "The hairy vetch we grow as a cover crop was developed in Minnesota by Jaime DeRosier in the 1980s, and is prized for its prodigious nitrogen-fixing qualities as well as controlling weeds. It's a great cold-hardy crop," Atina said, referring to the fields we had walked by earlier in the day.

"Even as late as the 1970s, many of the large-scale corn and soy farms in the Corn Belt relied on sustainable methods, not chemicals, to great success," Blobaum said. "These big organic farmers were going toe to toe on crop yields and profits with their chemical-reliant neighbors." When Rachel Carson's *Silent Spring* detailed the devastating impact of toxic farm chemicals on the environment and, at the same time, the price of oil spiked to historic heights, organic practices grabbed the attention of university plant researchers, farmers, and the media.

"Here's where it gets really interesting." Blobaum lit up as he relayed the following story. *The American Journal of Agricultural Economics* studied the differences between organic and chemical farming, measuring economic performance and energy intensiveness. "The organic group appears to be doing reasonably well despite the fact that they do not use the chemical inputs regarded as key elements in the productivity and prosperity of modern agriculture. In fact, for crop production alone, the two groups had the same average gross."

The *New York Times* picked up the story and it ran on newswires across the country. It also inspired the USDA director of science and education, Dr. Anson R. Bertrand, to study organic methods, despite disparaging comments from Earl Butz, President Nixon's secretary of agriculture, who said, "When you hear the word organic, think starvation."

The USDA study was the first and, for over thirty years, only serious attempt to understand the efficacy of organic methods. It reported that twenty thousand farms using organic practices were "productive, well managed and efficient. These organic farms have not regressed to agriculture pre-1930s. . . . They employ methods which have been cited as the best management practices for controlling soil erosion, minimizing water pollution, and conserving energy." The study recommended that the USDA provide farmers with more information about sustainable practices as well as financial support for chemical farmers interested in transitioning to organic methods.

Blobaum shook his head and said, "Ronald Reagan's secretary of agriculture, John Block, disowned the findings and he had the USDA strike the term 'organic' from any of the printed materials." The government had already printed and distributed ten thousand copies of this report to university-extension bureaus across the country, but it never went back to press. For the next several decades, the word "organic" was replaced by the less controversial "sustainable" and "low input" and "biological farming."

What's really important to note is that organic industry's tacit acceptance of the taboo on the "O-word" has diluted the concept of "sustainable agriculture," requiring farmers to redefine the systems they use. So the term "organic" has been perceived as a lifestyle choice, not as an entire system based in nature that considers the complexity of integrated relationships.

"Just imagine if this report had been more widely distributed. If the initial research into the true organic methods had inspired more study and informed more farmers," Blobaum said.

"Here's the thing," Atina added. "The information that was distributed to corn and soy farmers gave credit to the chemicals for the success these farmers were having with their crops. But in fact it wasn't the chemicals! It was the new seed varieties that created such great yields. The seeds and chemical fertilizers were developed simultaneously," she said. "The statistics used to argue against organic methods were drawn from older seeds and older methods, predating World War II. The newer organic methods with new hybrid seeds are as productive as the chemical methods. But the chemical companies took full credit for bumper crops."

Until the drought of 1988 hit, crop yields continued to grow at an astounding rate. And as farmers expanded production, they applied more chemical fertilizers to replenish the nutrients extracted from the land when the same crop was planted season after season. By 1995, plant breeders had taken the hybridization one step further by inserting a naturally occurring bacterium (*Bacillus thuringiensis*, or *Bt)* into the corn seed. "It is toxic to corn's biggest opponent, the highly damaging corn borer," Atina said. "The plant itself is a pesticide." But what's even more dangerous is the glyphosate in Monsanto's toxic herbicide, Roundup. Because Roundup kills everything it touches, Monsanto created a corn plant that will flourish while weeds die: Roundup Ready corn.

Recently the World Health Organization's cancer working group published a report that concluded glyphosate is "carcinogenic to humans." Seventy percent of the corn grown in the US is Roundup Ready corn. The corn borer is no longer a problem, but *Bt*-resistant rootworms are, and they've been devastating crops throughout southern Minnesota, where Roundup Ready corn is king.

University of Minnesota extension agents Ken Ostlie and Bruce Potter have presented their findings at agriculture conferences throughout the corn-growing regions in the state. "GMO Roundup Ready corn is basically backfiring. Instead of making things easier, we've just made corn-rootworm management harder and a heck of a lot more expensive. This bug damages the cornstalk's ability to absorb water just when it's needed most. Especially under drought conditions, when the roots are weakened, the plant is easily toppled by winds before harvest," Ostlie told Minnesota Public Radio. In addition, the corn doesn't decompose properly so the stalks stay in the fields longer and are so stiff and sharp they're puncturing tractor tires. Superweeds are becoming increasingly resistant to Roundup, so farmers supplement with even harsher chemicals.

Even if farmers go through the effort to find alternative seeds, they aren't always able to skirt GMO's reach. On the windy plains of corn country, it's impossible to keep corn from cross-pollinating, a.k.a. "GMO drift." "There are innumerable stories about pollen drift," Atina told me. "They're heartbreaking, and the farmers have no recourse, especially in court."

Two years ago, researchers discovered GMO contamination at an average level of about 70 percent in virtually all the non-GMO corn crops tested in the Midwest. Organic growers like Susan Fitzgerald, in Hancock, Minnesota, are especially vulnerable. The Fitzgeralds had managed to keep a hundred acres of open-pollinated, organic field corn free of GMO contamination for fifteen years. But surrounding farms planted with Monsanto's StarLink GMO corn, not approved for human consumption, contaminated some of her crop. The cost of the test, combined with having to dispose of the contaminated corn, cost the Fitzgeralds three thousand dollars—but more importantly, they might have lost their organic customers' trust.

Organic farmers in the Midwest, whose numbers have more than doubled since 1996, are in danger of losing their certification and a piece of the growing export market.

Since 1997, the European Union has barred everything but organic US corn imports over the possibility that GMO varieties have mixed with sanctioned crops. This has cost conventional American farmers access to a $200 million-a-year market.

When students ask me for "informational interviews," I know they are seeking a direct path to a career. But my work has itself been the sum of trial and error, of well-made plans ever revised. My days are not monotonous or routine and there is always something different on my calendar. I'm neither a journalist, nor a novelist, nor a home economist—no college offers a degree in cookbooks. Luck and happenstance have been my teachers and my research is driven by moments of serendipity, such as seeing the likes of a hand-painted sign—"Real Milk and Farm Eggs"—on a country road.

When I worked with Lucia Watson on *Savoring the Seasons of the Northern Heartland*, I read through most of the region's earliest cookbooks and they've greatly influenced my writing today. Take *Buckeye Cookery and Practical Housekeeping*. With chapters titled "Something about Babies," "The Arts of the Toilet," and "Accidents and Sudden Sickness," the book covers far more than recipes with step-by-step instructions for particular dishes. Estelle Woods Wilcox compiled solutions to everyday challenges that actually worked for a range of women and also included cheery encouragement: to make a good loaf of bread, "always be up in the morning early, just at the peep of day."

Wilcox's recipes provided approximate measurements: "a tea cup of sugar," "a coffee cup of flour," "a nutmeg of butter." Instructions for preheating the oven required a cook to insert her hand into the warm interior. If she could count to thirty-five before withdrawing her hand, the heat was "moderate"; if she had to take it out before thirty-five seconds had elapsed, the heat was high. And rather than prescribe exact timing, Wilcox describes what to look for in a finished dish. A sauce should be simmered until glossy and thick enough to generously coat the back of a spoon, and a loaf of bread is done baking if it sounds hollow when tapped. Such books have "voice," or personality, and reading them makes me feel the presence of the author; it's as though she's standing at my side, giving advice and encouraging me to think for myself. Made by two different cooks following Wilcox's pages, no two soups or loaves of bread will ever be the same. By comparison, today's cookbooks provide accurate measurements, precise timing, and rigid formats—and leave nothing to the imagination. They strive for consistency in flavor and presentation, standardizing the final results.

When I turned sixty, I squared off against all the daydreamy tomorrows of what I might yet become to face an absolute, irrefutable present. I have not cultivated one particular skill and so may be a master of none. But like those earlier cookbook writers, I seek a range of subjects, stories, and insights. I've let imagination into my life; I do not follow a recipe for my days. And I think I've come to embrace this. In a sense my approach is akin to that of organic farmers, who rely equally on science, intuition, and experience to cultivate vibrant fields and resilient lives.

Sometimes, of course, science and intuition seem at odds with each other. Is there real promise in GMO technology? Squash, sugar beets, tomatoes, and potatoes have all been approved for bioengineering. "Given the issues of drift, sweet corn from our local farmers' market may be double stacked with both genetically modified herbicide resistance and *Bt* traits," Atina said. The American Seed Trade Association recently asked the USDA to establish a tolerance level of 1 percent genetic contamination for seeds that are labeled nonmodified. "It's a pretty good clue that the seed companies can't manage what they're doing when they ask for a tolerance level," Fitzgerald quipped in a recent e-mail. "They've admitted that they can't guarantee non-GMO seed." The more GMO crops that are introduced into the environment, the less likely it is that the US will be able to produce any GMO-free produce—true organic produce—at all.

And here's the irony: huge seed corporations suffer from

GMO contamination, too. In a multijurisdictional federal lawsuit brought by Midwest farmers, Monsanto, and Cargill, the transglobal seed corporation Syngenta is being accused of contaminating the litigants' GMO corn with a variety not approved by the Chinese government. The contaminated corn rejected by the Chinese cost the litigants as much as $1.5 billion in export sales.

The way American corn is gathered, stored, and transported makes it impossible to segregate grain by source, and even a small quantity of a banned corn can quickly disperse through elevators, barges, and grain trains. Since the introduction of Syngenta's new corn, purchases of US corn have fallen by 85 percent, and corn prices have been driven to a five-year low.

GMO drift, a long-standing and long-disputed contention of anti-GMO activists, is now being addressed at a very high level, and the court's decision could eventually weigh in favor of organic corn farmers, whose crops and livelihoods have been destroyed by Monsanto. It may also support the GMO-labeling efforts in Minnesota, especially now that such legislation has been passed in Connecticut and Vermont.

The activists' issue is not with science or scientists, but with the universal claims made, based on insular data. Regardless of the carefulness of the research, it is just too hard to predict how a certain technology, tested in isolated laboratories, will perform in the world of interconnected and interdependent living systems. "The greater the rapidity of human-induced changes, the more likely they are to destabilize the complex systems of nature," wrote Aldo Leopold in *A Sand County Almanac.*

Time and again, experience shows that simple, low-cost, low-tech solutions like cover cropping produce better outcomes than what science has provided us. Critics of agricultural research question why money is going to labs and specialists. Why are scientists intent on solving problems in the most costly, complex ways imaginable, using the rationale of feeding the hungry to obtain funding?

The biggest criticism of the land-grant colleges' agricultural research regards its impact on small farmers and the American countryside. By putting its focus on high yields and high profits, the research has benefited nonfarming corporations at the expense of small farmers, who've had to "adapt or die."

"The monolithic nature of corn production presents a systemic risk to America's agriculture," said Jonathan Foley, executive director of the California Academy of Sciences. "It's important to distinguish corn the crop, from corn the system. As a crop, corn is highly productive, flexible, and successful. However, as a system it dominates American agriculture compared with other farming systems; it is not grown for food, it consumes natural resources, and it receives preferential treatment from our government through subsidies and crop-loss insurance."

Why are we growing so much corn? Economics. The production of corn has doubled over the past twenty years, and is worth $65 billion alone. Corn supplies a vast spread of industries—more than forty-five of the world's largest companies are in the corn production chain, accounting for about $1.7 trillion in earnings. Currently 40 percent of the crop becomes ethanol, 35 percent goes to animals, and the rest is processed into high-fructose corn syrup for soft drinks and other foods, or manufactured into plastics, even laundry detergents.

Between 2005 and 2010, US taxpayers spent $90 billion on corn subsidies, not including ethanol subsidies and mandates. In 2012, government-funded insurance payouts exceeded $20 billion. Federal subsidies, loose land-use policies, and demand for high-fructose corn syrup encourage farmers to grow more and more corn.

"If corn were actually grown for food, the average crop would sustain about fourteen people per acre. But because most of our consumption is in the form of high-fructose corn syrup and meat, it feeds merely three people per acre, lower than the average delivery of food from farms in Bangladesh, Egypt, and Vietnam," Foley said.

There is a real danger in relying on this one crop. With climate changes, volatile weather, superbugs, and superweeds, more corn crops fail every year and we taxpayers end up paying the bill. "This isn't rocket science," Foley added. "You wouldn't invest in a mutual fund that was dominated by only one company. That would be intolerably risky."

"To understand the risks, just look to the four-year corn-rust disaster of the 1970s," Atina commented. "We were growing just three varieties of corn, all of them susceptible to corn rust. For four years, farmers suffered devastating corn crop failure until wild corn varieties with rust resistance were bred back in."

Today, this $1.7 trillion industry—the equivalent of Australia's gross domestic product—is being threatened by water shortages, heat waves, and unpredictable rainfall, caused by climate change. It uses the most water for irrigation of any crop, and is raised in areas suffering drought—California's Central Valley and the high plains of Kansas and Nebraska. Ten percent of the fertilizer and the herbicide, like Roundup, equaling $420 million, is washed into the Gulf of Mexico, depleting oxygen levels and killing marine life. But corn's reign may be short lived. Increased temperatures and volatile weather are predicted to cause a decrease in corn crop yields by as much as 50 percent by 2065.

What would happen if corn growers shunned toxic glyphosate for organic methods? Would, as Monsanto claims, higher corn prices impact the affordability of our food?

Organic corn now costs between five and ten dollars more a bushel than conventional. But animal feed is a tiny part of our food cost. A bushel of corn will help produce two hundred eggs—less than two cents worth of corn per egg. So feeding those chickens organic feed raises the cost of the egg by a mere six cents. Higher corn prices won't raise the cost of staples, then—but they may raise the cost of sodas and processed food.

That's OK. The Department of Commerce reports that the indexed price of fresh fruits and vegetables has increased by 40 percent since 1980, whereas the indexed price of sodas has declined by about 30 percent. Fast food, snacks, and sodas are cheap, while fresh fruits and vegetables are not. Therein lies the relationship between poverty and diabetes and obesity. Government subsidies that depress the real cost of corn for processing cheap, unhealthy food are making one-third of America's children sick.

Here's a ray of hope: conventional corn farmers are adapting multicropping and soil-building techniques, planting prairie grasses between crop fields to absorb and filter water, and establishing hazelnut bushes along their borders for windbreaks. Secretary of Agriculture Tom Vilsack promises to ramp up support for conservation tillage, cover cropping, and diversification. All good ideas, but they lack economic incentive. What will convince farmers to do what is not in their financial interest? A single disaster, disease, pest, or economic downturn could cause a major disturbance in the global food supply.

Organic farmers reject GMO technology, but this does not mean that their methods conflict with a high-tech approach to agriculture improvement. The strong stand against GMO implies a thorough evaluation of the technological advancements in an ecological context. The US may be failing to pursue a sound strategy for meeting its environmental, agricultural, and economic goals unless it puts more muscle behind research into environmentally sound methods of growing corn. One group that does do this kind of work is the Organic Seed Alliance.

Working with Midwest corn farmers, the Organic Seed Alliance has developed open-pollinated corn varieties that can be saved and shared. Bill Tracy, a corn geneticist at the University of Wisconsin–Madison, and Martin Diffley have bred the first-of-its-kind, open-pollinated sweet-corn variety, which is getting high marks for tenderness and old-fashioned corn flavor. It's being released in the "Who Gets Kissed" variety line as Martina through High Mowing Organic Seeds. Martin, with his swarthy good looks and handlebar mustache, is a self-described old-farm-machine savant who can fix just about any tractor built before 1970 with a spare part he might happen to have in the shed—or he'll know where to find one. "Everything you need to know about a person shows up in their machines," Martin says.

"If they're angry, it's in the throttle—sticky and sputtering—uneven fuel delivery. If they are indecisive, the steering is sloppy. Lazy shows up in battery problems. Rebellion sounds out in the exhaust system."

"This corn will be as good, if not better, than any hybrid sweet corn on the market," he said during a dinner on the Diffleys' deck. "We've developed this corn so that the important traits will be retained, making it uniform enough for market. It will also have enough genetic variation to be resilient, allowing a farmer to further select and adapt the seeds to his or her local soil and climate conditions. The farmers who plant this corn will be helping to protect biologically diverse seed for future generations by simply managing this living resource." This is good news for a crop held hostage by science.

Martin showed us an ear of speckled gray-and-gold Mandan Bride corn. He was first given the seed at age ten by his uncle and he's been growing and saving the seeds ever since. "Every time I plant this corn, I think about the Indians and early farmers who did the same," he said. It's a ritual that ties Martin to his own memories of farming, and to his uncle, and to those who grew this corn for generations before him.

"We built our business by taking care of our soil, soil that grew the best corn in the region. People drove for miles to find it. Co-ops couldn't keep it in stock during the season," Atina told me the first time we met, some twenty-five years ago. "There are about fifty billion microbes in one tablespoon of living soil.

"The microbial life supports all living things," Atina continued. "Biological diversity is the key to keeping the balance on a farm." She picked up a handful of the black dirt and let it run through her fingers, adding, "Bugs pollinate crops, recycle nutrients, regulate animal populations, provide food for other animals. The friendly ones control pests. Organic farmers need to do a better job of communicating the real, tangible value of their production methods to society, caring for the foundation of our food, our lives by caring for the soil."

The value of delicious corn grown in well-cared-for soil extends far beyond sheer enjoyment at the dinner table. "Corporate farms exist to better the bottom line; they extract more than they put back in by using a shortsighted but effective profit-based business model," Atina said. But organic farmers are showing, through their work, that there are other, better ways to live in this world. "The opportunity to have a relationship with the farm has a value with a shelf life much longer than the produce the farmer sells. We've met so many people who express their aspiration to farm, and our success has served their dreams by showing another way to live, another paradigm. We gave them an example of a small, family-run business that was not based on corporate profit and fossil fuel, but on relationships— with the land, ourselves, our workers; with the co-ops and stores that sell our food; and with our customers, cooks, and chefs. Organic farming works, supports hope, and stimulates change."

In 2006, Gardens of Eagan was threatened with an eminent-domain suit from the Koch Brothers, whose pipeline company, the Minnesota Pipeline Company, LLC, proposed running a crude-oil pipeline across their land, threatening their soil health and organic certification. Gardens of Eagan intervened in the routing proceeding, becoming a party in the case and arguing that an organic farm provides ecosystem services through soil building and diversification. The court ruled that organic farms should be protected as a valuable natural resource. Thanks to the ruling, Minnesota's Agricultural Impact Mitigation Plan now protects organic soils and certification.

The Diffleys' attorney, Paula Maccabee, called the case "the perfect storm," and saw this as a defining moment for organic farmers across the country. Gardens of Eagan customers took the threat personally. "Even if they had never been to the farm, they felt a connection to our land," Atina said. "There was something about their relationship to our vegetables; to many it was our wonderful corn that sparked an emotional response." The area's natural-food co-ops launched a letter-writing campaign that generated over forty-eight hundred letters and e-mails to the administrative judge in support of Gardens of Eagan. Experts testified about the dangers of contamination and the environmental benefits of organic practices, parents told stories of the healing properties of organic produce, chefs presented the case for quality ingredients and flavor, neighbors exclaimed the farm's beauty and the people it employed.

The flavor and texture of the best corn has everything to do with the seed, and the attention given to growing and harvesting and transporting the crop; but the key is the soil. "Organic farming is present-tense farming; it relies on the sun and biological systems for fertility and pest control. When we use those toxic, petroleum-based chemicals, we are dipping into the past and burning up our future."

"We all felt endangered by this pipeline on many levels, most especially on a spiritual level," Atina said. "We don't like to use that term in this country, but it's important to discuss the spiritual aspects of food. When Martin plants Mandan Indian corn from the seeds he harvests year after year, I know that those corn plants will continue to go on evolving. The question is, will we?"

MILK

Just outside the tiny town of Grand Marais, you will find Lake View Natural Dairy off a long dirt drive, with rolling green pastures overlooking the blue expanse of Lake Superior. So quiet and peaceful, it's an unlikely battleground, and its farmer, David Berglund, is an unlikely warrior. But whether or not Lake View can continue to sell its raw milk, as it has for over three generations, is being decided in a contentious court case that pits the Minnesota Department of Agriculture against this small, rural community.

Lake View's customers typically help themselves to the jugs of whole, skim, and chocolate milk; yogurt; and butter from the cooler in the milk house, jotting down their purchases in a dog-eared ledger below the price blackboard and leaving their payments in a coffee can. The walls are plastered with pastel Post-its praising the milk and the dairy itself: notes of encouragement and love.

Catch Berglund between chores and dealing with his lawyers, and you'll find that he's soft spoken and patient, pausing thoughtfully in conversation—perhaps to slow down this city girl's rapid-fire questions. With a small copy of the Constitution tucked into the pocket of his work shirt and half-moon glasses sliding down his nose, he's professorial, confident, and clear. The case is about his right as a farmer to sell food that comes from his land; it's about the freedom of citizens to buy directly from a farm without government interference. The issue at hand is whether or not he has the right to refuse to allow Minnesota Department of Agriculture inspectors onto his farm. Under state statute, farmers may sell farm products directly from their farm without a permit, and so Berglund contends he's functioning within the law. The MDA contends that because some ingredients in Berglund's chocolate milk and yogurt do not come from the farm, he's selling food without a license. But the underlying issue is about raw, or real, or simply unpasteurized milk.

In the early 1800s Louis Pasteur discovered that heating milk to 161 degrees kills certain bacteria and disables certain enzymes. Today, dairies use ultra-high-temperature, short-time sterilization to create shelf-stable boxes of milk; ultra pasteurization for cartons of refrigerated milk; and vat pasteurization, the most gentle method, which takes longer but has less impact on the flavor of milk and is used by smaller dairies. While the process eliminates harmful bacteria that pose health risks—including *E. coli*, salmonella, listeria, and campylobacter—it destroys the beneficial bacteria as well. To some, pasteurization alters the milk's flavor, making it taste "boiled."

In the US, twelve states allow the sale of raw milk on store shelves. Twenty states ban it outright. The rest, like Minnesota, restrict the sale of such milk to the farm. But in the last two years, more than a dozen state legislatures have considered legislation that would make raw milk easier to acquire. So has the federal government: since May 2011, the US House Energy and Commerce Committee's Subcommittee on Health has had on its plate a proposal to legalize the traffic of raw milk across state lines. Currently it is the only food prohibited from interstate commerce.

It's legal to buy Lake View's milk from their cooler, but not from the Cook County Whole Foods Co-op just down the road in town. In Italy, Switzerland, Poland, and Slovenia, raw milk is sold in both specialized food stores and vending machines. I can bring the milk I buy at Lake View back to my Minneapolis kitchen, but not to our cottage on Madeline Island, Wisconsin, as that would be crossing state lines.

Why has raw milk ignited such a massive food fight between food-safety professionals and whole-food devotees?

Raw-milk advocates cite flavor, health-promoting properties, concern for the environment and the cows, and individual rights as their primary reasons for wanting this stuff.
The statistics used by both sides simply fuel the emotional
debate that underlies opposing beliefs. Are these regulations
protecting our health or regulating commerce?

The ruling by a judge in tiny Cook County is being
closely watched by thousands of Lake View customers,
especially the two hundred customers who showed up for
the hearing. Berglund has submitted to random inspections
in the past, but, he told me, "These are intrusive and unnecessary. I have a constitutional right to determine who steps
onto my property. People like my milk for a lot of different
reasons. They should be free to buy it."

"It's the fundamental right of citizens to engage in a
private transaction without having the nanny state peering
over our shoulder, saying, 'Thou shalt not do this,'" commented Berglund's lawyer, Zenas Baer. In a twist of fate, the
Cook County sheriff's deputy, responsible for enforcing the
inspection, is a fan of Lake View's milk. "I like the taste of it,"
Deputy Greg Gentz commented. "I am not a raw-milk advocate, I'm an advocate for people's individual rights and the
government respecting the limits of its authority." The Minnesota Department of Agriculture is concerned about Lake
View's raw yogurt and raw butter not sanctioned under the
unpasteurized-milk statute. "Lake View's customers know
the risk [of raw milk products]," Gentz added. "Requiring

Lake View to purchase pasteurization equipment for butter and yogurt would put the farm out of business and deny its customers freedom of choice."

Raw milk can taste a little sweeter and is usually creamier than pasteurized milk. Lake View's milk is especially clean tasting because of the cows' diet, as Berglund describes: "Our cows eat a lot of herbs and fresh greens that give the milk its mild flavor and a higher fat content." A Twin Cities chef, who asked not to be named, uses raw milk in desserts she caters. "Dairy is the single most delicate and sensitive indicator of terroir I have encountered. It's the purest taste of the land," she claims. As such, it is evidence of well-managed pastures and happy cows. Devotees describe the milk's "purity" with a hint of nostalgia for a lost agrarian, old-fashioned way of life.

But a good raw-milk dairy like Lake View will rely on state-of-the-art technology and equipment to keep the milk clean. At Lake View, Dave spray-washes the cows' teats with a bluish antiseptic cleaner and hooks them to stainless-steel suction cups, which draw the milk into a stainless-steel separator, which pipes the cream into one stainless-steel container and the milk into another. The cream is bottled or churned into butter. The skim milk is fed to the hogs.

Raw-milk advocates claim that pasteurization destroys milk's natural probiotic bacteria, along with vitamins B and C, calcium, and magnesium. Raw milk, they say, has been shown to help protect children against allergies—even the

FDA agrees with this last point. Pasteurization makes the lactose in milk more readily absorbable, explaining why individuals who are lactose intolerant have such a difficult time digesting commercial milk but can tolerate raw milk. In a Michigan study, 82 percent of those diagnosed with lactose intolerance reported they had no problems drinking raw milk.

"Of course I grew up drinking our farm's fresh milk," Berglund said. "So when I went to school and drank the milk from one of those small waxed cartons, I couldn't stand its taste. It made me feel sick. I discovered later that I am lactose intolerant and just didn't know it at the time."

Advocates also swear by the vitality, digestive vigor, strong teeth, and clear skin raw milk bestows. Charlie Wagner, a high-fashion yoga teacher, health advocate, and owner of the Juut Salons in Minneapolis and Los Angeles, attests that her husband, David, survived chemotherapy and radiation treatments for stage-four melanoma by drinking a gallon of unpasteurized milk a day. "It was the only food he could stomach," she said. "It tastes good and was soothing and it kept him from losing too much weight. The beneficial probiotic enzymes and vitamins gave him strength."

Many "rawists" view the bacteria in milk as a human ally and suggest that microbes are ubiquitous, necessary, and tasty—so why not collaborate with them? They claim that the friendly bacteria cultivate diverse intestinal flora and fauna that strengthen the gut wall and help prevent absorption of pathogens and toxins, while pasteurization—a mechanized method intended to prevent diseases—actually robs us of our power to prevent illness. "By engaging bacterial allies we are assuming responsibility for our own health," claimed Allie, a mom in the Minneapolis suburbs. Health inspectors raided her kitchen early one morning while she was in the shower and her teenage boys were finishing breakfast. She was being investigated as a "raw-milk drop-off site" for a "cow share" arrangement.

The quality of raw milk is directly related to the health of the cows, which, of course, depends on the conditions they're raised in. Until the mid-1800s, most families consumed fresh milk from their own cows. Before 1905, when zoning ordinances changed, St. Paul homeowners kept cows in their backyards. Bovines wandered through parks, yards, and streets without a second thought. While by today's standards the then-accepted milking practices might seem questionable, few health problems are recorded associated with the unpasteurized milk of that time.

The reason? The cows were healthy. They wandered outside in the fresh air, eating a diet of grass and hay. Healthy cows produce milk that contains multiple natural redundant systems of bioactive components that can reduce or eliminate pathogenic bacteria that could harm the calf. That milk is the best thing for calves, and it's good for people, too.

Dairy farming arrived in this region with Swiss, German, and Eastern European immigrants. As the wheat fields of Minnesota and Wisconsin became depleted, the Scandinavian settlers continued west in search of better soil, leaving behind grasslands that delighted the German settlers, who were used to a life "tied to a cow." In the late 1800s, William Dempster Hoard, a New York journalist and dairy farmer, recognized the region's potential and launched *Hoard's Dairyman* magazine, to educate dairy farmers. He also helped found the Wisconsin Dairyman's Association to set standards for milk, cheese, and butter, so they could be transported safely in ice-block-refrigerated railroad cars.

The Industrial Revolution dramatically changed the dairy landscape, while the midcentury Land-Grant Act established colleges of agriculture to breed and promote genetic selection for cows that produced more milk. Rural electrification provided light, which extended farming hours, as well as refrigeration to rapidly cool milk for safe storage.

But dairies began to take shortcuts as they increased production of milk to meet the needs of the burgeoning urban population. Most notorious was "swill milk," wretched stuff produced by huge milking operations that kept herds of perpetually sick cows chained in filthy sheds, eating brewery or distillery wastes. The swill milk was further whitened with plaster of Paris and sweetened with molasses.

Pasteurization, the heating of milk to kill all bacteria, became the most inexpensive means of sanitizing raw milk.

It was promoted by health officials throughout the Midwest. In Chicago, it proved effective: child-mortality rates from foodborne illness dropped 85 percent. But not everyone saw pasteurization as a magic bullet.

Initially, pasteurization was seen as a violation of a sacred substance, gambling with infants' lives. One Minnesota physician called the process "the best apology for dirty milk, a boon for those who used this new technology to camouflage poor dairy-management practices." In Minnesota and Wisconsin, the Board of Pediatricians favored the Certified Milk Program, with routine inspections of dairies and milk testing. But it was twice as expensive as pasteurization, and soon priced itself out of the market.

By the 1900s, demand for pasteurized milk soared. To meet the demand, the dairy industry underwent seismic changes to expand production. This required intense capital improvements that drove small independent farmers from their land or left them beholden to arrangements with commercial dairies and regional dairy cooperatives designed to pasteurize, homogenize, and distribute vast quantities of milk.

Homogenization puts milk through a machine that physically breaks up the milk's fat with heat. This disperses the fat into the milk so that it no longer rises naturally to the top. Homogenization allows milk to remain a consistent white color on the shelf. Not all pasteurized milk is homogenized; many small dairies that sell their milk off farm do not homogenize. But all homogenized milk must be pasteurized or will quickly turn rancid. (Unpasteurized milk will "clab-ber," a natural process of souring that turns the liquid into a thick, yogurtlike substance with a strong flavor and high acid content—it can be used as a leavener in baking. Pasteur-ized milk, however, simply spoils and becomes scummy.)

Today's dairy industry rests on extreme economies of scale that begin with the cow. A conventionally raised dairy cow produces four times as much milk as she did in the 1950s. High-energy, corn-based feeds, which increase milk yields, and Bovine Growth Hormone (BST), which increases lactation, strain the cows' metabolisms and diges-tive systems. To treat mastitis, a painful infection familiar to any woman who has nursed her child and stomach dis-orders, cows are doused with antibiotics that leach into the milk and eventually taint our water. Nearly 80 percent of the antibiotics used in the US are administered to farm animals, prompting the growth of antibiotic-resistant microbes, which already cause infections in more than one hundred thousand Americans annually.

"The customers who come to Lake View drive up from the Twin Cities and down from Thunder Bay, Canada, and they are, for the most part, educated people who have studied the issue and then realized the change it can make in their health," Berglund said.

Anyone researching raw milk with an open mind will quickly come to ask the simple question: if this stuff is so good for us, why is it so hard to obtain? "Much of the resistance to unpasteurized milk is being driven by the dairy industry—specifically the cheese industry," Berglund said. "They need cheap milk to keep cheese prices down." But this pressure is rapidly killing the institution of dairy farming.

"The average conventional farmer will receive about one dollar per gallon for milk, which is less than the cost of production. If a farmer wants to survive, she needs economies of scale, and methods that push cows beyond their nature. Raw milk currently goes for eight to ten dollars per gallon, and that money is paid directly to the farmer," Berglund said.

Natural dairy farming is unbelievably hard work and the legal barriers are immense. "We are not allowed to advertise," said Berglund. "And we don't get much walk-in traffic because our farm isn't near a densely populated area. It's a beautiful piece of land, and we've been approached by numerous developers, but we believe in what we are doing and don't want to sell."

The Farm-to-Consumer Legal Defense Fund represents real-milk farmers in legislative and judicial battles, and the Weston A. Price Foundation's national "Real Milk" campaign keeps consumers informed at the state and national levels, providing maps and resources and sponsoring scientific studies. But the legal fight has barely just begun.

Perhaps unpasteurized dairy is being scrutinized so carefully because of its increased demand. In the US about ten million people—about 3 percent of the overall population—drink raw milk, while sales of conventional milk have dropped by 3 percent, to the lowest point in history. Federal and most state governments continue to oppose raw milk. John Sheehan, the director of the FDA's Division of Plant and Dairy Food Safety, said, "Raw milk is dangerous; avoid it at all costs. Do not give it to your children." Yet he never mentioned the massive outbreaks caused by pasteurization slipups or recontamination of correctly pasteurized milk. According to the Center for Science in the Public Interest, unpasteurized milk and cheese did not even make the list of the top-ten most dangerous foods, falling far behind leafy greens and potatoes.

Is raw milk really worth the price or the fuss? If the herd is poorly managed and munches on skunk grass, the flavor of the milk can be terribly off. If cows are milked in a dirty barn or the milk is handled improperly, it may be contaminated. Yet all things considered, there have been no reported deaths from unpasteurized milk in the past quarter-century. And as the government tries to protect us from choosing raw milk, there's been little progress in reducing overall foodborne illness, reports the CDC.

Having met Berglund on his farm, and seen how his cows are treated and how he processes his milk, I trust that what I've pulled from his milk-house cooler is clean and healthy. I know that it has benefits beyond its flavor and health-giving properties. But Lake View is a good five-hour drive from our home, too far to go for an everyday food.

Milk is an intimate food, and the best milk is the result of a healthy relationship between the farmer and the cow, and the cow and the pasture. This is the quality that inspectors miss when they focus solely on the bacteria in the milk itself. Pasteurization destroys certain pathogens, but it can be a default for poor management and unclean conditions.

My group of friends in the Twin Cities are the smartest, kindest, funniest people I know—a lawyer, doctor, realtor, writer, journalist, teacher, filmmaker, chef, restaurant owner, gardener, poet, photographer, farmer, advertising executive, therapist, pastor, printmaker, yoga teacher, painter, and editor. There are no words of affection that can contain the whole of their wonderfulness. We hold hands through our lives' transitions—births and birthdays, illnesses and funerals, marriages and remarriages, and divorces.

We cook together for holiday gatherings, spending hours in each other's kitchens, baking cookies for teachers and neighbors, or jumping in to help prepare a friend's son's wedding banquet—Moroccan spiced lamb from a neighbor's farm, salads and pilafs from the friend's own splendid harvest. When one of us (finally) left an abusive husband, we raced over to help stock her new, empty pantry with her favorite spices; when another's son suffered a collapse at his college, we drove her to the airport (and tucked a baguette sandwich into her purse); when Kevin suffered a heart attack, these friends brought café au laits, muffins, and laughter into the hospital room, ran errands, and fetched medications. We've shared babysitters and cocktail dresses, morning coffee and happy-hour drinks; we've read each other's manuscripts, escaped to each other's cabins up north. We talk and text endlessly at any hour.

These women lead me to the greenest pastures and, thanks to these friendships, I graze on both possibilities and realities with more grace.

Loretta Jaus appreciates the things that bring people together, and the joy and progress that come out of knowing one another. A dairy farmer with her husband Martin, in Gibbon, Minnesota, Loretta is a statuesque woman whose greying blonde tendrils escape her loose bun, faded jeans hanging loosely on her rangy frame. "You can't separate things out," she told me over tea and ginger cookies in her warm, sunny kitchen. "Our farm, the cows, the land, the wildlife are a network. It's hard to appreciate all of them fully until you experience the place." Loretta and her husband, Martin, supply Organic Valley, the world's largest organic dairy co-op. It was founded in 1988, when eight farmers in southwest Wisconsin met in the shadows of a national farm debt crisis that had worn their community thin. Tens of thousands of farm families had gone bankrupt, many others had sold their land to pay bills, and foreclosure auctions threatened to end in violence. The eight founding farmers knew that the banks and government had encouraged farmers to take on too much debt and they realized that they needed to develop new marketing strategies to connect them to consumers. Today, nearly fifteen hundred participating farm members are creating almost $600 million in sales.

"We've been working with Organic Valley since the beginning and I've given talks all over the country about the importance of these practices, about the value of the work we do and the quality of our milk. It's time to bring this story closer to home and invite the neighbors in," Loretta said. "Given all the bad news about conventional farming and chemicals, I know these farmers feel defensive. We need to just get together and talk."

I'd first met Loretta at a party on the Diffleys' farm, and I'd been struck by her story. She and Martin had met while working in a wildlife sanctuary and they'd decided to return to his family's conventional farm and transition it to an organic dairy. A mother of four and grandmother of two, Loretta rises at 4:00 a.m. to milk her fifty-cow herd. In between all the farming chores, she sews her own curtains, knits shawls, paints the inside of her barn each fall, and pickles a year's worth of her garden's beans. At the Diffleys' party she played jazz piano until midnight. So when she shared her idea for a white-tablecloth, farm-to-table dinner for her conventional-farming neighbors and the city's local-food advocates, I was inspired, and said, "I'll cook."

Loretta carefully vetted the guest list of twelve. "There has to be a balance of interests, and no agenda except to share stories about ourselves and our lives." Word of the gathering leaked and several food celebrities began hinting that they'd like to be included. But Loretta drew the line. "This is an intimate affair. I don't want the neighbors to feel outnumbered," she said.

Loretta's farm is hemmed in by a neighbor's linear rows of tall, straight, brownish-green corn. The land is an oasis of verdant green, where cows and calves dine on a mix of grasses and wildflowers, and birds—bobolinks, Eastern bluebirds, sparrows, redheaded woodpeckers, mourning doves, yellow-throated warblers, owls, and red-tailed hawks—flutter and chatter over crops of hay, alfalfa, and buckwheat. Five acres of corn were planted just to feed deer, voles, mice, and pheasants. There's a small marsh that's perfect for frogs and a pond the size of a football field for ducks and splashing grandkids. "It took about five years for the frogs and toads to return," Martin said. "Growing up, we'd spend all day chasing them, but the farm chemicals wiped them out."

The Jauses' herd is a mix of Montbeliarde, Jersey, and

Holstein—some pure black and shiny, others with white faces and huge brown spots. The cows produce about fifteen hundred pounds of milk each day. That's not much compared to the eight thousand pounds of milk pumped from the average conventional farm's one hundred thirty five thousand head of cattle. "But it's enough," Martin said.

When Loretta and Martin moved back here, they didn't have the wildlife in mind. They just wanted to help the land heal from the damage caused by overtilling and toxic inputs. First they planted the windbreaks—a mix of crabapple, plum, pine, and oak—to both cut wind and stem soil erosion. The trees brought back the songbirds. Of the 410 acres, 105 are dedicated to pasture, divided into twenty-five paddocks for grazing. "We give our girls a smorgasbord. They pick and choose and just know what they need to eat," Loretta told me. She names each cow in her herd. Another 10 acres of trees and prairie grasses are in the federal Conservation Reserve Program, and 11 acres are left as seasonal wetland, with cottonwoods, willows, and marsh grasses.

Loretta's two daughters were on hand to help me prepare dinner and set the table. In the expansive kitchen, we cut sunflowers, foxgloves, and poppies to arrange in huge mason jars. We roasted a fennel-stuffed pork loin from a neighboring hog farmer, stirred up a farro risotto from a wheat farmer experimenting with the ancient grain, and sliced heirloom tomatoes, dressing them with homemade apple-cider vinegar and local honey. We filled cut-glass bowls with homemade pickles and chutney. We whipped cream and baked shortcakes to fill with just-picked raspberries.

Guests gathered at dusk at a table near the pond. Cows moved slowly and peacefully to the barn and doves cooed over the sound of clinking glasses. We poured wine and more wine; I settled in amidst talk of the blasting heat, early tomatoes, how to rid the garden of slugs, and who had good melons. We had place cards but I had trouble telling the different constituents apart. We shared recipes for raspberry jam and pickles with peppers, stories of children and grandchildren, how to clean copper, and where to find antique plates.

I'd driven down with Ellen, a public-health professional who had been gathering data on the region's spike in colon and breast cancer. She'd met Loretta at an organic-farming conference, and over lunch they'd become friends. Meg, an organic dairy farmer, holds an "off-farm job" with the Minnesota Department of Agriculture, and, like Loretta, has worked hard to earn the trust of her conventional-farm neighbors. Loretta's neighbor, Liz, who works in the office of Organic Valley, is raising two young kids and helping organize a natural-foods co-op in town. "Finding food in farm country is our biggest challenge," she said. "Sometimes we just have to stop at Walmart. It's the closest store around." Mavel, a gallant eighty-year-old in an orange hat, held a swollen arm to her side. "I'm almost done with chemo," she said. "Breast cancer." Judy, seated to my right, turned to me and whispered, "You know, it wasn't always this way. My husband died of lymphoma. I don't remember people ever getting so sick."

Though we'd never previously met, it felt as though I'd known these guests a long time. The conversation hummed among compliments and giggles. When I commented on Janice's pretty blue scarf, she said, "My hair is just growing back."

"I know it's how we're doing things, but we have so much money tied up in equipment and implements and I'm just too old to change," said Georgia, who volunteers at the local school's garden. She talked about helping kids pick the carrots they'd planted early in the spring for after-school snacks.

As we finished the shortcakes, we sat back in the velvety night. A slight breeze lifted the lily petals. Dippers and goldfinches and sparrows began to rustle through the grape-colored dusk. Just several miles to the north of these farms, the CDC had identified a "cancer cluster"; residents had started a Facebook page to share information. The prior spring, the National Cancer Institute had released studies that correlated breast cancer to exposure to the weed killer Atrazine, an endocrine disrupter, as well as twenty other pesticides linked to bladder and colon cancer, leukemia, and myeloma.

Yet in the gentle quiet, we did not talk of organic methods or toxic farm chemicals; no one used the words "sustainable" or "organic." No one said, "It doesn't have to be this way"; rather, we said, "Listen to those peepers," as the frogs' croaking swelled to triumphant crescendo.

Earlier in the day, as we had chopped onions, Loretta had told me, "I'm so happy these neighbors want to come tonight. When we first moved in, people were polite, but we were the outsiders, even though Martin grew up on this farm. We did things differently. They thought we were strange. I think they felt threatened." She paused. "Now I get asked questions in church and at the grocery store. People just seem more curious. Organic Valley provides us a stable price for our milk, we farmers elect the board, and we have some say in major decisions. The work is not easy, but farming is never easy and we are a viable business when so many small conventional dairies can't make it any more. Farm chemicals keep becoming more expensive and commodity milk gets cheaper all the time. We're really not a threat to any of these farmers."

It's a good two-plus hours from my home to Loretta's farm, the quiet of her pastures, her lowing cattle, the reflective blue of the iris-bordered pond. But I think of her every time I reach for that red-and-white carton of milk. And I can't help but recall Mavel's gravelly laugh or the pale, satiny skin on her "good" wrist as she reached to give me a farewell hug. The life stories of these hardworking women play out in my kitchen every morning.

In making my day-to-day choices, the lessons from

Loretta's dinner—with those chatty, laughing, question-ing women—are real. That evening, under the deepening indigo sky, a silence descended over us all; fireflies sparkled and stars pricked the sky with pinholes of hope. Together we watched the moon spread its light over the pond in the earth's blessed thrall.

Most of us wonder why our government is expending so much effort against small farmers working hard to sell good food to their small communities for very little profit. The clash is about two opposing worldviews, one that respects and honors local wisdom, another that puts faith in scientific methods and technological solutions. While the court cases focus on legal technicalities associated with permits and licenses, I can't help but wonder what might happen if the MDA inspectors, Deputy Gentz, and the moms and dads and kids who drink David Berglund's milk shared dinner together at a big table in Loretta's pasture, overlooking the pond.

CHEESE AND BUTTER

Whenever my dad came to town, the cheese platter we assembled resembled a map of the region. Creamy or tangy; aged or fresh; cow, sheep, goat, even water buffalo cheeses, all reflected the cheesemaker's skill and the area's particular conditions—its traditions, weather, environment, topography, animals—and the microbial activity that transforms milk into cheese. The French call this quality of particularity in a food *terroir*, and apply it to wine; the Italian term, *sotto il cielo*, translates to "under the sky".

Yet in our region, the concept of terroir differs from that of Europe. There, terroir is governed by bureaucracy and protected by "designation of origin" (DOC) laws that dictate how and where specific cheeses may be made. In the US, however, the place-based distinction implies that the product is so unique to one farm that it cannot be replicated anywhere else. Thus, in the US anyone can make a Colby; the name simply refers to the style of cheese, not the region or the animal's milk. In short, Americans celebrate variety, while Europeans applaud narrow tradition. But terroir also relates to the perceived value of a cheese to cooks who want food from an independent family farm, pastured animals, and working landscapes. Terroir suggests that buying this cheese is a thoughtful action, a means of supporting the places we all wish to live on or at least visit. For Europeans, the term refers to the past; for Americans, terroir is forward looking.

Terroir is too often incorrectly associated with elitism. Still its practical application is having a profound economic impact on our region. Artisan cheeses command a premium price, generating income that helps farmers stay on their land, revives rural communities, maintains the landscape, and protects the soil, water, and wildlife. Each cheesemaker is contributing in his or her own way to the local economy and the quality of our food. What word beyond "terroir" could better describe the taste of our fierce winters and blasting summers, lush prairies and dark forests, fast icy streams and deep cold lakes, as well as all the microbial life that dances the milk into cheese? Perhaps simply: "ours."

This region's artisans are working to redefine cheese as a handcrafted food, best enjoyed on its own, not as a cheap commodity melted in sandwiches and on casseroles. They are reclaiming the sense of place lost to commodity pricing, which has led to the collapse of small farms and their consolidation into huge industrial dairies. In this way, our generation of cheesemakers is investing locally, restoring land destroyed by the preceding generation. And this is in keeping with the traditions of farmers whose work has always relied on healing the land.

In the mid-1800s, when overplanting left wheat vulnerable to blight, the depleted fields of southern Wisconsin were converted to grass pastures for dairy cattle. Before that, cheesemaking had been the domain of farmwomen, whose "cheese and egg money" paid for small household luxuries like sugar and ribbons. But when the wheat crops failed, dairy products became many farmers' primary income. By the early 1900s, Wisconsin was home to some fifteen hundred cheese plants located at rural crossroads. Milk processing moved off the farms as farmers formed large cooperative dairies. The nation's first, Land O'Lakes, was founded in 1921 as the Minnesota Cooperative Creameries Association. It has grown from 320 dairymen to 32,000 members nationwide. It's one of seven multinational entities that produce about 80 percent of our country's dairy products; the growth is due primarily to the acquisition of smaller, local dairies. Industrial dairy plants pool milk from across the country, pasteurize it with ultra-high heat to standardize the flavor and color, and "culture" it with artificial ingredients. This explains why all commercial cheddar cheese tastes the same.

Since the early 1980s, the number of small, artisan cheesemaking operations has nearly doubled and Wisconsin leads the way. Specialty cheeses account for 25 percent of the state's overall production. Along with cow, sheep, and goat cheeses, we're now seeing water-buffalo cheeses, from a relatively new animal to this region. Each type of cheese is quite different—sheep's milk is high in fat and extremely rich and mildly sweet; goat's milk has a distinctive tangy taste; water buffalo's milk is especially mild and great for mozzarella; cow's milk can be slightly grassy and neutral.

There is nothing nostalgic in the American definition of terroir. It addresses the issues left in the wake of industrialization by focusing on appropriate tasks for small dairies, where the connection to the land is more important than any labels, such as "organic." The key is the relationship of the cheesemaker to the land, the animals, and the customers. Instead of "taste of place," the term might be better defined as "taste of a working landscape."

The nose-tingly quality of Shepherd's Way Farms' Big Woods Blue, named for the state park bordering the farm's rolling pastures, has much to do with the farm's location and cheesemaker Jodi Ohlsen Read's talents. But its success is the result of Jodi and Steven Read's persistence and resilience, and support from a community that cares about this farm and this family.

I'd met Steven at the Mill City Farmers' Market, where he and one of his sons were offering samples of their Frisago, a firm, nutty-tasting, Manchego-style cheese. Patiently and happily, he explained why farmstead cheese from pastured animals tastes so good and described the talents of his wife, who was the first to make sheep's-milk cheese in the state.

Though it's just a few miles outside the tiny college town of Northfield, less than an hour from the Twin Cities, the farm's verdant grasses, spanning under a wide sky, and nearby woods make it feel as though it's hundreds of miles away. As I stepped out of my car into a quiet September morning, a flock of hens scattered while snorting hogs raced to the edge of their pen. Jodi opened the creaky door of the farmhouse kitchen, the sun setting her honey-gold hair aglow. She's a small, handsome woman with keen blue eyes and a creamy complexion. A mother of four boys, she exudes a sense of purpose and calm. I'd come to learn how her beautiful cheese is made.

Shepherd's Way's plant is attached to the milk barn, and as I followed Jodi through the entrance, it took a minute for my eyes to adjust to the dark, cold corridor. Through the glass windows of the aging room, I could see stainless-steel shelves lined with wheels of cheese—small, pure, white orbs, golden rounds, and wheels dipped in black wax. In the cutting room, we scrubbed our hands and elbows; donned hairnets, rubber aprons, and boots that squeaked on the pristine concrete floor; then stepped into a tub of disinfectant before passing through a heavy plastic curtain to the cheese room. It's more workshop than "plant"; everything is small scale, with stainless-steel tables lowered to accommodate Jodi's five-foot frame.

We stood at a vat of sheep's milk; it glowed pale as moonlight and was warmed to baby-bottle temperature. Jodi added the starter bacteria to convert the lactose—milk sugar—into lactic acid, equalizing the pH level in the milk protein. The milk shuddered, divided, clumped, and separated, undulating, and then Jodi stirred in rennet, the chief enzyme that works in tandem with the starter. Jodi moved in ancient choreography, her steps measured and precise. She watched and put a hand in the milk to feel the process as the curds gathered into themselves. The liquid transformed, luminescent, and a white whale emerged from a sea of translucent whey. We took wooden-framed cutters and reached far into the vats to comb through the mass and slice it into squares, two-inch pillows that bounced and nudged each other and then bloomed and united to billow again. As instructed, I plunged my arms, elbow deep, into the silky mass and gently separated the curds with my fingers. We added handfuls of the salt she'd measured, stirred it in with large paddles, and reached in with our hands to swirl the mixture around again.

Next, the "hoops"—round, holed, metal cylinders—to mold and compress the curds as they drain. I scooped the curds from the vat with an enormous shovel to fill the hoops. Jodi reached in and, with a cupped hand, smoothed them out. I started to do the same, but she halted my effort with a light, firm touch and said, "I do this part." This is her final act before setting the cheese in the aging room to mature. "A prideful cheesemaker makes a bitter cheese," Jodi said. "I try and give a blessing to each cheese before it goes on its way."

We finished in silence. My hands became soft and pale from handling rich creamy curds and soft whey. Through the rest of the afternoon, we flipped the hoops several times, until the whey drained off.

In addition to this soft, mild, fresh cheese, called Shepherd's Hope, Jodi also makes several aged cheeses and a soft brie-like cheese that ripens from the inside out, with a "blooming" rind. When cut, it puddles all over the plate. Big Woods Blue, a Roquefort-style cheese, is similar to those you'd find in Europe, made of sheep's milk. Honoring the French tradition, Jodi folds the mold spores into the curds by hand.

It is against all odds that Shepherd's Way is still making cheese, and award-winning cheese at that. By now, Jodi, Steven, and their four boys should have returned to the Twin Cities and gone back to their former jobs, Jodi as a medical writer and editor, Steven as a teacher. Ten years ago, an arsonist's fire burned all of the Reads' outbuildings, killing more than five hundred East Friesian-cross ewes and lambs. It was devastating—the loss of life, a livelihood, a thriving business, and a future.

Occuring after midnight, in subzero temperatures, the event and its aftermath were horrific. So much damage was done. "Dairy sheep are socialized," Steven said shortly afterwards. "We feed them by hand after they're born. We touch them every day. We know each of them by name." Here's the thing: Steven began the huge task of cleanup and rebuilding, and Jodi went back to making cheese using purchased sheep's milk. Within a year, there was more demand for their cheese than Jodi and Steven could supply.

Cheese fans—chefs, co-ops, cheese shops, lawyers, bankers, businessmen—gave their time, money, and expertise. Steven salvaged a dairy barn from the nearby Nerstrand Big Woods State Park to replace the one they'd lost, launched an "adopt-a-sheep" program, sought small business loans, and sold CSA shares of cheese and meat delivered each month to drop-off sites throughout the Cities. Shepherd's Way created sheep products—woolen goods such as comforters, mattress pads, and pillows—the sons raised hogs for meat and chickens for eggs; and Steven had lamb sausage made.

Nationally, Shepherd's Way has become a cause célèbre of the Slow Money movement, founded by Woody Tasch, chairman emeritus of the Investors' Circle, a network of angel investors, venture capitalists, and foundations. Modeled on the Slow Food movement, Slow Money is a nonprofit that directs the flow of investment capital to small food enterprises. Its mission is to promote new principles of fiduciary responsibility, sustainable agriculture, and the emergence of a restorative economy as laid out in Tasch's book, *Inquiries Into the Nature of Slow Money: Investing As If Food, Farms, and Fertility Mattered.* "Through manpower and money, we're planting the seeds of nurture capital," Tasch has said. "What would the world be like if we invested 50 percent of our assets within fifty miles of where we live? What if there was a generation of businesses that gave away 50 percent of their profits? What if there was 50 percent more organic matter in our soil fifty years from now?"

Steven and Jodi created Farm Haven LLC, a financial vehicle to help bring the farm out of foreclosure, guided by a board of directors that included a restaurant owner, an attorney, a retired food-company executive, a banker, and a corporate CEO. The board shared their expertise in accounting, distribution, and packaging. Soon after, Jodi was able to make enough cheese to satisfy local customers as well as national accounts.

More recently, Shepherd's Way completed a successful Kickstarter campaign to fund a much-needed barn for lambing in the winter. "Traditionally, a farmer would get a farm loan for such a building. These opportunities aren't as easily available as they were before the recession, especially when you're still growing a business. The advantage of the Kickstarter, aside from the funding, is that we'll be able to draw in more people who are specifically interested in what we do," Steven said.

As a farmstead cheesemaking operation, Shepherd's Way has not lost sight of their sheep's importance. While purchased milk has allowed the business to continue, having a reliable source of milk from the farm's own herd is a core value of this enterprise. No doubt it's far easier and perhaps even less expensive to use purchased milk, but to do so betrays a fundamental tenet of the operation; the cheese must be made from the milk that comes from the sheep that are raised on this land, in these rolling fields. Single-source-milk cheese tastes of place. While in Jodi's gifted hands, any milk can still make award-winning cheese, fundamentally, it's just not the same.

These innovative funding sources are helping keep money within the region. They are the reverse of farm closures, signifying that this is what the land was meant to do. The Slow Money and Kickstarter contributions are investments in the Read family's work ethic and stewardship and represent an ethical commitment to the values that dictate place-making practices, practices that create delicious cheese.

The French term *affinage*, from the Latin *ad finem*, directly translates to "towards the limit," and describes the moment a cheese has reached perfection, before it turns overripe.

Relying on wild microbes that flourish in uncontrolled conditions, affinage explains the renowned flavors of Swiss Gruyère and French Mimolette, the latter of which benefits from cheese mites. And it describes the relationship the cheesemaker has with the microbial activity that creates world-renowned cheese, such as those from Love Tree Farm, near Grantsburg, Wisconsin.

Cheesemaker Mary Falk is one of the few in the US who practices the art of affinage. Mary does not pasteurize the milk for her cheeses aged in the caves she and her husband, Dave, built in the hillside of their land. Steven Jenkins, a noted industry authority and author of *Cheese Primer*, calls Falk "the most talented drop-dead cheesemaker in our country today. What she does to get her sheep's milk, my God."

What Mary does is carefully set the process in motion, and then get out of the way. She credits Love Tree's 130 acres of wild prairie, rolling hillocks, eight lakes, and spring-fed ponds for her herd's health and great milk. The land is a playground for trumpeter swans, ospreys, otters, eagles, wolves, and bears, and the sheep graze on lavender, bluestem, Indian paintbrush, and yellow birdsfoot. They are protected by tall loping llamas and feisty guard dogs—Spanish mastiffs and Polish Tatras that move with the sheep, and border collies that herd them into a flock when a coyote comes near. The Falks' fields, named Little Eden and Beer Can Stand, rustle with grasshoppers, ladybugs, and bees.

In the 1980s, Mary moved to St. Paul from California for an office job, and on a hike through the back woods of Wisconsin met Dave. He was owner of "the prettiest farm I'd ever seen," she told me. Short version: they fell in love and married. A self-described "old hippie," with curly blonde locks that she flicks out of her eyes with a bob of her head, Mary is as outspoken, bawdy, and quick to laugh as Dave is quiet and wry. She'd experimented with making her own cheese back in California, so after she married Dave, she started applying her self-taught skills to their sheep's milk.

After completing the Master Cheesemaker Program at the University of Wisconsin–Madison, Mary won a grant to explore the cheesemaking Basque region of Spain, with a similar climate and topography to the Falks' farm. On her return, she applied her knowledge to breeding the same type of hardy sheep she'd seen and creating her signature cheeses with affinage.

She and Dave dug an aging cave into the red-clay hillside of their farm, a round concrete room with ventilation pipes running up through the earth into the woods. Each morning the tule fog from the surrounding ponds, damp and fragrant with meadow, drifts over the cheese.

Trying to explain the flavor of Love Tree's cheese is like trying to count angels on the head of a pin, or mites on the rind of that Mimolette. The medium for Mary's art is the raw milk from her sheep. Just that. She uses the whey as the culture to begin the process and ages her cheese the required sixty days. Though she gently pasteurizes her milk for the fresher cheese, she told me, "Just think of how much more delicious young cheeses would be if they could be made from real milk. Milk left in its natural state so all the fresh flavors are allowed to shine."

One May morning some ten years ago, I arrived at the farm with a station wagon full of sixth-graders who galloped through the fields like so many lambs. After visiting the curious big-horned highland cattle that provide milk for Love Tree's sheep–cow's milk blends, we stretched out on the grass near a picnic table. The kids took turns bottle feeding an orphaned lamb and devoured cups of Mary's yogurt drizzled with Love Tree honey.

"There is no reason we can't use raw milk for all cheeses," Mary told me. "I test every batch of milk and mine is cleaner than most milk from large processing plants. Our equipment is spotless, and I handle everything carefully. The cleaner the milk, the better-tasting the cheese will be." Mary and like-minded raw-milk-cheese advocates say that raw milk is the best and safest host to the important agents of change in making great cheese. Just as the sheep munch the grass—and eagles pick off the voles, and mice eat the grasshoppers—the microbes feast on the bacteria in raw milk, transforming the cheese's texture and flavor as it matures. The Falks' caves provide the perfect environment for the molds and spores that give Love Tree Farm cheese its character. While these clouds of microbes spook health inspectors, they give life to Mary's cheese.

In Europe, raw-milk cheeses are the pride of each country, crafted to reflect centuries-old regional traditions. In an effort to ensure that these raw-milk cheeses are safe, the European Union has established guidelines, requires training in best practices, and sends inspectors to visit cheese-making facilities to ensure food safety and quality. Defending raw cheeses to the European Union, French agronomists credited the economic and cultural value of flavor: "The interaction between indigenous raw-milk microflora and starter bacteria are extremely important in the ripening process and subsequent flavor and texture of the cheese. Raw milk cheeses (Swiss, Manchego, Raclette and Saint-Paulin) develop their characteristic flavor sooner and the flavor is stronger, richer, and more diverse (less uniform) than that of the same cheeses made from pasteurized milk. The diversity that comes from raw milk is a direct consequence of variation in the conditions of milk harvesting and transformation. This diversity is sought by both the producers and the consumers because it is a special feature of traditional cheeses." After much debate, the EU voted to sanction raw-milk cheeses.

"What most people don't understand is that pasteurization is no magic bullet," Mary told me. "Milk and whey contain competing bacteria. Left in its natural state, the health-promoting bacteria will preside over the harmful bacteria."

The USDA is currently considering even more restrictive laws in cheese production. The existing sixty-day rule was premised on the belief that bacteria become inactive after that time, but back in the 1940s many of the more dangerous pathogens had not yet been identified. The biggest concern is listeria—but most outbreaks have been traced to deli meats and raw poultry, not to raw-milk cheese. Most health-related issues with cheese are the result of improper handling and storage after the cheese leaves the dairy. Further restrictions on raw-milk cheeses beyond the sixty-day rule would be devastating for the entire artisan-cheese industry. "We're all pretty worried about this," Mary said.

"No other cheese tastes like mine, and none of mine ever really taste the same," Mary said. "Each wheel is different because each sheep is different and the flavor will also depend on where the sheep graze. The cheese made in the spring will not be the same in autumn, because the sheep are eating different grasses, even though I haven't altered the recipe. Finally, our caves are the perfect environment for aging: damp and cool, just right for the beneficial microbes that transform each wheel into something special."

Like many artisan cheesemakers, Mary is constantly being inspected. "It's disruptive, and I really don't understand why. I pasteurize my milk for fresh cheeses and age the others for sixty days or more," she told me as we headed through the prairie flowers toward her caves. "Instead of spending so much time and energy monitoring artisans, wouldn't it make more sense to establish raw-milk-cheese standards and train people in best practices? The EU has created directives that all raw cheesemakers must follow. These represent a collective agreement and methodology for assuring the safety of Europe's raw dairy products. And they protect the art of making good cheese."

I followed Mary into her cave that sunny afternoon. Damp and eerily dark, deeply silent, it smelled of wet earth, hay, and cream. As my eyes adjusted to the dimness, I took in the shelves lined with rows of cheese—rough, uneven, and brown or ashy orbs, some streaked with tiny pinpoints of red, lacy mold, others burnished gold—all created by this artist. "In France, they understand the value of microscopic life," Mary said. "They even have a silver spoon designed for scraping off and eating the mites from Mimolette."

In the dim, drippy quiet, I could feel the beat of my own heart match the pulse of so much earthly life. Is this what scares us most about bacteria? Is it the mystery of decay? Does pasteurizing away all the microbial activity separate me from this vibrant community? As Mary and I emerged back out into the soft afternoon, light gilded the tall grasses, waving in the breeze. Sheep bleated and the dogs barked in answer and a flock of schoolkids frolicked after that bottle-fed lamb.

In Love Tree's cheeses Mary extends to us the wonderment of diversity, the range of tastes and textures she shepherds through her craft and knowledge. She is meshed in the ecology of the farm, the prairie grasses, the sheep, the guard dogs, and the magical microbial activity in those caves. The cheeses Mary offers at the farmers' markets are all part of a glorious loop, a network that supports and nurtures these relationships. Every week, when I see Mary and taste her cheese, I connect with her, the sheep, her land, the life in her caves. Places are made through human practices. Our cheesemakers are weaving together the biophysical, cultural, and economic senses of locale that resonate through every encounter I have with Mary Falk and Love Tree Farm cheese.

When my father was ill and could no longer swallow, he still liked the smell of the "stinky cheese" from Mary's farm that I'd tuck into my carry-on for the flight back to New Jersey. Though he could no longer help me as I chopped and sizzled dinner for him and my mom, he'd watch and comment from his wheelchair. He took great delight in this chair, the latest model, and he'd zigzag down the street with his small white terrier mutt, Bandit, on a leash, waving to neighbors and annoying delivery drivers and those harried commuters dashing to get to their New York trains. My dad had already been "grounded" several years earlier, no longer able to fly or hang out with other amateur pilots at the tiny airport where he'd once kept his plane—but he still loved speed and movement.

His was a slow and frustrating lung disease and he battled it with admirable dignity and characteristic wit. One night, he fell off his bed and we called "the squad." But he perked up as soon as he heard the siren, and when the EMTs arrived he greeted each one by name, offering coffee. "How 'bout a Scotch?" he asked. No matter his pain, he was happy they'd "dropped in."

Through his last year, he'd bravely rally then slide— seem stable and better, and then sink very low again, unable to sleep, unable to talk. All through this ordeal my mother remained very much present, attentive, and gracious, managing the children, grandchildren, relatives, friends, neighbors, and business associates who all flowed through the front door, eager to be with him.

Ten years later, I still long to have been with him the morning he took his last breath. We'd just talked on the phone, my sister holding a family album and turning the pages as he named each child, grandchild, sister, and brother-in-law, one by one, page by page. I should have known he was saying good-bye.

Later that afternoon, I got the call at the Land School, where my junior-high students were celebrating the last day of class with a picnic and games in the fields. I stood in June's hazy sun, prairie grasses pulsing, the wind rustling, bugs buzzing. While a fly lazily circled my forehead, I focused on the words "your father is dead." For an eternal instant, all the whirring, hopping, and chirping ceased; the great world stopped spinning. And then—and then—I could take a breath.

The economic assets of terroir shine through in buttermaking creameries, providing jobs at small processing facilities and a market for grass-fed milk from nearby farms. Take Hope Creamery. The sweet tangy flavor of its butter caught the attention of Lucia Watson in a butter tasting she held for the cooks at her restaurant. It contains none of the ingredients found in most commercial butters—no stabilizers, dried milk, or annatto, a natural yellow dye—and along with its flavor, its higher butterfat content makes it especially useful in piecrusts, croissants, and cakes.

Like so many creameries in Steele County, Minnesota, Hope stood as a testament to the hard work of the state's dairy cooperatives, dating back to the 1920s, when the region produced more butter than any in the country. Hope Creamery hit maximum production in the 1980s, but by the end of the century, its volume had been cut by two-thirds. In early 2000, Hope was put up for sale.

Victor Mrotz bought Hope in 2001, for a lot of good reasons. He wanted to raise his two kids in the place he loved and had grown up in; he was ready to leave his nine-to-five job in St. Paul and the commute to a suburb. He knew that the economic future of the town relied on reviving the creamery: "Hope Creamery is a big part of this place. Right after we moved back, an older gentleman came up to me to tell me he met his wife of fifty years at a town meeting in the creamery." The second floor of the plant was once the town hall, too.

"Hope was infamous when I was a teenager, a place with two bars and a grocery store. Now it's just two bars. It's gotten better or worse depending on your perspective," Mrotz joked.

A solid guy with a thick, gray ponytail pulled tight off his broad forehead, Victor is straight talking and humble, but unabashedly boastful about his butter. "Our butter is better than anything coming from France and Vermont because we use the highest-quality milk from farms down the street and we deliver it the same week it's made. It doesn't sit around in a warehouse. And unlike corporate butter producers, we don't freeze it to hold when the price drops, then release for sale when it rises; temperature fluctuations affect flavor. That's why you can actually taste the difference."

And that difference in this butter's flavor, churned from the fresh milk of pasture-raised cows and delivered quickly to stores and restaurants, is the reason its sales have skyrocketed. This means jobs for residents, a market for the nearby dairy farms, and sales for local stores and restaurants. In "Finding Food in Farm Country," economist Ken Meter calculates that every dollar spent on local food returns four dollars to the local economy.

When Mrotz bought Hope, the hundred-year-old business employed two people and sold about thirty thousand pounds of salted butter a year to a few local grocers. Mrotz began making deliveries in his wife's old green Volvo 240 station wagon. "I'd load it up in the early morning, put a quilt over the case of butter in the back of the car and take off. The first time I drove up to the Twin Cities, I had four cases and brought home none. Pretty soon it got to the point where we had to take the seats out of the car to make room for the cases; then I bought a truck, and I thought we'd never be able to pay for it. But six months later, we had to buy another one, a bigger one.

"Lucia's Restaurant's commitment to Hope was our leg into the business," he said. Within the next fifteen years, Hope Creamery grew from two employees to twelve, and now produces about three hundred thousand pounds of butter a year. Land O'Lakes, for comparison, produces about one million tons per year.

When the Lunds & Byerlys stores approached Hope Creamery, they asked Mrotz to use one of their distributors to make their ordering and delivery easier. He balked. A middleman would take too large a cut of the profits. But more importantly, Mrotz insists that his butter is handled properly and that he is there to answer questions and address concerns right away. "The chefs and grocers I work with are independent businesspeople; they want to work with other independent businesses; they like the trust and accountability," he said. "Most of my deals are sealed with a handshake." So he offered to also deliver locally produced milk, eggs, and meat, thus supporting wider distribution for his neighbors, too.

In an industry that prides itself on consistency, artisanal butter shines for its variety. Its flavors and colors reflect the changes in the milk and cream as the cows move through the season. In the summer, their diet of grass brightens the butter to a deep yellow, and in the winter, when the cows eat hay, the butter is a paler golden hue.

Hope Creamery's milk, from nearby dairies, is trucked into Hope's brick building and pasteurized with low heat for minimal impact. Hope processes about five thousand pounds of butter a week, compared to huge operations that churn out four hundred thousand to a million pounds of butter daily. To do so, operations like Land O'Lakes source milk from across the globe and process it quickly at very high temperatures. This process, while less expensive, flattens the flavor.

Gene Kruckeberg has been working for Hope since 1958, and oversees the buttermaking process. A quiet, slim, precise man, he walked me through the evolution of cold milk into rich butter. Shouting over the clanking and sounds of swooshing milk, he explained how the cream is skimmed off and pumped into the nine-hundred-gallon churn to mix with well water. As the small curds of butter begin to separate and become heavier, the churn turns more slowly. Then the buttermilk is drained. It's thin and watery, quite different from the thick, cultured product on supermarket shelves.

We drank a coffee mug of it, icy cold; it's sweet, refreshing, and light. "It's too bad we can't sell this in our markets," he said. The USDA regulates fluid milk differently than butter, and selling it would require Hope to invest in equipment for bottling and storage. Instead Hope sells its buttermilk to animal-feed manufacturers.

Kruckeberg intently watched and listened for sounds that gave clues as to the butter's progress. "As soon as the water has worked into the butter, and it's become solid, you've got to quit rotating it, otherwise the butter gets sticky. You have to keep an eye on it, you just can't walk away and come back," he told me. "I make sure to flush the milk solids out because they'll give the butter a stale flavor and they'll also burn when a cook goes to make a sauté. Large manufacturers have continuous churns; the cream goes in one end and comes out as a ribbon of butter. It's fast," Kruckeberg admitted, "but it's a process that can alter the texture and butter's clean taste."

To test the butterfat content, Kruckeberg removed a small tin cup of butter and weighed it on an antique scale. Using a blowtorch, he melted the butter and brought it to a boil to evaporate the water. Then he weighed the clarified butter and calculated the result, aiming for 80 percent butterfat. If it was too low and the butter was too moist, he would keep churning.

Gene added salt to a batch of salted butter and a culture to an unsalted batch. Years ago, butter was salted to add flavor as well as help prevent spoilage. But salt also masked the flavor of a butter that was beginning to turn sour. The tang in cultured butter hearkens back to a time when butter was churned from the cream collected through several milkings and had begun to sour. These days, because commercial butter must be made from pasteurized cream, which does not sour gently, a culture is added to give it the distinctive, slightly fermented note. Hope also makes a super-rich 85 percent milkfat butter for commercial bakers. It is the key component in flaky croissants, scones, and pound cakes.

Once the churning was finished, Kruckeberg and his crew dipped their arms into a trough of water and sanitizer before scooping up great hunks of butter by hand to plop into the old-fashioned wrapping machine's square mouth. A scent like that of buttered popcorn wafted through the air as each pound of butter was pressed and wrapped into a waxed-paper block and stamped with Hope's simple label.

To Hope's residents—creamery employees and several farmers—Mrotz is a hero. "It's too strong a word," he said. "Heroes are people who run into burning buildings. I ran into a falling-down building." Now that that building has been renovated and cleaned up, there are plans to refurbish the second floor, too, for community events.

To area chefs and home cooks, Hope butter is the gold standard. Mrotz distributes his salted, unsalted, organic, and high-fat butter no further than a seventy-five-mile radius. "Beyond that is too far away to be considered local.

We make what we know we can sell and retailers move it out right away."

Kruckeberg is training younger workers in the butter-making trade, showing them what to listen for, how to tell when the butterfat is right, and how to wrap pounds efficiently. These are skills no calculator can mimic, no computer can accurately reflect.

Mrotz is awed by Hope's success. "What amazes me is that people are willing to invest time and energy and spend a little more on a local product, to care where it comes from. They could easily go to Cub and buy butter for about half the price. We're fortunate to be in this place at this time." Mrotz is a rural entrepreneur, ecological steward, sustainable developer, and local citizen who supports conscientious farmers. He's invested in a rural locale that has regained its significance and relevance.

In my kitchen, I keep an old-fashioned butter dish on the counter, just as my grandmother did, so that my Hope butter stays soft and spreadable and doesn't develop that "ice-boxy" taste. It works wonders in mashed potatoes, roasted sweet potatoes, and piecrusts.

You could say that butter put Hope back on the map.

TURKEY

When I think of my New Jersey family's Thanksgiving feasts, it's hard to recall the actual taste of the turkey itself, but the presentation was always spectacular. A big, bronzed hero, the turkey was carried to the table by my dad on a silver platter, and met by the diners' applause.

Roasting the turkey, however, drummed up family drama. Every year, my mom tested a different method she'd discovered in *Good Housekeeping* or *Gourmet*. She'd rise at 5:00 a.m. to preheat the oven and debate my aunt on whether to stuff the bird or bake the stuffing alongside. The roasting methods varied from year to year as she tried to keep the white meat moist while the dark meat finished cooking. One year, she draped the turkey with cheesecloth doused in butter, but it clung too tightly and tore off the crisped skin; the next, she shrouded the bird in aluminum foil that trapped in too much moisture, so the skin didn't brown and the meat was soft. Then she tried roasting the turkey in a brown grocery bag that caught fire and set off the smoke detector. Firemen, axes raised, stormed into the kitchen. (Dad gave them all a beer.) And when she tried Butterball's internally basted turkey, it overcooked because the pop-up thermometer didn't pop up.

My grandmother took charge of the gravy, but her decisions did not go unquestioned. She insisted on making a roux, whisking flour into the hot pan drippings before adding stock. My mother argued that cornstarch gave a glossier finish and lighter result. They both agreed to add a splash of Kitchen Bouquet, however, to bring the pale stuff "up to snuff."

But for all the jostling about the oven temperature, stuffing, gravy, and carving, no one ever talked about the turkey, the animal, itself. We didn't consider that this was once a live creature that ran and pecked and clawed the earth. We did not ask about the breed, where it came from, how it was raised or slaughtered. I learned from my dad how to carve breast meat and separate the leg from the thigh to keep the "pope's nose" for myself. But I understood nothing about the animal we were cooking, eating, and celebrating. I'm surprised, because as a kid, I was the one always asking annoying questions. Once I finally had a kitchen of my own, though, my previous lack of curiosity about Thanksgiving turkeys caught up with me.

One of my first jobs after our move from New Jersey to Minnesota was with a marketing firm, working on a promotion campaign for a large turkey producer. My first week on the job, I toured the processing and packing plant, my first glimpse into how my Thanksgiving turkeys came to my table.

The turkeys arrived at the plant in stacked cages, trucked in from Concentrated Animal Feeding Operations (CAFOs), where workers moved with efficiency and precision. Men in face masks and rubber aprons snatched each turkey from its cage and hooked its feet onto a conveyor belt so that it hung upside down. Its throat was slashed before the turkey moved along to vats of boiling water and an enclosed drum tumbler to be defeathered. A line of women yanked out the guts and placed the necks, gizzards, and hearts into the cavity of the whole bird to seal in plastic bags. The other birds moved on to be cut into pieces, then Cryovac sealed. Lit with gloomy, flickering fluorescent lights, the plant smelled of eye-burning, nose-singeing chemical cleanser. When running 24/7 at full tilt, the plant could process one hundred fifty thousand turkeys per day.

Not far from this turkey plant, the Land School raises chickens primarily for eggs. But one year, inspired by a neighboring farm, the junior-high students took on a "poultry project," raising and butchering chickens to sell to the school community. Using funds from bake sales, they purchased a "poultry tractor." This rolling wire-mesh barrel allowed the chickens to peck at fresh grass while protecting them from coyotes and raccoons. Michael, the project leader, decided poulet rouge chickens were the best choice and organized classmates and parents to help with the slaughter. We set a cutting board on an old tree stump, put a huge kettle of water to boil over an open fire, and readied the garden hose and plastic bags.

It was a bright, moist, cool spring morning, with the lilacs just out. I won't tell you that chopping off a chicken's head is not bloody and unsettling. But the students gathered around Michael as he grabbed the chicken and clasped its wings closely to his chest, while our farmer, Andy, tied its feet together and then slipped a bright orange cone over its head. Michael held the bird steady while Andy slit its throat, then laid its neck on the cutting board and with one swift cut removed the head. Working in a line, we submerged the birds in hot water and plucked out feathers, so that they no longer resembled their former fluttering, squawking selves, but packaged supermarket chickens. Michael reached into each with one hand to gently fish out the guts and heart, and then set the body into a tub of ice water.

We worked quietly, music wafting from an iPod speaker,

the mood somber and focused. The afternoon began to get chilly, and the competing emotions of thrill and terror dissipated in the slanting sun. That night, we grilled chicken skewers over an open fire and no one resisted or protested; in fact, ironically, the whole process and our physical exhaustion seemed to add a certain savor to the meal.

The students had done their research into best practices for slaughtering poultry. They'd found independent lab results showing that poultry slaughtered outside, using the proper methods, is actually cleaner and safer than the poultry slaughtered inside. Yet the US government literature states that unenclosed slaughtering places are unsanitary, and that fresh air and sunshine are the source of dangerous pathogens. The experience these students had, raising and slaughtering chickens, seemed to dispute the government's guidelines.

They knew these chickens, named them, chased them in play, fed them food scraps with their hands, and seemed to know what made the birds happy. The Land School, with its generous apple tree and waving sunflowers, is an aesthetically and aromatically pleasing place. The animals thrive in the open air and sunshine—nature's number-one sanitizer. The dangerous diseases that spread so quickly in close quarters don't stand a chance when animals live freely outside, where they're not breathing in the fecal particulate that irritates their respiratory membranes and causes infections. They get plenty of exercise, so their muscles are strong and their meat is firm. Their diets are naturally healthy, not laced with antibiotics, chemicals, or fertilized feedstuffs.

There is nothing ugly or repugnant about this kind of slaughter. In raising and being responsible for the chickens we grilled that night, the students had engaged in the entire process. There was reverence; the sacrifice had profound emotional ramifications. And the chickens had played an important role on the farm before they became dinner. They ate pesky bugs and kitchen scraps, and contributed their waste to compost, which enriched the soil that grew the lettuces and peas for our meal.

In accepting total responsibility for this dinner, we shifted from being eaters reliant on unknown, unseen entities that use troubling mechanized processes to participants in the drama of life and death. When we took part in the killing we were no longer observers, but responsible actors. I suspect that this experience will help inform the major decisions these students will make throughout their lives; it certainly has in mine. Those of us at the Land School that day will never look at packaged chicken or turkey in the grocery store the same way again.

My world didn't end when my father died or when, shortly after, our first son left for college, followed by the next and the next. One by one, they packed their clothes and cleats, left their trophies, yearbooks, concert tickets, and posters of rock stars, soccer and lacrosse heroes taped to the walls: their stuff, my memories.

It wasn't the rambling empty house, but the empty rooms in my head and heart that haunted me. I missed the long phone calls with my dad; the endless sports practices, teachers' meetings, plays and games and music performances, graduations, and parties; the screen door banging with friends coming and going, and driving carpool and eavesdropping when no one thought I was listening. I missed those mornings when I'd wake before sunrise just to savor the quiet, the whole house tucked in sleep, breathing in unison.

But then what happened? Our third son harvested his memories of sailing with my dad off the coast of New Jersey to create a college essay; our eldest son, inspired by my mother's volunteer years with her town's ambulance, tacked on part-time work as an EMT and firefighter to his teaching day job. Our middle son, who found his voice debating politics at family gatherings, teaches high school social studies and is in an improv troupe. The empty rooms, stripped of those fading posters, have been repainted for visiting friends and colleagues. And we say "yes" to more dinners, plays, movies, lectures, and gallery openings.

I won't pretend it's been easy to witness each son cross the threshold into adulthood. But when they come home, and they do come home, they bring their bright shining stories and crushing disappointments, their views of the world's future and their place in it.

And, as much as I miss my father, we still engage in long rambling conversations, just not over the phone, but when I'm off on a run. My brother, I've come to realize, is a very good listener, having inherited my missing patience gene. In my grief, I was numb and detached—but I also allowed others to step in and bring more of themselves to the glorious banquet of our shared lives.

We all come to the table to savor, and the quality and variety of turkey meat depends on the breed of the turkey and how it's raised. Brandon Severson, a high-school senior in Good Thunder, Minnesota, sells his heritage breed of turkey through the Wedge Co-op in Minneapolis. Severson, a member of 4-H since grade school, is a linebacker on his school's varsity football team. When we met on his farm, he was leaning against his pen's fence, chatting at the birds while texting on his cell phone. Severson is near six feet tall, with freckles, a shy smile, and the reserve of most teenage boys—until he starts talking about his birds. He's putting the money he earns from these turkeys into a college fund and his goal is medical school. He wants to return to his hometown as a doctor. His younger sister, Nora, raises chickens for meat and eggs.

As far as turkeys go, Severson's black Spanish are good-looking creatures. Their glossy, dark-green feathers gleam as they strut and gobble and rush to the edge of the pen when Severson calls. "People think turkeys are dumb, but they're responsive and I am pretty sure they know what's up. They're very social creatures." Severson cleared the fence with a leap, scattering the birds, to show me how friendly they are. "When I gobble at them, they'll gobble back." He started strutting, sticking his neck out and high-stepping. Pretty soon the turkeys gathered close to him again. "One of the turkeys bonded with our dog and followed him around; another seemed to attach to a chicken and the chicken to her. That chicken would hitch a ride on the turkey's back," Severson said.

Severson's turkeys are closer to "wild" birds, smaller than commercial turkeys. "Commercial broad-breasted whites are bred to have big breasts and small legs. They're top heavy and their legs are so short, they often topple over; they have an odd, off-kilter, waddling gait," Severson said.

"The gene pool for commercial turkeys has become so narrow that vets are noticing heart problems, leg failure, and suppressed immune systems," he continued. "If you don't have a varied gene pool the animal will have real problems. Industrial turkeys could be wiped out by a virus or stress—it's one of the things we covered in bio class."

This encounter with Brandon dates back to 2013. In 2015, avian flu wiped out nearly five million industrially raised turkeys in Minnesota (and a total of nine million nationwide).

Commercial birds are fed a mix of GMO corn and soy, laced with antibiotics to prevent diseases that are ripe in unsanitary conditions, and they grow to up to forty pounds. "They literally eat themselves to death and are so heavy and lopsided they can't fly." Severson's turkeys could take off at any time but choose not to. They forage for grubs and bugs and dine on the corn and grain he mixes specially for them.

To be registered as "heritage," the turkeys must be able to breed naturally and grow slowly, so their meat is firmer, darker, and richer tasting than that of commercial birds. Slow Food selected heritage turkeys like Severson's black Spanish for Ark of Taste, an initiative to protect heritage and endangered foods threatened by agricultural standardization. By creating awareness and driving demand, Ark of Taste is attempting to ensure these foods will remain in our kitchens.

"Heritage turkeys can be tricky to cook," Severson said. "They are small, and lean, and can dry out quickly." Brining overnight in a solution of saltwater, peppercorns, and herbs helps to keep them moist and tender. "We drape our turkey with lots of bacon, and baste like crazy."

Toward the middle of November, Severson trucks his turkeys to a Minnesota-certified slaughterhouse about thirty miles from his home. It's a much smaller plant than the corporate processor I once toured. Unlike that huge operation, where the caged birds are often left waiting outside for several days, this processor receives Severson's turkeys immediately. He's one of the luckier growers in the country.

Processing and distributing meat is the biggest link missing from our local food chain. Many independent plants have either been absorbed by larger operations or closed. Minnesota raises the most turkeys in the country and is home to Jennie-O, the world's second-largest turkey producer, now owned by Hormel. Jennie-O was founded in Willmar, Minnesota, in 1940 by Earl B. Olson and named for his daughter. In the 1990s it was the first company to market cuts of turkey meat the same way pork and beef producers packaged and marketed their cuts of meat. The Turkey Store brand, an innovative marketing move, was soon copied by Cargill Value Added Meat's Honeysuckle White and Shady Brook Farms brands. But many of Minnesota's turkeys are processed in North Carolina, where labor is cheaper and transportation time to the dense urban centers of the East Coast is shorter.

Failing to find a turkey from his family's farm in his hometown of Cannon Falls, Minnesota, John Peterson created the first farm-to-turkey store, Ferndale Market. "When I returned home after college, I searched the local grocery stores and not one sold our turkeys." He had not known that his family's turkeys were processed in plants back east, where state of origin is not added to the label. So it was impossible to tell where the turkeys sold in the Cannon Falls stores had been raised.

With his wife, Erica, Peterson created a market that carries his family's turkeys as well as foods from neighboring farms. Ferndale Market, named for John's parents—Fern and Dale—has become the area's source for hearth-baked breads, artisan pastas, premium sauces, preserves, milk, eggs, meat, and turkey from local producers. Now in his early forties, Peterson retains the blonde good looks of his college self and the upbeat energy and grace of the athlete he still is. "As soon as we opened, we were astounded by the variety of the food grown and produced right here," he said. "Before the store, no one could find these things unless they went to each of those farms."

By providing this community with a source for local food, Ferndale Market has become a gathering place, offering cooking classes and seasonal events. The store's Thanksgiving festival draws hundreds of people with music, crafts, sampling, and, of course, the sale of its Thanksgiving birds.

Peterson Farm's white Holland turkeys, an old-fashioned breed, were made famous in Norman Rockwell's painting Freedom from Want. "We raise these birds humanely, without antibiotics or hormones, and they spend lots of time outside. We operate on a smaller scale and just can't get by with the dollar a pound commercial producers charge," Peterson said. "Our turkeys cost a little more, but people have never complained and they're pleased with the quality of turkey that comes from a farm that's nearby."

Ken Meter, an economist and journalist who covered the 1980s Farm Crisis for the Wall Street Journal, told me,

"If each of us in this region spent just five dollars per week buying food from a local farm, we'd generate a 20 percent increase in farm revenue. It's getting easier and easier to do this every year. But the barriers to meat processing are harder to crack than for other foods. Here's another reason we need to rethink the farm bill's system of farm support. Rather than make policy using abstract formulas, Washington policymakers should look to those who know the intricacies of a given region. Farm supports should not go to individual farmers, but to rural communities that can create their own credit base." This way, neighboring poultry farmers could work cooperatively to build plants that suit their needs, provide jobs, and keep money within a locale.

Meter is founder of Crossroads Resource Center, a nonprofit organization working with communities to foster democracy and local self determination and build capacity. Having grown up on a farm in rural Minnesota, Meter is an avid gardener and great cook. Dressed in blue jeans and fleece, his gray hair brushed back, he looks like he just stepped off a tractor. But in fact, every day he is planting ideas by speaking at organic farmers' conventions and consulting with city planners, politicians, and academics. With graphs and flip charts and spreadsheets, he's making the case for communities to support independent meat processors and distributors.

Throughout the region, older plants are facing a shrinking labor market and rising costs. Building new facilities is daunting, given health codes and regulatory barriers. Money is tight, and the economy is uncertain. Farmers have few processing options because the large, federally-inspected poultry plants won't take small quantities of birds. Doing so interrupts their production schedules, and their equipment is geared to standard-sized commercial turkeys, not the variations in size and weight of free-range turkeys.

Local, free-range poultry "is still a small niche," said Ron Barlet, who raises three thousand turkeys on his farm in Grimes, Iowa, and teaches in the local high school. "Now that the plant in town just closed, I have to drive my birds several hours away. It takes so much time, and the miles I cover will have to be reflected in a higher price. If it gets too hard, I'll quit altogether. It's the consumer who is going to miss out, because those free-range local turkeys and heritage chickens just won't be available anymore."

"No pun intended but this is a chicken-and-egg dilemma," said Arion Thiboumery, whose doctoral research at Iowa State's Leopold Center for Sustainable Agriculture inspired him to found the Niche Meat Processor Assistance Network, the most comprehensive stakeholder network in livestock agriculture. Energetic and articulate, with bright blue eyes and square-jawed good looks, Thiboumery might easily be mistaken for an investment banker or hedge-fund manager. And in fact, he's hoping that this fast-growing industry sector will attract "smart young Ivy Leaguers looking for an alternative to Wall Street." The afternoon we toured the Lorentz Meats processing plant in Cannon Falls, Minnesota, Thiboumery said, "Thanks to technology, we're connecting nationwide. We're sharing innovative solutions, best practices, alternative pricing structures, cost-structure spreadsheets, and all the practical tools for growth. The more we work on these issues collectively, the better off we'll all be." Take the new Valley View Poultry Processing, one of Iowa's two state-inspected processing plants, in the largely Amish town of Bloomfield. It's employing local women interested in part-time work and schoolteachers who want to earn income through the summer months. "These processors have to be nimble," Thiboumery said.

Callister Farm in West Concord, Minnesota, has brought the processing issue home. "My dad was adamant about not buying meat when you didn't know where it came from," Lori Callister told me one morning at her St. Paul Farmers' Market stall. "We never bought margarine or fast food, but we sure ate well." Plainspoken and thoughtful, her blue jeans rolled up and her blonde hair tied up in a bun, Lori is proud of her farm's role in advancing local food. She and her husband, Alan, began selling chickens and turkeys to their neighbors nearly twenty years ago and then started bringing the poultry to the farmers' markets. "We didn't realize how popular our meat would be. People are just now rediscovering clean, good-tasting meat."

Lori credits Thiboumery for his advice and encouragement when a certified USDA processor nearby closed down several years ago: "Arion helped us decide to expand. We really want to support local food and local producers." Now the Callisters employ six full-time people and process about one thousand chickens a week and sixteen hundred turkeys during the holidays for farmers' markets, restaurants, co-ops, and other institutions.

Further outstate, poultry farmers have begun sharing mobile poultry-processing units, or MPPUs. These slaughterhouses on wheels travel from farm to farm, processing poultry for a fee. Farmers can invite volunteers and CSA members to engage in the work. The farmer benefits from the free labor and volunteers learn about their meat. "It reminds me of my childhood, when we'd go to my grandparents' farm with all my relatives to butcher turkeys for Thanksgiving," said Florence Hastings, of Baldwin, Wisconsin. "Here we are, helping my daughter slaughter chickens for their CSA farm. But with its steel countertops, hot-water-pressurized sinks, and big tubs, this is easier and cleaner."

"Farmers need to link with cooks and eaters," said Lori Callister. "Many of our neighbors that produce commodities don't appreciate the relationships they have with their animals, the land, and their customers. They just keep everything separate." Callister Farm, Peterson Farm, and Brandon Severson cultivate these relationships.

Given the complexities of meat production, there's a lot to be said for becoming a vegetarian or vegan, a decision that releases one from engaging in the morally questionable aspects of agriculture. Yet many small farmers in our region will argue that a farm needs animals to complete the nutrient cycle and that those animals are going to die, regardless of timing. Doesn't it make sense to end their lives gracefully and with purpose?

In these small, diverse, and integrated operations, managing relationships is the key to success. "We're interested in producing good food that makes healthy, happy customers," said Lori. "One of the reasons we wanted to process our own turkeys is because that's always been embedded in farm life. It's part of the integral work of the farm, not a separate business."

When animals are conceived, birthed, and reared on a farm, then it makes sense to end their lives on the same farm, not in a distant processing facility. In a farm's choreography, turkeys help dispense with harmful pests by pecking at the ground outside and contribute manure for compost.

The Callisters offer butchering classes on their farm to help their customers connect directly with their food. It's a way to educate those customers and help them to appreciate the beautiful, healthy animals the Callisters have raised with such care. Historically, people, plants, and animals were not segregated. Their lives intertwined. The idea of slaughtering an animal that has a name and follows you around may seem difficult, but all life comes from the sacrifice of another life.

WILD RICE

One balmy autumn morning, as the maples tipped red, I drove north to Lake Chippewa, near Hayward, Wisconsin, to help Nick VanderPuy with the harvest at his "rice camp." Every late August through September, VanderPuy hauls in over two hundred pounds of green rice that he'll winnow into one hundred pounds of finished wild rice to sell and to stock his own larder. Wild rice is the region's most important food and central to Native American culture. It's indigenous, nutritious, versatile, and delicious. Important in both Native and European traditions, it's also been nettlesome, a source of conflict.

True wild rice isn't rice at all, but the kernel of a wild grass the Ojibwe call *manoomin*, meaning "good berry" or "good seed." In Ojibwe origin stories, a series of prophecies led the tribes from the Atlantic coast westward in search of food. "It was foretold that as the ice melted we were to move westward and food would be provided for us. That's what happened, when tribes moved into Minnesota, we found the food that grows on water," says White Earth elder Earl Hoagland. "*Manoomin* is a gift from the creator, and it's sacred. Since the beginning of time, this aquatic plant has been central to our ceremonies and a source of sustenance."

Wild rice contains about twice the amount of protein of brown rice and is far richer in vitamins than wheat, barley, oats, or rye. Because it stores well, it was the primary staple for the Ojibwe before the European settlers arrived, especially towards the end of winter, when game and fish were scarce. As wild rice cooks, it swells to about four times its original size, earning it the name "pocket money" among early traders, who realized a handful could feed a lot of hungry men. It continues to play a significant role as a staple in the Ojibwe diet and is always served at weddings and funerals. Wild rice is often cracked and boiled into a healing gruel for babies, the elderly, and the infirm.

To find VanderPuy's rice camp, I followed a rutted dirt road off the state highway, parked my car at a fallen tree, and hiked into a shade-dappled quiet that opened to the shore. An aluminum canoe rested near VanderPuy's faded-green army tent and campfire ring, strewn with dented aluminum pots. Mounds of what looked like grass clippings, piled on canvas tarps, drew flocks of diving red-winged blackbirds.

VanderPuy is a law-school dropout turned wilderness-hunting-and-fishing guide, freelance radio journalist, and substitute elementary-school teacher. He has been living off the land for the past thirty-five years: fishing; hunting venison, birds, and bear; and foraging berries and mushrooms. The most important element in his diet is his wild rice. He's a rangy, fierce-looking sixty-something, but despite his gnarly appearance, he weeps easily when recalling a conversation with his grandfather or a poignant moment with one of his sons.

I picked up a brown stalk from the matted pile of green rice and peeled back the spiky shaft to reveal a chartreuse grain that glowed in the sun. At the season's end, Vander-Puy will return to his home in Mellen, Wisconsin, to parch or roast the dried green rice in huge aluminum kettles over an open fire, and hull it in a rotating drum to remove the chaff. (In traditional ricing ceremonies, an adolescent male or young woman wearing special moccasins dances on top of the rice to the beat of a drum, crushing away the hull.) Finally, VanderPuy and his friends will winnow baskets of rice by tossing them in the air, sometimes near huge fans, to separate the lighter stalks and chaff from the heavier kernels.

On that morning, Lake Chippewa's sky-blue waters rippled to the edge of the waving, green rice field. The lake is the spring-fed source of the Chippewa River, which flows about one hundred eighty miles through northwestern and west-central Wisconsin to the Mississippi. Since the early

1900s the Wisconsin DNR and the Great Lakes Indian Fish and Wildlife Commission have protected this lake, and over forty-seven other lakes and five hundred miles of riverbeds, from development. Unlike many lakes to the south and east, Lake Chippewa remains unpolluted by lawn fertilizers, septic runoff, and motorboats, which churn up lake bottoms and leak gasoline.

VanderPuy handed me two long, tapered "rice knockers" he'd whittled from birch, to tap the rice into the canoe. As soon as we pushed offshore, VanderPuy dug into a tiny leather pouch he keeps on his belt and sprinkled tobacco into the water, as an offering. We entered the tall, spiky grass, and VanderPuy stood up in the stern to pole, using an old curtain rod with a metal "duckbill" on its end to grip the lake's mucky bottom. It took a while to get the hang of harvesting, bending the grass stalks over the boat with one knocker, then, with the other, gently tapping the top of the seed head. Each tap sent a rain of husks, spiders, and tiny wriggling rice worms onto my lap. "Careful, they bite," VanderPuy laughed.

As the sun arced across the turquoise sky, we glided through the tall swishing stalks, our tap-tapping echoed by other ricers bent to their own music, the plunk of jumping fish, and an occasional honk of wild geese. "The Indians know how you follow the dictates of dreams and honor the spirits," wrote Thomas Vennum Jr., an anthropologist and musicologist who studies Native American drum ceremonies.

Wild rice is so significant to the Ojibwe that the lands with the best rice stands, including Big Rice Lake, Lake Winnibigoshish, and Nett Lake are reserved for ricing by Native Americans alone. The land beyond reservation borders was transferred to the US government, but the rice was not. In a 1837 treaty, the Ojibwe ceded nearly fourteen million acres of Wisconsin and Minnesota but retained "the privilege of hunting, fishing, and gathering the wild rice . . . included in the territory ceded." Federal and Supreme Court cases, including the 1990 Mille Lacs case, have upheld the rights of the Ojibwe to traditional land use outside the reservations.

Only residents of Minnesota and Wisconsin can obtain a license to harvest wild rice. On reservations, like White Earth, wild rice generates an important income and residents enter a lottery that allocates permits. The White Earth Land Recovery Project, in Callaway, Minnesota, processes rice at a small mill using old, creaky equipment, some of it handmade: a 1940s Clipper fanning mill, a handmade thrasher, a set of banged-up 1980s metal parching drums, a 1950s gravity table. In White Earth's community, ricing is a vocation as well as a way of life. "I grew up ricing," says Joe Fineday, a tribal elder. "You get to visit people you haven't seen for a whole year, because just about everyone goes ricing. We call the season Wild Rice Moon, *Manomminike Giizis*. And at the end, we hold a feast to honor the Great Spirit."

Some fifty years ago, Minnesota farmers started planting a domesticated variety of wild rice in flooded paddies. Hard, black, and shiny, paddy rice is nothing like the true wild rice, a fact more apparent in the kitchen than on the stalk. Paddy rice, sold in supermarkets as well as bait shops and gas stations, requires a good hour or more of simmering before the kernels open up. It's tough, chewy, and relatively flavorless—but it sells for about a third of the price of real wild rice, which is a variegated brownish black and cooks in about twenty minutes. The flavors of the real thing carry the notes of the cedar forest and woodsmoke from roasting.

To most Ojibwe, the idea of cultivating wild rice is anathema; it implies interrupting the natural cycles of the rice. Harvesting the rice by hand with poles or knockers helps reseed the crop because many of the grains miss the canoe and land in the water. But intentionally sowing rice would imply taking control of this process and risk offending Mother Earth.

What is meant by a "sacred food?" In my family's Christian tradition, we consume the host as the Body of Christ, but of course I'd never serve those wafers at a dinner party, or Easter dinner; they are distributed only in church. For the Ojibwe, however, wild rice is both an ordinary staple as well as a ceremonial dish that weaves members into the tribe's history, ecology, and community. How could it be anything but sacred?

Wild rice grows only in this particular watershed, lying

within the ancestral homelands of the Anishinaabeg—the Odawa, Ojibwe, and Algonquin First Nations in Ontario—whose languages all reflect Algonquin origins. The word Anishinaabeg means "good people"—those on the path given by the Creator, *gichi-manidoo*. Ojibwe scholar Basil Johnston explains the name in a creationist context: the Anishinaabeg are "Beings Made Out of Nothing" or "Spontaneous Beings," created by divine breath and made of flesh and spirit.

The Anishinaabeg, writes Robin Kimmerer, "understand a world in which all beings were given a gift, a gift that simultaneously engenders a responsibility to the world. Water's gift is its role as life sustainer and its duties are manifold: making plants grow, creating homes for fish and mayflies." As VanderPuy's canoe coasted through the tall grass, we dipped our hands into the water to cool our necks and sip directly from the lake. VanderPuy recited the Ojibwe thank-you (*miigwech*) prayer:

We offer our prayers, tobacco, and our hearts.
Thank you for the Grandfathers and Grandmothers of yesterday, today, and tomorrow.
Thank you spirits of the winds, water, fire, and earth.
Thank you spirits of the north, east, south, and west.
Please help us to live a good life.

"Our work now is to protect our land, our water, our food," says Winona LaDuke, Native American activist, former Green Party vice-presidential candidate, and founder of the White Earth Land Recovery Project. "We won't allow what the Creator gave the Anishinaabeg to become a profit-making enterprise for others," she told me one sunny afternoon on the shore of Madeline Island, near the Bad River Reservation's rice sloughs. Tall, strong, dark-haired and handsome, LaDuke has been working to reintroduce healthy indigenous food to the Native American diet, overrun with cheap, processed American junk food. She helped found Native Harvest, a co-op that harvests and processes wild rice and hominy corn using traditional methods, for sale online and through retail outlets. While she recognizes the potential for Native American food businesses, she is adamant that their practices "honor the earth"—a phrase she bestowed on her nonprofit, whose mission is to create awareness and support for Native American environmental issues. "In the 1950s University of Minnesota researchers embarked on a mission to domesticate *manoomin* and 'create' strains of rice for cultivation," she said. "That crossed the line."

Ervin Oelke, a University of Minnesota scientist, began the process, using germplasm collected from twenty-four natural wild-rice lakes to create a hybrid strain that ripens simultaneously and has a harder hull, so that it is both predictable and easy to harvest. It has been cultivated in paddies, flooded fields that can be drained to allow access with a combine. By 1968, Minnesota's paddy wild rice had become a commodity, mass marketed and packaged by Uncle Ben's, Green Giant, and General Foods.

In 1977, the Minnesota legislature designated wild rice the official state grain and the U of M received state funds to aggressively promote the domesticated version, which soon glutted the market. In 1995, California's NorCal company received a patent for a hybrid wild rice, laying ownership to this Ojibwe food. By the early 1990s California had become the largest producer of cultivated wild rice in the world, dominating the market so that much of the rice sold in Minnesota was shipped in from the West Coast. Native Americans were offended by the Ojibwe images California and Minnesota corporations used on packages of this cultivated rice, and fought back. In 1988, Minnesota passed a labeling law requiring cultivated rice to indicate its source, but the statute doesn't apply in California. The vast majority of the California exports to Minnesota continues to be sold with deceptive packaging.

Later, when the U of M sought options to genetically engineer wild rice, the tribes were able to craft legislation that prohibits the introduction of any genetically engineered wild-rice paddy stands without a full environmental-impact assessment. "We Ojibwe are determined to protect this sacred plant's DNA from being exposed to public use," LaDuke said.

Wild rice is a cash crop for dozens of Minnesota farmers, who produce about $40 million worth of paddy rice in a good year. But California has an easier time growing paddy rice, and since they do so more efficiently, they beat Minnesota farmers on price. The biggest issue for Minnesota's paddy-rice farmers is the region's wind, which knocks ripened rice off the plant and often reduces yield by 50 percent. Ironically, the wind is great for real wild rice, since it reseeds the crop.

Raymie Porter, a University of Minnesota researcher in Grand Rapids, is breeding strains of wild rice that don't fall off the plant as easily as natural wild rice does. Although he uses a genetic map, he contends that he is doing what others have done for centuries: "It's traditional plant breeding."

But most Native Americans disagree. "Wild rice is not like wheat," says Jill Doerfler, who grew up on the White Earth Reservation and now teaches in an Ojibwe-immersion elementary school. "Our Western society has a hard time understanding that other societies have different values. We are not concerned with crop uniformity and yields. Our wild rice should not be scrutinized or altered in any way. Our view is just as valid and just as useful as the Western view of agriculture."

Years ago, a friend who saw me struggling to carry one of our toddlers on my shoulders commented, "You look like you have your dad on your back." And I answered, "Oh, you are right in innumerable ways." Each of our sons, to varying degrees, resembles my father. Most strikingly, they all have his clear blue eyes and bright smile; most movingly, they help continue my father's favorite family traditions. And they've inspired new rituals as well. Our holiday solstice fire near Lake of the Isles always illuminates our shared prayers for past trespasses and aspirations for the coming year. And when each of our sons turned thirteen, he and Kevin took a "coming-of-age" kayak camping trip through the Apostle Islands.

Recently, Kevin refinished the drop-leaf table from my grandmother's home and reread the legend she left in the side drawer: crafted in 1860, the table has served in family dining rooms and kitchens through five generations. It will go to one of our sons, and to his son or daughter. This remarkably beautiful, sturdy, and useful table is so like my grandmother—a reminder of her values, her approach to life.

Our sons have surrounded themselves with strong women as friends and partners, women who dream big dreams, cultivate good close friends, and who enjoy my company as much as I treasure my time with them. On the evenings we make dinner together, they'll talk about their work and play, whether or not it involves my sons. Long after the dishes are put away, we sip tea and talk about movies, and politics, and how to make a great piecrust. These women are straightforward, warm, independent, smart, resourceful, and optimistic. They have questions and I am now old enough to know not to answer them. But I love those endless questions anyway—the need that inspires them, as we forage for goodness in our lives.

The debates over wild rice's "sacred nature" are coming to a head across the Lake Superior region, with proposed sulfide mining in Michigan's Keweenaw Bay, the northern regions of Wisconsin, and the Boundary Waters of Minnesota. Mining proponents seek to rewrite laws to allow for sulfide discharge into pristine wetlands, streams, and rivers, all of which ultimately drain into Lake Superior. The resulting sulfuric acid changes the pH of the water system and liberates heavy metals, including mercury, from rock. Despite having spent more than $20 million on their projects, the mining companies have yet to receive a clean bill of health from the Environmental Protection Agency.

Wild rice is like the proverbial canary in the coal mine. It will not grow if the water is out of balance. When we lose the wild rice, we lose much of the aquatic and wildlife, as well as the Native Americans who depend on it. There's no doubt that the clean water is critical to the region's tourist economy, too.

In the St. Louis River, which runs into Lake Superior in northeastern Minnesota, the Department of Natural Resources has seen a spike in sulfates south of the Partridge

River. "Above the river it's choked with wild rice, and of course flocks of ducks. When you get to the Partridge, you get to the end of the wild rice. That's when the first mining-impacted water hits the St. Louis River," notes Glen Anderson, a quiet, precise man who teaches science in a local high school.

In efforts to reverse the damage, the Minnesota DNR is partnering with more than fifteen local agencies and organizations, including the Fond du Lac Band of Lake Superior Chippewa (Ojibwe), to restore habitat on the Lower St. Louis River estuary. Work is underway to support the growth of twenty acres of wild-rice beds in various locations.

As Mary Annette Pember wrote in *Indian Country Today*, among the "remote and beautiful . . . Penokee Hills, a range of mountains that ride the Northern Continental Divide," the battle lines were clear. Pember notes that one side "measure[d] the earth's resources in terms of jobs and money," while the other side sought to protect those resources and considered it "a sacred responsibility to preserve both for future generations." The issues at stake, according to Pember, were "tribal sovereignty, economics, political and environmental responsibility and the very survival of a people and their culture."

The twenty-five miles of elevated land—hardwood forest, rivers, streams, and wetlands—is home to wolves, eagles, songbirds, and rare plants, as well as the wild rice. Nicknamed "Wisconsin's Everglades," the Kakagon Sloughs was designated a National Natural Landmark in 1973. According to a study carried out by the Sierra Club, "large-scale taconite mining would have threatened local communities' air and water. The area's surface and groundwater provides drinking water for the cities of Ashland, Mellen, Highbridge, Marengo, Odanah and Upson."

For two full years, a group of nearly one hundred protesters lived in wall tents at the Penokee harvest camps, surviving subzero winters—temperatures dropped to thirty degrees below—and summers of blasting heat. They cooked together and hosted seminars with university professors, researchers, and tribal elders. Each morning, Bad River elders raised the Lac Courte Oreilles tribal-nation flag and made an offering of tobacco. "We want to tell our future generations how to use Mother Earth in the right way," said tribal elder Joe Rose.

Pember notes that although Bad River takes its name from "French explorers vexed by how difficult the river was to navigate, the Ojibwe call this place *Mashkiki Ziib*i, Medicine River, because of the vast store of medicinal plants growing along its banks." To the Native Americans who gathered to protest the mines, wild rice is far more than just a food. Its prophecy spurred the movement of tribes to this area. "Wild rice is the nourishment for spirits and hearts, and it reminds us all that we are joined to this earth, this place," Joe Rose has said.

The mining company sent guards armed with automatic

machine guns to the proposed drill site, housing them in a construction trailer. Before long, the camp protesters invited the guards to their feasts and ceremonies. "Because they wouldn't join us, one of the women brought them a dish of cooked wild rice and the chicken we roasted over an open fire," VanderPuy said. "She tasted it in front of the guards to reassure them it was OK. It's the way the Ojibwe do things. We all got a kick out of it when we saw the guard, machine gun slung over his shoulder, return the empty Tupperware dish to her tent. Maybe we'll get somewhere if we can keep this up."

They did keep it up, and finally, after endless contentious and often tedious county-board meetings, Gogebic Taconite closed its office and put a hold on building the open-pit mine. The mining debate helped create new and surprising alliances between tribal groups and local citizens and even those who, at first, were in favor of mining. Activists worked to educate opponents about the real cost of the mine to the environment as well as the tourist industry that draws visitors to hunt and fish, sail and hike.

During a presentation about the impact of mining on wild rice, a board member asked, "What exactly is the economic contribution of wild rice to the county?" The Native Americans then explained the cultural and environmental value of this sacred food and why it's worth protecting. Consequently, the board agreed to strengthen the county's mining regulations, making it far more difficult and more expensive for Gogebic Taconite to comply.

It's too easy to see this conflict as an isolated effort by a handful of people trying to protect an obsolete livelihood. Wild rice signals the health of the water as well as the fish, waterfowl, wildlife, and people it nourishes.

Ricing, like all of the Native American harvest rituals, repeated over countless generations, is the essence of community and of faith. In relying on a food that appears year after year, without any intervention, the gathering of rice is a celebration of the trusting relationship the Ojibwe have with the earth, predicated on a willingness to let go and to pay attention to nature's gifts.

What if we all learned to forage some of our food? Looking for wild mushrooms in the forest, sorrel along the edge of a soccer field, watercress clinging to rocks in an icy stream, sweet-tart blueberries on a sandy shore, or those wild strawberries that hide underneath daisies on a dusty path—these humbling reminders of Mother Earth's unrequited gifts are all here for us if we pay attention and look more closely for the goodness right under our feet.

COOKING MY WAY HOME

The first, fat snowflakes of the year are falling slowly and gently, covering the faded backyard as night presses in. Memory and anticipation swirl with the steam of cranberries simmering and chestnuts roasting, glazing the windows with a lacy sheen. As I await the arrival of our three sons, from Colorado, Iowa, and across town, I punch down the bread dough with a yeasty thump-whap and begin shaping the loaves. The flour, from the Mill City Farmers' Market, was milled the day I purchased it from Sunrise Flour Mill's Darrold Glanville, and it has dusted the kitchen table and countertop.

The potatoes are cooked and tender; they're ready to mash. I recall that damp, misty morning I pulled up to Featherstone Farm, to find Jack Hedin looking over his verdant fields. And so I've left a few of his Alby's gold Ranger Russet and Yukon gold spuds unpeeled, to give the dish texture and the haunting flavor of the rich, dark soil from that lush, quiet place. Working in lumps of golden Hope butter, I heed my grandmother's advice: "Too much butter will make this dish too heavy; too little and it will fail to satisfy." So I try and strike a balance, whipping starchy carbs to be at once fluffy and very rich. Blissful mashers will soak up the gravy, the turkey, the cranberries, the stuffing bite by bite.

The chestnuts are roasted, their skins peeled back, ready to shuck. There is no recipe for the stuffing; my grandmother hardly ever wrote anything down, and when she did, it was "a coffee cup of flour" or a "teacup of sugar" or a "nutmeg of butter"—like Estelle Woods Wilcox, another woman of an earlier time—calling for a pinch of this, a little of that. So I toss together the cubed toast, crumbled herbs, stock, cream, and peeled, chopped chestnuts, feeling my way and tasting as I go. But what is fixed in my mind's eye is the chestnut farmer, Philip Rutter, standing in his cathedral of chestnut trees, preaching their virtues, proclaiming their promise for our soil's salvation, their potential to heal stripmined land and protect farmland—all the while, in the distance, came the timeless clap-clap of horses pulling an Amish cart down the road. In that unlikely enclave, heritage knowledge and cutting-edge science foster gorgeous, healthy chestnut trees. Just yesterday, in a phone conversation, that humble hero sighed in frustration and exclaimed "Dagnabbit!" when his computer unexpectedly shut down.

In my refrigerator, two little turkeys—one a black Spanish heritage bird from Brandon Severson, now a pre-med major in college—are brining. The first time I tried to cook such a turkey it emerged from the oven shriveled, dried out, a pitiful thing. Heritage turkeys are lean and in need of a lot of bacon or butter and plenty of basting as they roast in low temperatures. Brining them first helps them retain moisture and stay plump. The bigger bird, from John Peterson's farm, will be treated to high heat. That technique seals in the juices and helps to keep the meat from drying out as the turkey cooks quickly. I'd ordered this turkey from Ferndale Market, about an hour from home. To pick it up, I stood in line during the fall festival, sampling local cheeses, beers, and baked treats.

On the counter, brilliant scarlet cranberries shine in a white crockery bowl. On the day I visited the bogs, autumn's sun glinted off Sandhill cranes as they balanced on awkward, bent-back legs and dipped their graceful necks. Once the cranberry, orange, and ginger relish is done, I'll set it in a cut-glass bowl, to serve alongside the pickled carrots and dilly beans. Opening their jars releases nose-tingling notes of vinegar and hot pepper, assuring me there will be some spice in this meal.

Goodness knows, I really don't have to cook every component of this Thanksgiving dinner. But doing so is calm-

ing, and it's gratifying watching the potatoes from Featherstone turn from ivory to gold in the pot; tasting the sticky,
tangy cranberry jam; smelling the toasty scent of baking
bread. If nothing else, all this says "welcome home" to our
sons, to our friends, and to me. I cook to work through gratitude and worry, history and joy, through my hands. I like
rubbing butter into flour to make tart and piecrusts. It often
takes days to get the bread dough from under my fingernails.
The food I'm serving comes from the people I know, the
farms I've walked, the kitchens where I've shared coffee and
pie. I learned more about how apple trees grow from Dan
Bussey, the afternoon he introduced me to his orchard, than
from any book. I remember the names of the tastiest apples
because of the tales he shared.

When it comes to assembling the cheese plate, Mary
Falk's nutty and buttery hard cheese sits next to Jodi Ohlsen
Read's sharp, assertive blue. As I tasted their cheeses, met
their animals, and helped make cheese, I've come to respect
all the unseen life that gives our food flavor.

When Atina Diffley let a handful of rich, black dirt run
through her fingers, releasing its fragrance of warmth, must,
and mineral, I could feel her connection to that microbial
life. "It's not the GMO plants that will do us in," she said.
"It's the chemicals used to grow, the Roundup that destroys
everything else on the land except those plants that are engineered to withstand toxins."

Taking toasty corn sticks from the oven, crisped around

the edges and split on top, I am reminded of Atina's lesson in fertility. "There are over one billion bacteria, fungal filaments, protozoa in a teaspoon of soil," she said. "Soil is alive; it's a healthy jungle of voracious creatures that eat and reproduce and create fertility. The base of our food web is organic matter, material derived for living entities. It's clear when you walk a chemically treated field that everything is dead. We need to protect this soil, this life."

Peeling sweet potatoes from Mhonpaj, the Hmong organic farmer, I recall her telling me how, as an adult, she'd understood that farming was in her DNA, part of her identity, and that she'd learned her family's stories out in the field. Slathering the sweet potatoes with my father's special mixture of maple syrup, whiskey, and butter, and already thinking about leftovers, I recall those years he'd come to our home; how we'd sneak down to the kitchen in a conspiracy of late-night hunger and talk, eating leftovers while he told me of his years in the war.

Through these thirty-five years, the Thanksgiving seating arrangements have grown to make room for a burgeoning family and broadening collection of friends. The old card tables are secured with duct tape for last-minute guests, each bringing a sampling from their own childhoods. The kitchen counter, crammed with platters and bowls that brim with good food—as though they, like us, were filled with happiness. Cooking and sharing well-loved dishes is a source of glorious, yet strangely humbling pleasure.

These days, there's so much enthusiasm for "reading" our plates, for wanting to know where our food comes from and how it gets to our tables. The talk of local food is both old and new. Old in that the local-food movement, slow eating, and the explosive growth of farmers' markets and CSAs continues to be reported by the national press so extensively that it's nearly cliché. The number of farmers' markets has doubled across the country since we moved here some thirty-five years ago. And the term "CSA" is so familiar that the acronym no longer needs an explanation. Yet the coverage never strays too far north. The more temperate regions of our country—New York's Hudson River Valley, northern California, Oregon, all of it—are all considered the country's culinary centers. Luminaries such as Alice Waters in Berkeley, Deborah Madison in Santa Fe, and Dan Barber in New York—these chefs, educators, writers, and teachers work in temperate climates. Yet the stunning variety of our bounty here reflects a place that is simply unparalleled in its diversity and too often ignored.

It's taken me years to fully appreciate what it means to live in this region that gives its food so reluctantly. Unlike those who live with moderate temperatures, we are governed by distinctly different seasons. The dramatic weather shapes our physical and emotional landscapes. We celebrate the year's changing riches: the autumn's crisp air, brilliant colors, and snappy apples; winter's bluster and those simmering and warming stews. We yearn for spring's tender greens and pink rhubarb and delight in summer's golden corn. Come July, the perfect juice-split tomatoes reward our January patience. We take so little for granted, and it's by getting to know the people who grow my food that I've come to better appreciate its real value and the role it plays in my life.

I credit these regionally distinctive conditions for cultivating the Upper Midwest's philosopher-poets—Wes Jackson, Fred Kirschenmann, Aldo Leopold. Our long, dark winters nurture solitude, inquiry, and creativity. It's during the fallow seasons that organic farmers continue to gather to share their experiences, knowledge, and wisdom about work on the land. Throughout our history, they've forged networks and founded organizations such as the Midwest Organic and Sustainable Education Service (MOSES), which hosts the country's largest organic-farming conference.

When asked "Can local food feed the world?" I can only reply, "Why do we think it should?" Its role is not to deliver the most food at the lowest cost, regardless of flavor or nutrient content. Its value cannot be measured in pounds harvested or money saved. In this system, decisions are made with an eye to the soil's fertility, human health, fair wages for workers, and the animal's welfare. Its highest consideration is the future, not the immediate impact on the bottom line.

It's only within my short sixty-year life span that gardening and cooking have become recreational skills. But local food isn't a novelty; it's going to be increasingly important when energy prices begin to soar once again and unstable weather is the norm. When we look for local ingredients, at the farmers' markets, through CSA memberships, in the co-ops, we are creating friendships that extend well beyond our zip codes.

The better we get to know our food, the more likely we are to understand the impact our local and national policies have on our farmers and producers. We can see first hand how the Farm Bill hampers growers like Jack Hedin; why Atina Diffley's work on open-pollinated seeds is so necessary; how Nick VanderPuy's efforts to protect wild rice are urgent. When we cut into Cress Spring Bakery's dense and crusty heritage loaves, we taste our region's potential for reclaiming our position as a "milling capital" for heritage flour and the real "breadbasket of the world."

As I prepare this year's Thanksgiving dinner, I revisit my dad's question: "Do you know where you are?" In my kitchen, informed by past conversations on farms, in co-ops, with butchers and friends, I continue to seek the answer from the food that delights, nourishes, and does us all good. To learn about this place is to savor every season as it unfolds anew.

Every year, this journey around my Thanksgiving table helps me understand what a vibrant, viable, and delicious local-food system looks like in a climate where the land freezes hard for six months a year, a land where industrial farms and global food companies are front and center in our economic, political, and physical lives. Yet here, in this place, by connecting with small farmers and growers, through our own gardening and foraging, we're rediscovering the beauty and pleasure in nature's bounty that may inform different and more positive decisions as we cook meals, vote for our leaders, and engage with each other.

Tonight, as I chop and stir and set the table, I wander through memories of conversations with orchardists, butchers, cheesemakers, my grandmother, and my dad, and revisit those sticky, dog-eared pages of *The Joy of Cooking*. While I may be by myself in the kitchen, I'm really not alone. Every part of this meal tells a story of our region's food, steeped in the flavors of the past and enriched with the present knowledge that will nourish the future.

Perhaps most encouragingly, the people who will gather tomorrow will need no explanations as to why local kale has replaced the frozen creamed onions, or a smaller turkey now sits in place of the huge factory bird. The younger generation has been raised on this food. They know it and watch appreciatively as I carve the turkey with my dad's bone-handled knife. For a moment before the meal, we hold hands and are silent, and let Thanksgiving speak for itself.

RECIPES

APPLES

The quality of an apple is most apparent in applesauce, and the more varied the apples, the more interesting the sauce will be. Good applesauce is made solely of apples, never flavored with vanilla or lemon zest. Applesauce can be sweetened with a little sugar, honey, or maple syrup, but never too much. Savory applesauce, with fresh rosemary, sage, or thyme, makes a fine companion to pork and game. Don't puree the sauce; it should be lumpy.

Applesauce
MAKES ABOUT 1 QUART

To vary the sauce, add a cinnamon stick and a little freshly grated nutmeg.

2 pounds apples, peeled, cored, and coarsely chopped
½ cup apple cider
1 to 2 tablespoons honey or maple syrup, to taste

Put the apples and cider into a large saucepan and set over high heat. Bring to a boil, reduce the heat, and simmer until the apples are very tender and the sauce is thick, about twenty minutes. Cool a little and sweeten to taste with the honey or syrup.

SAVORY APPLESAUCE VARIATION: Omit the honey or syrup and add 1 to 2 tablespoons chopped fresh sage or a sprig of fresh rosemary.

APPLE BUTTER: Continue cooking the sauce over low heat, stirring occasionally so that it doesn't stick to the bottom of the pot until very thick and caramel colored. Depending on the quantity of sauce in the pot, this may take anywhere from twenty minutes to an hour.

BREAD

After our third son was born, I came to realize that baking bread didn't require being housebound, and that dough is far more flexible and forgiving than I had once believed. I am master of my dough, not it of me. The dough can be stored in the refrigerator, where it will rise slowly and patiently until I am ready to make bread or pizza. This allows time for the gluten proteins to develop so that the bread rises more evenly and has a good, firm texture. During a longer, slower rise time, the dough ferments a little to impart a tangy sourdough flavor.

Daily Bread

MAKES 3 TO 4 SMALL LOAVES OR 2 LARGE LOAVES

This remarkably straightforward recipe makes dough that's equally as good for baguettes as it is for cinnamon-raisin loaf. The idea is to make a starter dough that provides the base for several loaves through the week.

6 to 7 cups flour (use a mix of all-purpose and wheat flours)

2 ½ to 3 ⅓ cups very warm water (about 120 to 130 degrees)

3 tablespoons honey

2 packages regular yeast (about 4 teaspoons)

1 tablespoon coarse salt

Oil or soft butter for greasing the bowl

Put 3 cups of flour, the water, honey, and yeast into a large bowl and whisk together. Allow to stand about fifteen to twenty minutes, until the mixture begins to bubble. Beat in the remaining flour and salt, and stir briskly to make firm dough. Lightly grease a large bowl and place the dough in it, then set this aside and allow to rise for about one hour at room temperature. Punch the dough down and allow to rise a second time, for one hour.

Generously dust a countertop or board with flour and flour your hands. Knead the dough by pushing from the middle outwards, folding the dough over, then pushing outwards again, adding more flour if it seems sticky. After several turns, you should have a firm, pliant dough. Continue kneading until the texture is as smooth and soft as an earlobe or baby's bottom.

Preheat the oven to 425 degrees. Shape the dough into two baguettes, two loaves, or three long strands to braid together, and set onto a greased baking sheet. Allow the dough to rise until doubled, about thirty minutes. Then bake until it's toasty brown and the bread sounds hollow when tapped, about thirty-five to fifty minutes depending on the size of the loaves.

RAISIN-LOAF VARIATION: After kneading the dough, roll it out into a rectangle about five inches across and eight to ten inches long. Sprinkle a handful of raisins, a little brown sugar, and ground cinnamon over the dough. Starting at the narrow end, roll the dough up and seal it with a little water. Allow it to rise again until doubled, about thirty minutes. Bake the bread until it's crusty and sounds hollow when tapped, about twenty to twenty-five minutes.

DINNER ROLLS: After kneading the dough, shape it into balls, about three to four inches in diameter. Allow these to rise until doubled, about twenty minutes. Bake until they're crusty and sound hollow when tapped, about fifteen to twenty minutes.

POTATOES

The most memorable mashed potatoes manage to be both fluffy and buttery at once. Too much butter and they're heavy; not enough and they'll seem wimpy. Here's where choosing the right spud for the job really matters. The texture of a potato after cooking depends on its structure and moisture content. Some varieties, such as Idaho bakers, have low moisture and cook up to be light and airy. Beaten with butter and cream, they make a fluffy mash. High-moisture potatoes, such as red potatoes or new potatoes, can turn "gluey" when beaten. But because they have such a distinctly earthy, nutty flavor, I like to add just one or two to the pot.

Best Mashers

SERVES 8

Use a mix of baking and boiling potatoes. I like to use Idaho bakers, big russets, and Yukon gold. Always mash potatoes by hand with a potato masher or big spoon. Do not whip or put into a Cuisinart, as this results in a gluey, dense mash.

3 pounds potatoes (2 pounds bakers, 1 pound mix of red
    bliss and Yukon gold), about 6 to 8 medium spuds
2 tablespoons salt

1 cup whole milk
½ cup heavy cream
Coarse salt and freshly ground white pepper
2 to 3 tablespoons unsalted butter

Peel the potatoes, cut into quarters, and put into a large pot. Add the salt and enough water to cover the potatoes by about two inches. Bring the water to a boil, reduce the heat, and simmer until the potatoes are very tender, about fifteen to twenty-five minutes.

Tip the pot to drain off all but about a ½ cup of water. Return to the heat and mash the potatoes, then add the milk and cream, adding more cream if necessary. Season with salt and pepper to taste, and finish with a few pats of butter.

PICKLED GINGER CARROTS

These are quick and easy enough to make the night before serving, but they also keep beautifully, and can be refrigerated for several months.

Pickled Ginger Carrots

MAKES ABOUT 2 PINTS

1 pound carrots, cut into four-and-a-half-inch sticks

1 ¼ cup water

1 cup white-wine vinegar

¼ cup sugar

3 cloves garlic, crushed

¼ cup thinly sliced fresh ginger

2 tablespoons kosher salt

Bring a medium pot of water to a boil and blanch the carrots until they're bright orange, about one minute. Drain and refresh under cold water. Transfer the carrots to clean canning jars or a glass container with a lid.

In a medium saucepan, bring the water, vinegar, sugar, garlic, ginger, and salt to a boil. Reduce the heat and simmer for two minutes. Pour the hot liquid over the carrots and let cool, uncovered. Then cover and chill before serving.

SPICY DILLY BEANS

Here's my grandmother's dilly-bean recipe, perked up with red-chili flakes. My grandmother used this brine for beans, cauliflower, carrots, broccoli, asparagus, and cucumbers. . . it is the universal pickle.

Spicy Dilly Beans

MAKES 4 PINTS

4 cloves garlic, peeled

4 heads of dill or 5 teaspoons dill seeds

1 teaspoon red-chili flakes

2 pounds fresh green beans, tailed and cut to fit pint-size jars

2 ½ cups white-wine vinegar

2 ½ cups water

4 tablespoons kosher salt

Wash four pint-size jars. Put a garlic clove and head of dill or teaspoon of dill seeds, plus a pinch of chili pepper, into each jar. Fit the beans into the jars, allowing about half an inch of headroom at the top of each jar.

In a medium pot, bring the vinegar, water, and salt to a boil. Pour over the beans, filling to within a quarter-inch of the rim. Fasten the jar tops according to manufacturer's directions and either allow to cool and then refrigerate, or process in a boiling-water bath that covers the lids with two inches of water for five minutes, remove, and cool.

SWEET POTATOES

The vast array of sweet potatoes at the farmers' market brings a whole new range of flavors to the traditional family dish. The drier varieties, kotobuki and Hannah, taste of chestnuts, while the yellow Jersey is golden and brown-sugar sweet. One of my favorite ways to serve sweet potatoes is to roast, peel, slice, and drizzle them with a little balsamic vinegar and a very light drizzle of honey.

Old-Fashioned Maple Sweets

SERVES 6 TO 8

You can make the entire dish ahead of time and simply warm it in the oven before folks arrive. It's almost sweet enough to be served for dessert!

3 pounds sweet potatoes, about 6 to 8 medium sweet potatoes

¼ cup maple syrup

2 tablespoons unsalted butter

1 teaspoon ground cinnamon

Pinch freshly grated nutmeg

Splash of whiskey, optional
Salt and pepper to taste
Butter for the baking dish

Preheat the oven to 400 degrees. Wash the sweet potatoes, poke lightly with a fork, and roast in the oven until the skins are shriveled and the potatoes are very tender, about forty-five to fifty minutes. Remove and allow to cool enough to handle. Peel and set aside. Lightly butter a medium baking dish.

Reduce the heat to 300 degrees. In a small saucepan, heat the maple syrup with the butter and stir in the cinnamon and nutmeg. Season with whiskey, salt, and pepper to taste. Slice the potatoes and layer, brushing the maple-syrup mixture between the layers. Pour any remaining syrup over the potatoes. Bake until the potatoes are glazed and hot, about twenty minutes.

FRESH CRANBERRIES

You can serve turkey and mashed potatoes at any time of year, but it seems to me that cranberries make the Thanksgiving dinner. Colorful and tangy, they spark the blander dishes. I prefer organic cranberries when I can find them; they tend to be drier and more flavorful.

Fresh Cranberry Relish

MAKES ABOUT 2–2½ CUPS

Make this in a food processor or blender. It will keep several days in the refrigerator.

3 cups fresh cranberries, rinsed and sorted
2 tablespoons orange zest
¼ cup fresh orange juice
¼ cup chopped crystallized ginger, optional
½ cup sugar or honey, to taste

Place all of the ingredients into a blender or food processor and chop until fine. Store in a covered container in the refrigerator.

Cranberry Sauce

MAKES ABOUT 2 CUPS

Do not add the sweetener until after the berries have popped open, as it will make them tough. This sauce keeps beautifully in a covered container in the refrigerator. Add a chopped apple or pear for variety.

3 cups fresh cranberries, rinsed and sorted
½ cup apple cider or orange juice
½ cup sugar, honey, or maple syrup, to taste

In a medium saucepan, bring the cranberries and cider or juice to a boil. Reduce the heat and simmer until the berries have popped open, about three to five minutes. Stir in sugar, honey, or maple syrup to taste—about half a cup should be plenty.

CHESTNUTS

When roasting chestnuts, be prepared to have your fingertips singed and to lose a few chestnuts from overcooking or because they've dried out; they do not store well. But they are worth the effort and it's always fun to roast them in a fireplace to eat warm. Creamy, nutty, and slightly sweet, they lift this stuffing from—well, just stuffing—to memorable.

Old Fashioned Chestnut Stuffing

SERVES 8

My grandmother never used recipes and neither do I when making this dish. Follow the simple guidelines below to create your own variation, using the bread, herbs, and spices you like best. Do not use olive bread or herb bread in this—the flavors are overwhelming. If the bread is not stale, pop it in an oven at low heat for a few minutes, to dry it slightly. This recipe is easier to follow if you have everything organized and set out before you begin.

1 pound chestnuts, roasted and peeled*
6 slices slightly stale bread (whole wheat, white or
    baguette), cut into half-inch pieces
2 chopped onions

2 chopped celery sticks

6 tablespoons chopped herbs (use a mix of sage, thyme, and parsley)

1 cup chicken stock

1 stick (½ cup) melted butter

¼ cup heavy cream or more as needed

Salt and freshly ground black pepper to taste

Butter for the baking dish and aluminum foil

Toss everything *except* the stock, butter, and cream together in a large bowl. Add the stock, then the butter, tossing to coat all of the ingredients. Then add enough cream to make a moist but not wet stuffing.

Generously butter a three-quart baking dish and fill loosely with the stuffing—do not pack it in. Cover the dish with buttered foil and bake for about twenty minutes. Remove the foil, baste with turkey juices, and continue baking until the top is crusty brown, another ten to fifteen minutes.

TO ROAST CHESTNUTS: With a small paring knife, score the chestnuts by making an X on the flat of the nut. Then place on a baking sheet and set in an oven set to 350 degrees. Alternatively, put the nuts at the edge of a fire. Roast until the shells pull back, about ten to fifteen minutes. When the nuts are cool enough to handle, peel off the shells, being careful to remove the dark-brown pith that covers the nuts as well.

CORN AND CORNMEAL

Riverbend Farm in Delano, Minnesota, is the source of beautiful golden cornmeal, ground from organic flint corn. Opening the bag releases a milky, sweet scent that will take you right back to a hot summer in August. Because this is a little coarser and moister than most commercial cornmeal, the resulting cornbread or corn sticks tend to be denser and richer tasting.

Golden Cornbread

SERVES 8 TO 12

If you're in possession of an old-fashioned cast-iron corn-stick pan, by all means use it. A cast-iron skillet works nicely as well.

6 tablespoons unsalted butter

1 cup fresh cornmeal

¾ cup flour (either all-purpose or a mix of whole-wheat and all-purpose)

1 teaspoon baking powder

½ teaspoon baking soda

½ teaspoon kosher salt

1 ½ cups buttermilk

2 eggs

2 tablespoons honey

Preheat the oven to 375 degrees. Put the butter into an eight-to ten-inch dish or divide into twelve corn-stick or muffin pans and place in the oven to melt. Remove and pour most of the excess butter into a medium mixing bowl. (This way, the pan is actually greased while you're melting the butter.)

In a large bowl, whisk together the dry ingredients. In the bowl with the melted butter, whisk together the buttermilk, eggs, and honey. Fold the wet ingredients into the dry ones and stir lightly, until just smooth.

Pour the batter into the buttered skillet or the prepared pans and place in the oven. Bake until lightly browned and springy when touched, about fifteen minutes for the corn sticks and muffins and twenty-five minutes if using the large pan. Serve warm.

FALL FRUIT TART IN A BUTTER CRUST

Butter is the essential ingredient in a fine, rich tart crust. Adhering to my Dad's dictum "Apple pie without the cheese is like a hug without the squeeze," we serve a good sharp Wisconsin cheddar with this favorite tart. But go ahead and whip up cream, laced with whiskey, to dollop on top.

Fall Fruit Tart

SERVES 8 TO 10

Be sure to use real, unsalted butter in the tart dough and chill it well. Allow the dough to rest in the refrigerator so that the gluten relaxes a bit, making it easier to roll out.

RICH TART PASTRY

1 cup unbleached all-purpose flour

½ cup unsalted butter, chilled and cut into small pieces

1 tablespoon sugar

Pinch of salt

2 to 3 tablespoons ice water

FILLING

5 medium tart apples, peeled and cored

½ cup fresh cranberries, rinsed and sorted

4 tablespoons unsalted butter, cut into small pieces

1 tablespoon brandy or applejack, optional

2 tablespoons sugar mixed with ½ teaspoon cinnamon

GLAZE

⅓ cup apple or apricot jam or jelly

2 tablespoons brandy or applejack, optional

PASTRY: Put the flour, butter, sugar, and salt into a large bowl and cut in the butter with a pastry cutter, two knives, or your fingertips, until the mixture resembles coarse meal. Using a fork to toss, drizzle in the water a little at a time, adding just enough to create a stiff dough. Gather the dough, shape it into a ball and flatten slightly, wrap it in waxed paper, and chill in the refrigerator for at least an hour or overnight.

Roll out the dough on a lightly floured surface, forming a twelve-inch circle. Line a nine- to ten-inch tart pan with the dough. Trim and crimp the edges and prick the bottom of the dough with a fork. Preheat the oven to 400 degrees.

FILLING: Slice the apples thinly and arrange in concentric circles around the dough. Toss the cranberries over the apples, then place dots of butter over the fruit. Brush with the brandy and sprinkle with the sugar. Set the tart on a baking sheet and bake until the apples are caramelized and the crust is well browned, about fifty minutes to one hour.

While the tart is baking, put the jam, and brandy if using, into a saucepan and set over medium heat, cooking until the mixture is melted and smooth. Spoon the glaze over the tart and allow to cool a little before slicing into wedges to serve.

TURKEY

Early European settlers chose turkey for Thanksgiving for reasons that still make sense today. These birds are big enough to satisfy a crowd; easier, and more economical, to slaughter than cows or hogs; and in line with British holiday customs imported to the new world.

Fresh free-range turkeys are the best all-around choice for this meal. A wild turkey is delicious, too, but usually so small and lean that it needs to be brined and basted frequently so that it doesn't dry out. We'll sometimes roast both a domestic free-range turkey and a wild turkey to offer a variety of choices.

Simply Roast Turkey

SERVES 8 TO 10

Be sure to allow the turkey to rest at room temperature before carving; you'll have a juicier, tastier bird. This is because the heat of the oven draws the juices up to the surface; those juices will be released if the turkey is cut while still hot. When the meat cools, the juices retract back into the turkey, so it remains juicy.

8 tablespoons unsalted butter

Zest and juice of 1 lemon

2 teaspoons chopped fresh thyme leaves

1 10- to 12-pound turkey

Coarse salt and freshly ground black pepper

1 large bunch fresh thyme

1 large bunch fresh parsley

1 whole lemon, halved

1 large white onion, quartered

1 head garlic, cut in half crosswise

Preheat the oven to 350 degrees. Melt the butter in a small saucepan and add the lemon zest, juice, and thyme leaves. Set aside.

Remove the turkey giblets and wash the turkey inside and out. Trim any excess fat and pinfeathers, and pat the inside and outside of the turkey dry with a paper towel. Place the turkey in a large roasting pan and sprinkle with generous amounts of salt and pepper, inside and out. Put the thyme, parsley, lemon, onion and garlic into the cavity of the bird. Brush the outside of the turkey with the butter mixture and sprinkle with salt and pepper. Tuck the wing tips under the body of the turkey.

Roast the turkey until the juices run clear when you cut between the leg and the thigh, for about 2 to 3 hours. Once the turkey is removed from the oven, the temperature will continue to rise to the FDA benchmark for food safety, 180 degrees. Remove the turkey from the roasting pan and set on a platter; let the turkey rest for about twenty minutes before carving, while you make the gravy.

Turkey Gravy

MAKES ABOUT 4½ CUPS

4 cups homemade chicken stock or reduced-sodium chicken broth
¼ cup all-purpose flour
1 tablespoon fresh chopped thyme leaves
Salt and freshly ground black pepper to taste

Leave the drippings from the turkey in the pan and place the pan over medium heat. Add the stock and wine and whisk together, scraping the bottom of the pan until all of the bits have come loose. Bring to a boil and cook until the liquid has reduced by about one inch in the pan. Transfer the liquid to a fat separator and allow to separate, about five minutes. Scoop out about ⅔ cup of the fat and return to the roasting pan, discarding the rest. Whisk in the flour and cook over medium-low heat, until the mixture thickens and becomes smooth, about three minutes. Slowly add the stock mixture back into the pan and whisk until the gravy's thickness is to your liking, about five to eight minutes. Stir in the herbs and season with salt and freshly ground black pepper.

WILD RICE

No wonder the voyageurs called wild rice "pocket money." A handful of raw rice swells as it is cooked and can feed eight hungry men. It's a treasure of flavor. Real wild rice grows in shallow lakes, and is hand harvested in canoes. When parched, toasted, and winnowed, it expands to four times its original size and fills the kitchen with the aromas of the forest—mushrooms, damp leaves, pine. It cooks quickly, so I have to be vigilant once the pot comes to a boil. The age of the rice, how well it's been parched, and how long it has been stored all determine how long it will take to cook. It's ready when a few kernels begin to curl and are just tender.

True wild rice may seem pricey, at three times more per pound than cultivated rice, but it is the best choice. It tastes better and cooks far more quickly. Paddy rice is shiny, hard, and black, grown from a seed that's been hybridized for consistency and ease of harvest. Real wild rice can be speckled black and dark brown or tan. It's low fat, high fiber, and loaded with protein and minerals, and its flavor is slightly nutty and smoky, the taste of the woods.

Basic Wild Rice

MAKES 4 CUPS, SERVES 8

1 cup real wild rice

4 cups water (or enough to cover the rice in the pot by
two inches)

Salt to taste

Wash the rice thoroughly by putting it in a colander and running under cold water until the water runs clear. Turn the wild rice, water, and salt into a large, heavy saucepan and bring to a boil. Reduce the heat and simmer about twenty to forty minutes, or until the rice has puffed. Be sure it doesn't become too mushy. Fluff the rice with a fork and let stand a few minutes before serving.

Notes

INTRODUCTION

XXIII *The first community supported agriculture*   Community-sup-
ported agriculture (CSA) first appeared in the US in the 1970s,
but dates back to the early 1900s in Japan and Europe. The
movement was influenced by the eideas of Rudolf Steiner, an
Austrian writer, educator, and social advocate, related the ecology of the farm-organism to that of the entire cosmos. Nearly
all CSA farmers work with nature to keep their land in balance,
using intensive composting practices and friendly pests in lieu
of petrochemical inputs.

Steiner's work helped shaped the identity of CSAs as an economic arrangement that connects farmers with "sharers" to
address human needs, eradicate poverty, and forward social
equity, while improving the environment.

In the CSA arrangement, consumers "subscribe" to a farm and
receive a portion of the farm's harvest each week. Initially, most

CSA farms offered vegetable shares, but many have evolved to include eggs, dairy products, meat and poultry, honey, syrup, and fruit. The cost varies from farm to farm, with shares purchased in advance.

In the Twin Cities, the number of residents with CSA memberships has nearly tripled over the last ten years. Twenty years ago, there were two CSA farms in the region; today there are more than eighty.

APPLES

5   *Up until the 1960s*   Tom Burford, *Apples of North America: 192 Exceptional Varieties for Gardeners, Growers, and Cooks* (Portland, OR: Timber Press, 2013).

5   *Since the 1960s*   Gary Paul Nabhan, ed., *Forgotten Fruits Manual & Manifesto: APPLES* (Renewing America's Food Traditions Alliance, 2010).

5   *Forty-five percent of*   Gary Paul Nabhan's official Web site, "Place Based Foods," http://www.garynabhan.com/i/place-based-foods (accessed 1/9/2010).

6   *Gary Paul Nabhan—a founder*   Gary Paul Nabhan, ed., *Renewing America's Food Traditions: Saving and Savoring the Continent's Most Endangered Foods* (White River Junction, VT: Chelsea Green Publishing, 2008).

6   *Cider production rose*   www.beerinstitute.org cited in Jonathan Frochtzwajg, "America's Hard Cider Boom Has One Problem: Not Enough Apples," *Modern Farmer*, April 23, 2014.

7   *It describes the varieties*   The series will be published by JAK KAW Press in 2016. Many of the fifteen hundred illustrations selected for the book are archival watercolors, created a century ago by artists at the USDA. The Ceres Trust, an environmental nonprofit, funded the production and the print run; the encyclopedia will be offered for free to the nation's agricultural libraries.

9   *A diverse orchard is a secure*   As Michael Pollan notes in *The Botany of Desire: A Plant's-Eye View of the World* (New York: Random House, 2001), "As we go about selecting the tastiest apple and sending it around the world, we are also shrinking the species' genetic diversity by grafting the same plant over and over, restricting its natural ability to keep adapting its defenses against the pests that prey upon it. Most of the apples grown today have been grafted from the same five or six parents. That has allowed the apple's natural insect and viral enemies to gain on it, requiring farmers to apply ever-greater amounts of pesticides to keep the predators at bay." A diverse orchard, is a beautiful orchard hosting trees that flower differently and successively.

15   *Dr. David Bedford, a U of M*   John Seabrook, "CRUNCH: Building a Better Apple," *New Yorker*, November 21, 2011. Seabrook tells the story of how the SweeTango evolved from the Honeycrisp to become the country's first "managed variety" or "club apple."

15 *Now ranked America's favorite* Rick Moore, "The Apple, Rebooted," University of Minnesota Discover, May 29, 2014, http://discover.umn.edu/news/food-agriculture/apple-breeding-program-continues-shine. According to Moore, the Honeycrisp, the fifth-highest-selling apple in the world, is "the most desired apple in America. It's being grown in seven different countries, with imports flowing back to the states from New Zealand and Chile." In 2006, it was named the Minnesota state fruit.

16 *The Association of University* John Motoviloff, "The Honeycrisp: A Sweet, Tart Jump-Start for a Sagging Limb of the Apple Industry," in *Technology Transfer Stories: 25 Innovations that Changed the World: The Better World Report* (Northbrook, IL: Association of University Technology Managers, 2006).

16 *a "persnickety apple"* Christina Herrick, "The Dark Side of Honeycrisp," *American Fruit Grower,* January 2015.

16 *a concept introduced by* Australia's apple program is an initiative of the Apple and Pear Australia Limited (APAL), an industry body that also provides leadership and funding to Horticulture Innovation Australia (HIA), a nonprofit, grower-owned research-and-development corporation. APAL and HIA fund the work to breed, market, and sell apples such as Pink Lady. Funds generated by sales the two groups.

17 *Angered by exclusion from the* Harry Hoch, "News from the Orchard," Hoch Orchard, September 14, 2009, http://www.hochorchard.com/wp-content/uploads/Sept-14-2009.pdf. This issue created a buzz in the news outlets of apple-growing

areas of Wisconsin and Minnesota. Hoch wrote that the number
of SweeTango trees he was allowed to plant in his organic orchard
was limited. For more on the controversy, see Renee Montagne,
"Want to Grow These Apples? You'll Have to Join the Club,"
The Salt, National Public Radio, November 10, 2014, http://
www.npr.org/templates/transcript/transcript.php?storyId=
358530280.

Richard Lehnert, "Stemilt to Manage New Minnesotan Apple,"
Good Fruit Grower, October 15, 2014, http://www.goodfruit.
com/stemilt-to-manage-new-minnesota-apple/. More recently,
the University of Minnesota has loosened its restrictions on
Minnesota growers, allowing them to produce fruit without any
restrictions. The MN 55, a new apple that ripens earlier than the
Honeycrisp and the SweeTango, has been licensed to Stemilt
Growers of Wenatchee, Washington. Stemilt will help guide
national marketing and growing efforts—outside Minnesota. "It
will be available to all Minnesota growers who wish to plant it
and who can market it with few restrictions," David Bedford said.

20   *The Environmental Working Group*   Environmental Working Group, "Apples Top Dirty Dozen List for Fifth Year in a
Row," February 25, 2015, *http://www.ewg.org/release/apples-
top-dirty-dozen-list-fifth-year-row*. "Apples," the report reads,
"turned up with the highest number of pesticides for the fifth
year in a row, while peaches and nectarines moved up to the
second and third spots. Nearly two-thirds of produce samples
tested by the U.S. Department of Agriculture and analyzed by
EWG for the 2015 Shopper's Guide contained pesticide residues—a surprising finding in the face of soaring consumer
demand for food without agricultural chemicals."

21   *But there's no proof*   Michael Phillips, *The Apple Grower: A Guide for the Organic Orchardist* (White River Junction: Chelsea Green Publishing, 2005).

21   *Currently SweeTango apples*   Richard Lehnert, "SweeTango's Saga," *Good Fruit Grower,* May 29, 2014 http://goodfruit.com/sweetangos-saga.

WHEAT

26   *This iconic crop is*   "Ears of Plenty: The Story of Man's Staple Food," *Economist,* December 20, 2005.

27   *Wheat, derived from wild*   Abdullah A. Jaradat, "Ecogeography, Genetic Diversity, and Breeding Value of Wild Emmer Wheat," *Australian Journal of Crop Science* 5, no.9 (2011).

28   *Through harvesting and sowing,*   Eli Rogosa, "Restoring Ancient Wheat," Heritage Grain Conservancy, 2009, http://growseed.org/wheat.html.

28   *These early strains of wheat*   Abdullah A. Jaradat, "The Vanishing Wheat Landraces of the Fertile Crescent," *Emirates Journal of Food and Agriculture* 26, no.2 (2014).

29   *Farm journals of that era*   Merrill E. Jarchow, "King Wheat," *Minnesota History* 29, no.1 (March 1948).

30   *the more quickly the crew*   Carrie Young and Felicia C. Young, *Prairie Cooks: Glorified Rice, Three-Day Buns, and Other Reminiscences* (Iowa City: University of Iowa Press, 1993).

31   *late into the night*   Ibid.

31   *Following World War II*   William Cronon, "Lecture #9: The Machine in the Garden: Agricultural Revolutions," http://www.williamcronon.net/handouts/460_handout_09_ machine_in_the_garden.pdf. University of Wisconsin professor William Cronon writes, "Since in the US land is cheap and unskilled labor is dear, American farmers were motivated to buy labor-serving machinery. Our faith in technology has become the foundation for our commitment to progress and improvement, increasingly involved in replacing human energy with nonhuman energy. Thus we are more inclined to conserve labor rather than resources.

34   *In our region's first*   Estelle Woods Wilcox, *Buckeye Cookery and Practical Housekeeping* (Minneapolis: Buckeye Publishing Company, 1877). Wilcox moved to Minnesota with her husband, the publisher of the *Minneapolis Daily Tribune*, and published this recipe book, gathered from women in her former home of Ohio, through the newspaper's press (hence the name Buckeye). The book became so popular that it was republished for settlers in German, Swedish, and Norwegian.

34   *In those days*   The story of the Washburn Roller Mill is sourced from Alison Watts, "The Technology that Launched a City: Scientific and Technological Innovations in Flour Milling during the 1870's in Minneapolis," *Minnesota History* 57, no. 2 (Summer), and from Robert M Farm III, Mills, Machines and Millers: Minnesota Sources for Flour, Milling Research," *Minnesota History,* 46, no 4 (Winter 1978).

36   *Just as Washburn was building*   Sylvester Graham, *A Treatise on Bread and Bread-Making* (Boston: Light & Stearns, 1837). Ralph Waldo Emerson dubbed Sylvester Graham "the prophet of bran bread." In his *Treatise on Bread and Bread-Making*, Graham wrote about the connections between diet, health, and mortality, and called for bread to be made with whole wheat.

38   *Borlaug, known as the*   Prabhu L. Pingali, "Green Revolution: Impacts, Limits, and the Path Ahead," *Proceedings of the National Academy of Sciences* 109, no. 31 (July 31, 2012). This detailed retrospective of the Green Revolution reviews its achievements and limits in terms of agricultural productivity and its impact on society, the environment, and the economy. Pingali outlines strategies for a "Green Revolution 2.0," with integrated environmental, social, economic, and agricultural impact.

38   *Yet analyses of the*   Whole Grains Council, "Research Sheds Light on Gluten Issue," January 25, 2012, http://wholegrainscouncil.org/newsroom/blog/2012/01/research-sheds-light-on-gluten-issues. The issue is controversial, but according to the Whole Grains Council, a consumer-advocacy group, the biggest difference between heritage varieties of wheat and modern wheat is in levels of gliadin, one of the proteins in gluten. Older wheats have fewer chromosomes and tend to have less gliadin.

38   *they need excessive amounts*   Sense about Science, "Are There Dangerous Pesticides in Our Bread?" July 17, 2014, http://sensaboutscience.org/resources.php/159/are-there-dangerous-pesticides-in-our-bread. Some of the chemicals used on commercial wheat include disulfoton, methyl parathion,

chlorpyrifos, dimethoate, and dieamba. They contribute to the overall toxic load in our bodies and increase our susceptibility to neurotoxic diseases as well as cancer.

39   *that irradiated foods may*   P. R. Shewry, "Wheat," *Journal of Experimental Botany* 60, no. 6 (2009).

39   *The changes in this wheat's*   Hetry C. van den Brueck and others, "Presence of Celiac Disease Epitopes in Modern and Old Hexaploid Wheat Varieties: Wheat Breeding May Have Contributed to Increased Prevalence of Celiac Disease," *Theoretical and Applied Genetics* 121, no.8 (November 2010).

39   *According to Dr. William*   Dr. William Davis is author of *Wheat Belly: Lose the Wheat, Lose the Weight, and Find Your Path Back to Health* (New York: Rodale, 2011), which explains the adverse effects of modern wheat on human health.

40   *Nearly twenty million people*   Michael Specter, "Against the Grain," *New Yorker*, November 3, 2014.

45   *At stake is the*   Bill Donahue, "The Search for Monsanto's Rogue GMO Wheat," *Bloomberg Businessweek*, June 20, 2013.

45   *US government studies have*   Beth Hoffman, "GMO Crops Mean More Herbicide, Not Less," *Forbes*, July 2, 2013.

49   *seeking wild plants that*   The spring 2013 issue of the *Land Report*, a magazine for American landowners, was devoted to 'Kernza', the natural perennial wheat developed by the Land Institute and the University of Minnesota. Interest in the plant

is high. While it is not yet perfect for commercial production—the kernels are plump, uneven, and yield a heavy, bran-laden flour—'Kernza' has become more uniform and easier to harvest. Growers anticipate it won't be long before 'Kernza' is milled into flour and stocked in stores.

50   *Ford has been profiled*   Christine Muhlke, "Grain Elevator," *New York Times Magazine*, October 7, 2009.

50   *by the legendary mason*   Alan Scott and Daniel Wing, *The Bread Builders: Hearth Loaves and Masonry Ovens* (White River Junction, VT: Chelsea Green Publishing, 1999). Scott, who passed away in 2009, is considered the most influential builder of masonry ovens in America. *The Bread Builders* is far more than a how-to manual; it's a treatise on the history of ovens and the physics of baking and provides detailed instructions on how to create the best dough for the perfect loaf of bread.

54   *Its production leads all*   B. C. Curtis, "Wheat in the World," in *Bread Wheat: Improvement and Production*, ed. B. C. Curtis, S. Rayarama, and H. Gómez Macpherson (Rome: Food and Agriculture Organization of the United Nations, 2002).

POTATOES

55   *Come summer, she steamed*   Potatoes are categorized by starch content, determined by both moisture level and the structure of the flesh. High-moisture, low-starch potatoes have a waxy flesh and hold their shape when cooked. They are good for gratins and salads. High-starch potatoes bake and roast up to be fluffy and mash beautifully. There are also, of course, plenty of medium-starch potatoes. To evaluate the starch content of a potato,

draw a knife through it. If the knife emerges with a "potato slick," or white chalky smear, on the blade, it's low starch.

55   *The story of the potato famine*   Michael Pollan, "Playing God in the Garden," *New York Times Magazine,* October 25, 1998.

58   *The Center for Food Safety*   Andrew Pollack, "USDA Approves Modified Potato. Next Up: French Fry Fans," *New York Times,* November 7, 2014. A new GMO potato, named 'Innate' by its creator, Simplot, is engineered to brown slower than non-GMO potatoes and bruise less easily. It also contains less of a probable carcinogenic compound known as acrylamide that appears when potatoes are fried at high temperatures.

McDonald's announced that it will not be sourcing these GMO potatoes despite an existing relationship with Simplot. McDonald's buys 3.4 billion pounds of potatoes annually. According to a recent company press release, "McDonald's USA does not source GMO potatoes, nor does it have plans to change sourcing practices."

59   *In collaboration with the*   Sara Briles, "A Spud in the Spotlight," *Wisconsin Natural Resources Magazine,* August 2004. http://dnr.wi.gov/wnrmag/html/stories/2004/aug04/spud.html.

63   *Featherstone's practices are inspired*   "[A. P. Anderson's] *The Seventh Reader* gives a rich glimpse into this man's curiosity and generosity of spirit . . . qualities which we try and bring to the present twenty-first-century Featherstone Farm," Jack Hedin told me.

65 *The food was given*   Daniel Imhoff, *Food Fight: The Citizen's Guide to the Next Food and Farm Bill* (Healdsburg, CA: Watershed Media, 2012).

66 *SNAP underwrites school*   Whether to continue to separate SNAP from the Farm Bill is being debated in the US House of Representatives as of this writing.

66 *It would be hard to*   Jim VanDerPol, *Conversations with the Land* (Belleville, WI: No Bull Press, 2011). VanDerPol farms and writes in western Minnesota, a world very different from the one in which he was raised, in the 1950s. Agribusiness has replaced the small, diversified farms and tight-knit communities of his youth. In *Conversations with the Land*, VanDerPol offers clear, down to earth ideas for ways to recreate a food system that respects the environment and the people who live and work in it.

67 *The insurance program is*   Nancy Watzman, "Farm Bill Allows Congress to Keep Crop Subsidies Secret," Sunlight Foundation, February 7, 2014, http://sunlightfoundation.com/blog/2014/02/07/farm-bill-allows-congress-to-keep-crop-subsidies-secret.

68 *It also includes increased funding*   Organic Farming Research Foundation, "2014 Farm Bill a Victory for Organic Farming," February 4, 2014, http://www.ofrf.org/news/2014-farm-bill-victory-organic-farming. The 2014 farm bill expanded funding to provide reimbursement for organic certification costs of up to $750 in thirty-five states. While this is helpful, the bill also cut billions from conservation programs that protect national resources and the environment.

68 *By contrast, European governments* Mathias Stolze and others, *Organic Farming in Europe: Economics and Policy: The Environmental Impacts of Organic Farming in Europe* vol. 6 (Stuttgart: University of Hohenheim, 2000).

69 *more than even the defense* Ron Nixon, "Senate Passes Long-Stalled Farm Bill, With Clear Winners and Losers," *New York Times,* February 4, 2014.

69 *By contrast, organic farmers draw* Wes Jackson, Wendell Berry, and Bruce Colman, eds., *Meeting the Expectations of the Land: Essays in Sustainable Agriculture and Stewardship* (New York: North Point Press, 1985).

70 *Hedin wrote in a* Jack Hedin, "An Almanac of Extreme Weather," *New York Times,* November 27, 2010.

72 *After the latest bill's passage* Floor Statement by Senator John McCain on Farm Bill Conference Report, February 3, 2014.

BEANS AND CARROTS

77 *By providing fresh produce* USDA Agricultural Marketing Service, "Food Deserts," http://apps.ams.usda.gov/fooddeserts/fooddeserts.aspx. Food deserts are defined by the USDA as "urban neighborhoods and rural towns without ready access to fresh, healthy, and affordable food. Instead of supermarkets and grocery stores, these communities may have no food access or are served only by fast food restaurants and convenience stores that offer few healthy, affordable food options. The lack of access contributes to a poor diet and can lead to higher levels of obesity and other diet-related diseases, such as diabetes and heart disease."

79   *which teach kids to grow*   Tamar Haspel, "Farm Bill: Why
Don't Taxpayers Subsidize the Foods That Are Better for Us?"
Washington Post, February 18, 2014.

80   *By the 1930s, 40 percent*   "Mass Exodus from the Plains,"
American Experience, Public Broadcasting Service, http://
www.pbs.org/wgbh/americanexperience/features/general-ar-
ticle/dustbowl-mass-exodus-plains/

"1800-1990: Changes in Urban/Rural U.S. Population" http://
www.elderweb.com/book/appendix/1800-1990-changes-ur-
banrural-us-population

81   *By 1943, these local*   Rae Katherine Eighmey, *Food Will Win the
War: Minnesota Crops, Cooks, and Conservation during World
War I* (St. Paul: Minnesota Historical Society Press, 2010).

81   *Before the end of the war*   Rose Hyden Smith, *Sowing the Seeds
of Victory: American Gardening Programs of World War I* (Jef-
ferson: McFarland & Company, 2014).

85   *Youth Farm and Hopkins Public Schools*   "Protecting the
U.S. Food Supply from Agroterrorism," *Homeland Security
News Wire,* November 12, 2014, http://www.homelandsecu-
ritynewswire.com/dr20141112-protecting-the-u-s-food-sup-
ply-from-agroterrorism. Tommy Thompson addressed issues
of food security in his 2004 farewell speech as US Secretary
of Health and Human Services: "For the life of me, I cannot
understand why the terrorists have not attacked our food supply because it is so easy to do." Materials found in a 2002 US
military raid on an al-Qaeda warehouse included outlines for

attacking tomato canning and processing plants in Sacramento, California, among other food sources.

86   *Three-fourths of America's*   William H. McMichael, "Most U.S. Youths Unfit to Serve, Data Show," *Army Times,* November 3, 2009, http://archive.armytimes.com/article/20091103/NEWS/911030311/must-u-s-youths-unfit-serve-data-sheet.

86   *Forty percent of the vegetables*   Susan Levine and Rob Stein, "Obesity Threatens a Generation," *Washington Post,* May 17, 2008.

86   *the toll of their poor health*   Harvard T. H. Chan School of Public Health, "Obesity Prevention Source: Economic Costs," http://www.hsph.harvard.edu/obesity-prevention-source/obesity-consequences/economic.

86   *If a foreign power were*   Mark Bittman and Michael Pollan (*Food for Tomorrow Conference*, Stone Barn Farms, Pocantico Hills, NY, October 20-21). Mark Bittman said in a speech, "Much of what the current food system produces pollutes, sickens, exploits and robs." He and speaker, Michael Pollan made the case that if a foreign power were to threaten our health, our land, and our environment the way our industrial food does, we would declare war.

87   *Our food is too cheap* Allison Linn, "Food Bill Rising? At Least You're Not French," CNBC, May 1, 2014, http://www.cnbc.com/2014/05/01/food-bill-rising-at-least-youre-not-French.html. According to data from the USDA, Americans spend 6.6 percent of their household incomes on food. The next lowest country is Singapore, at 7.3 percent. The highest country is

Pakistan, 47.7 percent. Canadians spend 10 percent, Japanese spends 14 percent, and Russians spend about 32 percent.

91   *she sparked our collective*   Michelle Obama, *American Grown: The Story of the White House Kitchen Garden and Gardens Across America* (New York: Crown, 2012).

92   *And when* Savoring the Seasons   *Savoring the Seasons of the Northern Heartland* was a finalist for the James Beard Award in 1997. It was one in a fifteen-book series called *Knopf Cooks American,* the brainchild of legendary editor Judith Jones. Each of these books focuses on an American culinary tradition. *Biscuits, Spoonbread, and Sweet Potato Pie* by Bill Neal, for example, is devoted to Southern baking, while Janie Hibler's *Dungeness Crabs and Blackberry Cobblers* covers the whole Northwest.

92   *The demand for this program*   Ilene Pevec, "The Ethical Responsibility to Provide Youth with Access to Gardens" in *EDRA 40: Re: The Ethical Design of Places*: *Proceedings of the 40th Annual Conference of the Environmental Design Research Association*, ed. Janice Bissell and others, (Edmond, OK: Environmental Design Research Association, 2009).

92   *Science supports what we intuit*   Mark Schatzker, *The Dorito Effect: The Surprising New Truth About Food and Flavor* (New York: Simon and Schuster, 2015).

SWEET POTATOES

95   *Until the advent of the local*   To some extent, the local-food movement began as a reaction to the shift in federal farm policy

in the 1970s that drove the farm crisis. Farmers filed for bankruptcy and left their fields; small farms, purchased by corporations and incented by commodity price support, grew corn and soy. "Hippies" and "back-to-the-landers" created food-buying clubs and then co-ops to purchase food from nearby sources.

95   *How the marshmallow-topped*   Lesley Porcelli, "How Sweet It Is: The Perfect Sweet Potato Casserole," *Saveur,* October 25, 2011.

95   *Yet marshmallows aside*   The Center for Science in the Public Interest, a consumer-advocacy group focused on health and food, ranked the sweet potato number one in nutrition of all vegetables. Sweet potatoes have more than double the nutrients of the runner-up, the potato.

100   *I also saw the importance of*   Pakou Hang, "Transforming Hmong Farming," BlueCross BlueShield, Minnesota Center for Prevention, December 2, 2014, http://www.centerforpreventionmn.com/newsroom/news-articles/real-stories-pakou-hang.

105   *Hmong growers represent about*   Kevin Giles, "Minnesota Among Nation's Farmers Market Hot Spots," *Minneapolis Star Tribune,* July 20, 2009.

108   *Hmong farmers have contributed*   Bruce P. Corrie and Sarah Radosevich, "The Economic Contributions of Immigrants in Minnesota," Minnesota Chamber of Commerce, September 2013.

108   *No two families sweet pork*   Sami Scripter and Sheng Yang, *Cooking from the Heart: The Hmong Kitchen in America,* (Minneapolis: University of Minnesota Press, 2009). *Cooking from the Heart* is the most comprehensive existing guide—at least that I've encountered—to Hmong cooking and traditions, including spiritual practices, medicinal herbs, and celebrations.

108   *Whether you eat or not*   Christine Wilson Owens, "Hmong Cultural Profile," EthnoMed, June 1, 2007, www.ethnomed. org/culture/hmong/hmong-cultural-profile. EthnoMed, oriented toward immigrants in Seattle, supplies this advice: "It is considered impolite to simply decline a drink, food or gift offered to you. Refrain from quickly saying 'No.' When entering a Hmong home during mealtime, guests will be invited to join the family in eating. Whether the guest wants to eat or not, he or she should take part in the meal, just taking a bite or two will make the family happy. Otherwise, the family will stop eating and will talk to the guest until he or she leaves."

Refugee Educator's Network, "Hmong Proverbs," http:// www.reninc.org/reading-resources/hmong-proverbs.pdf. The Sacramento-based Refugee Educator's Network provides the translation in text, as well as the original: "Noj tsis noj kuj tuav diav, / Luag tsis luag kuj nxti hniav."

112   *In Hmong, our healing herbs*   Emily Romatoski and Dan Hager, "Green Medicine: From the Mountains of Laos to the Labs at UW Oshkosh," Beyond Classroom Walls, University of Wisconsin Oshkosh, May 8, 2015, http://www.uwash.edu/ beyondstories/green-medicine-main. Sitha Thor, a biology graduate student, and Dr. Teri Shors, a biology and microbi-

ology professor, are studying the potential of Hmong herbs to combat viruses and infections.

CRANBERRIES

114 *Wisconsin is the fresh cranberry* Wisconsin State Cranberry Growers Association, "About Cranberries," Wisconsin Cranberries, http://www.wiscran.org/cranberries.

117 *These findings are notable* Jeffery S. Pettis et al., "Crop Pollination Exposes Honey Bees to Pesticides Which Alters Their Susceptibility to the Gut Pathogen *Nosema ceranae*," *PLOS ONE* (July 24, 2013), http://journals.plos.org/plosone/article?id=10.1371/journal.pone.0070182.

This study shows that neonicotinoids aren't the only pesticides that might be undermining bee health—a pair of fungicides are actually of most concern. "While Neonics get a lot of attention and a lot of research dollars and no doubt play a role in CCD, our research shows we need to be looking more broadly at the pesticides bees are exposed to," writes Dennis vanEngelsdorp, one of the paper's authors.

117 *Dining on cranberry flowers* Over the past decade, soy and corn farmers have been planting neonicotinoid-treated seeds as a preventative measure against pests but the flowers are also toxic to bees. Bees are exposed to the toxin by a number of other sources as well—sprays, dust, residue from plants, contaminated pollen and water. And even by their own kind—their abilities to gather pollen, navigate, return to hives, and reproduce suffer when residues are introduced by bees returning from collecting foods. Furthermore, There is little evidence

to show that this treatment benefits production. Even the
EPA concludes that "in most cases there is no significant difference in soybean yield when the soybean was treated" with
these chemicals. Environmental Protection Agency, "Benefits
of Neonicotinoid Seed Treatments to Soybean Production,"
http://www.epa.gov/pollinator-protection/benefits-neonicoti-
noid-seed-treatments-soybean-production.

124 *But the government denied*   Kim Severson, "Cranberry Growers Search for Ways to Share Their Bounty," *New York Times,*
November 26, 2014.

124 *In the past ten years, about*   Center for Land Use Education,
"Wisconsin Land Use Megatrends: Agriculture" University of
Wisconsin, Stevens Point, 2010.

125 *Stauner, with his son Ben*   Of the nearly 17,700 acres of
marshes in cranberry production in Wisconsin, just 165 acres
are organic.

CHESTNUTS

135 *Those who know anything*   Phil Rutter, in-person conversation
with author, October 2009.

135 *Americanoid chestnut trees grow*   William Powell, "The American
Chestnut's Genetic Rebirth," *Scientific American* March 2014.

139 *As we toured his grove*   The phrase "woody agriculture" was
coined by Rutter to differentiate between perennial woody crops
and agroforestry that relies on annual planting and tilling.

139   *The chestnut tree's deep, permanent*   G. Tyler Miller and Scott
       Spoolman, *Environmental Science* (Boston: Cengage Learn-
       ing, 2013). Chestnut trees help preserve topsoil in numerous
       ways: they act as a windbreak to prevent winds from blowing
       the soil off cropland, retain moisture, and provide habitats for
       birds and insects that help with pest control and pollination.

139   *Through erosion and runoff, we're*   John Crawford, interview
       by *the* World Economic Forum, "What If the World's Soil Runs
       Out?" *Time*, December 14, 2012.

139   *Chestnuts return more nutrients*   Ferris Jabr, "A New Genera-
       tion of American Chestnut Trees May Redefine America's For-
       ests," *Scientific American*, March, 2014.

144   *The chestnut tree's revival*   Society for Ecological Resto-
       ration, "SER International Primer on Ecological Restoration,"
       October, 2004, http://www.ser.org/resources/resources-de-
       tail-view/ser-international-primer-on-ecological-restoration.
       The Society for Ecological Restoration defines "restoration
       ecology" as an "intentional activity that initiates or accelerates
       the recovery of an ecosystem with respect to its health, integ-
       rity, and sustainability."

145   *By growing a vast mix*   Bill Mollison, *Introduction to Perma-
       culture* (Tasmania: Tagari Publications, 1997). As restoration
       ecologists, Rutter and Brandon practice permaculture, "a philos-
       ophy of working with, rather than against, nature; of protracted
       and thoughtful observation rather than protracted and thought-
       less labor; and of looking at plants and animals in all their func-
       tions rather than treating any area as a single product system."

145 *It's a great source for clean* Susan Freinkel, *American Chestnut: The Life, Death, and Rebirth of a Perfect Tree* (Berkeley: University of California Press, 2007).

146 *Fast-growing chestnut trees* Jabr, "A New Generation of American Chestnut Trees May Redefine America's Forests." Scientific American, March 1 2014, Jabr writes, "In 2002 Charles Rhoades of the U.S. Forest Service's Rocky Mountain Research Station traveled to West Salem [Wisconsin] and gathered dirt and leaf litter from areas surrounding 20 chestnut trees and from 20 different spots where other kinds of hardwood trees grew. Later, in the lab, he analyzed the chemistry of these samples. Chestnut leaves had more nitrogen, phosphorus, potassium and magnesium than leaves from other species, and sandy soil beneath chestnuts had as much as 17 percent more carbon and nitrogen as well as a little more moisture. In sandy soils chestnuts were returning more nutrients and life-building molecules to the earth, where they would be available to numerous other plants, animals and microorganisms."

CORN

151 *Atina's memoir,* Turn Here Atina Diffley's *Turn Here Sweet Corn: Organic Farming Works* (Minneapolis: University of Minnesota Press, 2013) won the Minnesota Book Award for memoir and creative nonfiction.

153 *It replaced wheat, oats, and barley* Michael Pollan writes in an editorial, "When a Crop Becomes King," *New York Times,* July 19, 2002: "80 million acres of corn [are planted] . . . an area more than twice the size of New York State. . . . We douse it with chemicals that poison our water and deepen our dependence on

foreign oil . . . We eat it as fast as we can in as may ways as we can—turning the fat of the land into, well, fat. One has to wonder whether corn hasn't at last succeeded in domesticating us."

154 *studied the differences between organic* Robert Klepper et al., "Economic Performance and Energy Intensiveness on Organic and Conventional Farms in the Corn Belt: A Preliminary Comparison," *American Journal of Agricultural Economics* 59, no.1 (September 1, 1976. wwwajae.oxfordjournals.org/content59.

David W. Crowder and John P. Reganold, "Financial Competitiveness of Organic Agriculture on a Global Scale," *Proceedings of the National Academy of Sciences of the United States of America* 112, no.24 (June 16, 2015).

This report finds that organic farming is more profitable than conventional farming thanks to higher prices per product.

Tom Meersman, "Organic Farmers See Green Both in Sustainability and Profits," *Minneapolis Star Tribune*, June 12, 2015. Robert King, a University of Minnesota professor of applied economics, commented on the report, "The costs for each system are pretty much a wash." Meersman notes that the Crowder and Reganold study does not capture all the benefits of organic farming, however: "equal or more nutritious foods with less or no pesticide residue, improved soil quality, greater plant and wildlife diversity, and less pesticide and nutrient pollution of ground and surface water."

155 *The study recommended that the* USDA Study Team on Organic Farming, "Report and Recommendations on Organic Farming," July 1980, http://www.nal.usda.gov/afsic/pubs/

USDAOrgFarmRpt.pdf. In 1980, Bob Bergland, then secretary of agriculture, charged Anson Bertrand, the head of the USDA's Science and Education Administration, with putting together a USDA Study Team on Organic Farming. It was estimated that there were at least twenty thousand organic farmers in the United States. In his foreword to the report, Bergland wrote, "We need to gain a better understanding of these organic farming systems—the extent to which they are practiced in the United States, why they are being used, the technology behind them, and the economic and ecological impacts from their use. We must also identify the kinds of research and education programs that relate to organic farming."

155 *despite disparaging comments from* Earl Butz, several 1970 speeches, quoted in Mark Lipson, *Searching for the "O-Word": Analyzing the USDA Current Research Information System for Pertinence to Organic Farming* (Santa Cruz: Organic Farming Research Foundation, 1997).

156 *So the term "organic"* Ibid.

157 *Recently the World Health* International Agency for Research on Cancer, IARC Monographs Volume 112: Evaluation of Five Organophoshate Insecticides and Herbicides," World Health Organization, March 20, 2015, http://www.iarc.fr/en/media-centre/iarcnews/pdf/MonographVolume112.pdf.

157 *Ostlie told Minnesota Public Radio* Mark Steil, "Corn Farmers Struggle to Cope with Rootworm Resistance," Minnesota Public Radio, August 3, 2012, http://www.mprnews.org/story/2012/08/03/regional/corn-rootworm.

158   *Two years ago, researchers*   Carey L. Biron, "U.S. Farmers Report Widespread GM Crop Contamination," *Inter Press Service News Agency,* March 3, 2014, http://ipsnews.net/2014/03/tamars-adress-u-s-data-gap-gm-crop-contamination.

161   *In a sense my approach is*   In *Fields Without Dreams: Defending the Agrarian Idea* (New York: Simon & Schuster, 1996), Victor Davis Hanson, a grape farmer and Greek scholar, argues that the decline of working farmers results in a diminished connection to the virtues and work ethic upon which our democracy rests. Hanson considers the independent and self-reliant farmer as the "brakeman" on an affluent, leisured, and rootless society.

162   *corn prices have been driven*   Ron Meador, "Corn Farmers Say Syngenta's GMOs Have Cost Them the Chinese Market," *MinnPost,* October 9, 2014, https://www.minnpost.com/earth-journal/2014/10/corn-farmers-say-syngentas-gmos-have-cost-them-chinese-market. This contamination happened in transport, however not in the field.

162   *The activists' issue is not*   Kenneth A. Dahlberg, ed., "Introduction," *New Directions for Agriculture and Agricultural Research: Neglected Dimensions and Emerging Alternatives,* (Totowa, NJ: Rowman and Allanheld, 1986). As early as the 1970s, the National Academy of Sciences and the Rockefeller Foundation released reports arguing that public agriculture research had become highly insular and largely divorced from the frontiers of knowledge in the basic biological sciences. Both were strongly critical of what they perceived to be the dominant thrust of US agricultural research geared toward commodities.

163   *wrote Aldo Leopold in*   Aldo Leopold, *A Sand County Almanac* (New York: Ballantine Books, 1986).

163   *Why are scientists intent on solving*   Union of Concerned Scientists, "Genetic Engineering in Agriculture," http://www.ucsusa.org/our-work/food-agriculture/our-failing-food-system/genetic-engineering-agriculture

163   *the research has benefited nonfarming*   Jim Hightower, *Hard Tomatoes, Hard Times: Failure of the Land Grant College Complex* (Cambridge, MA: Schenkman Publishing Company, 1973). Hightower writes, "Corporate agriculture's preoccupation with scientific and business efficiency has produced a radical restructuring of rural America that has been carried into urban America. . . . Today's urban crisis is a consequence of failure in rural America."

163   *said Jonathan Foley, executive*   Jonathan Foley, "It's Time to Rethink America's Corn System," *Scientific American*, March 2013.

164   *it receives preferential treatment*   Ibid.

165   *But corn's reign may*   Suzanne Goldenberg, "Climate Threat to America's 'King Corn,'" *Guardian*, June 11, 2014.

166   *Higher corn prices won't*   Dan Weissmann, "If Animal Feed Were Organic, Could We Afford Eggs?" *Marketplace Money*, March 23, 2015, http://www.marketplace.org/topics/sustainability/if-animal-feed-were-organic-could-we-afford-eggs.

166 *promises to ramp up support*   Tom Vilsack, keynote address (Ag Outlook Forum, Ohio State University, Columbus, OH, February 2013).

168 *Rebellion sounds out in*   Diffley, *Turn Here Sweet Corn: Organic Farming Works.*

MILK

174 *most gentle method, which takes*   University of Minnesota Associate Professor of Veterinary Public Health Jeff Bender is currently experimenting with sonication, using sound waves to kill microbes, which relies on far less energy and doesn't alter milk's flavor.

175 *The ruling by a judge*   Bob Mercer, "Legislation Would Give Raw Milk a Place of its Own at State's Table," *Aberdeen News,* January 28, 2015, http://www.aberdeennews.com/news/politics/legislation-would-give-raw-milk-a-place-of-its-own/article_9fcb7889-9264-504a-b56e-6eecc740c58b.html. In April 2015, South Dakota Governor Dennis Daugaard signed Senate Bill 45, makes it possible for raw milk to be purchased by consumers from retail outlets. As legal products, raw milk and raw cream will be regulated by the state just as is grade A milk.

175 *I am not a raw-milk advocate*   Brady Slater, "Cook County Dairy Farm Locked in Legal Battle with State," *Duluth News Tribune,* March 4, 2015.

176 *Raw Milk, they say*   Marco Waser et al., "Inverse Association of Farm Milk Consumption with Asthma and Allergy in

Rural and Suburban Populations across Europe," *Clinical and Experimental Allergy* 37, no.5 (May 2007). The USDA rebuts these findings in, "The Dangers of Raw Milk: Unpasteurized Milk Can Pose a Serious Health Risk," http://www.fda.gov/Food/ResourcesForYou/consumers/ucm079516.htm.

177   *In a Michigan study, 82 percent*   Ted Beals, "Pilot Survey of Cow Share Consumer/Owners Lactose Intolerance," Campaign for Real Milk, March 2008, http://www.realmilk.com/health/lactose-intolerance-survey.

178   *claimed Allie, a mom in*   Allie asked that her real name not be disclosed.

178   *She was being investigated as*   Allie was a member of a "cow share" arrangement, where members contribute to the cost of an animal's purchase price and upkeep. As co-owners with the farmer, the members are entitled to the cow's milk and pick it up in the nearest town, instead of having to drive miles from their homes to a farm.

180   *One Minnesota physician called*   John Spargo, *The Common Sense of the Milk Question,* (New York: The Macmillan Company, 1908).

181   *A conventionally raised dairy*   Don P. Blayney, "Statistical Bulletin Number 978: The Changing Landscape of U.S. Milk Production," Economic Research Service, USDA, June 2002, June 2002, http://www.ers.usda.gov/media/488847/sh978_1_.pdf.

183   *According to the Center for Science*   Center for Science in the Public Interest, "The Ten Riskiest Foods Regulated by the

U.S. Food and Drug Administration," http://www.cspinet.org/ new/pdf/cspi_top_10_fda.pdf.

183   *And as the government tries*   Stacy Crim et al., "Incidence and Trends of Infection with Pathogen, Transmitted Commonly through Food—Foodborne Diseases Active Surveillance Network, 10 U.S. Sites, 2006–2013," Morbidity and Mortality Weekly Report, Centers for Disease Control and Prevention, April 18, 2014, http://www.cdc.gov/mmwr/preview/ mmwrhtml/mm6315a3.htm.

CHEESE & BUTTER

193   *laws that dictate how and where*   "Consorzio Del Formaggio Parmigiano Reggiano Succesfuly Defends Parmigiano Against Infringement," November 15, 2015, http://www.parmigianoreggiano.com/news/2005_3/46dd930f52b24dfb894b-8f9aa187ee4a.aspx. To be labeled Parmigiano-Reggiano, the cheese must be produced in the provinces of Parma, Reggio Emilia, Bologna (but only the area west of the river Reno), or Modena (only the area south of the river Po). Outside this region, the name Parmesan can be applied to cheeses similar to Parmigiano-Reggiano.

196   *the number of small, artisan cheesemaking*   Matthew Rubiner, "The Big Cheese," *The American,* Americas Enterprise Institute, November 23, 2007, https://www.aei.org/publication/ the-big-cheese.

196   *Specialty cheeses account for*   National Agricultural Statistics Service, "Wisconsin Speacialty Cheese Production up 5 Percent," *Wisconsin Ag News: Specialty Cheese*, United States

Department of Agriculture, May 6, 2014, http://www.nass.usda.gov/Statistics-by-State/Wisconsin/Publications/Dairy/2015/WI-Specialty-Cheese.05.15.pdf.

196   *Along with cow, sheep, and goat*   There is one water-buffalo rancher in Plain, Wisconsin, whose milk is processed into mozzarella by Cedar Grove Cheese and Landmark Creamery. Given the adaptability of these animals to the region and the demand for artisan mozzarella and burrata, we should expect to see more water buffalos on our farms.

196   *the connection to the land is more*   To be labeled "organic," a cheese must come from a certified organic cow not given growth hormones or antibiotics. The cow's feed must be 100 percent organic and the cow must graze on untreated pastures at least 120 days a year, receiving 20 percent of its nutrition from grazing. The label does not regulate the size of the farm or the number of cows.

201   *Its mission is to promote new*   Gary Paul Nabhan's official Web site, "Slow Money's Pivotal Role in the Next Stage of the Local Food Movement," http://www.garynabhan.com/i/place-based-foods (accessed 11/30/2012). Since 2010, Slow Money has helped to funnel $25 million into nearly two hundred food enterprises; Slow Money comprises sixteen domestic chapters and one in France, six investment clubs, and Gatheround, a new crowd-funding platform. "It's really not about building a better financial base but about building community," says Gary Paul Nabhan.

206   *This diversity is sought by both*   Rémy Grappin and Eric Beuvier, "Possible Implications of Milk Pasteurization on the Man-

ufacture and Sensory Quality of Ripened Cheese," *International Dairy Journal* 8, no.12 (November 1997).

207   *The biggest concern is listeria*   Bill Marler, "Why is Listeria so Deadly Dangerous?" *Food Poison Journal*, September 10, 2011, http://www.foodpoisonjournal.com/food-poisoning-information/why-is-listeria-so-deadly-dangerous/#.VgzFoY9Viko.

212   *In "Finding Food in Farm Country,"*   Ken Meter and Jon Rosales, "Finding Food in Farm Country: The Economics of Food & Farming in Southeast Minnesota," Crossroads Resource Center, 2001, http://www.crcworks.org/ff.pdf. Ken Meter, "Local Food as Economic Development," Crossroads Resource Center, 2008, http://www.crcworks.org/1feed.pdf. These articles are among first and most comprehensive evaluations of the impact local food has on rural economies. Meter argues that every dollar spent on local food returns four dollars to the community.

213   *Land O'Lakes, for comparison*   Caroline Fairchild, "Portraits of the 500: Inside a Land O'Lakes Dairy Farm," *Fortune*, June 11, 2014.

TURKEY

222   *They'd found independent lab results*   Joel Salatin, interview by Tracy Frisch, "Sowing Dissent: Lunatic Farmer Joel Salatan Digs In," *Sun*, October 2012. Salatin says, "Chickens from the supermarket averaged 3,600 colony-forming units of bacteria per milliliter. The chickens from our farm [processed in an open-air facility] averaged 133 units."

222   *Yet the US government literature*   Laura Kingsbury, "Comparisons of Microbial Counts in Organic and Commercially Processed Chickens" (master's thesis, University of Wisconsin, Stout, 2006). Farm or small-plant-processed organic chicken meat has fewer *E. coli*, listeria, and salmonella pathogens. This may be due to the fact that the chickens are raised in cleaner conditions, are healthier, and are handled by fewer people.

226   *it's one of the things we covered*   Robert Wallace, "Midwest Bird Flu: A Diseconomy of Industrial Poultry" (lecture, Institute for Agriculture and Trade Policy, Minneapolis, MN, June 11, 2015). My encounter with Brandon dates back to 2013, two years before avian flu wiped out nearly five million industrially raised turkeys in Minnesota (and a total of nine million nationwide).

While the poultry sector has laid blame on farm workers and wild waterfowl, H5N2 Bird Flu Virus demonstrates the poultry sector's dysfunctional economy of scale. Wallace said, "Industrial poultry production survives solely by externalizing the damage it causes producers, consumers, workers, governments, and the environment. In a market economy, the effect would hit a company's margins ending the industry as we know it."

226   *Commercial birds are fed a mix*   National Research Council, *The Use of Drugs in Food Animals: Benefits and Risks* (Washington, DC: National Academies Press, 1988). Nearly 80 percent of the antibiotics used in the US go into meat and poultry production. The National Research Council, part of the National Academies of Sciences, Engineering, and Medicine, concluded that "a link can be demonstrated between the use of antibiotics in food animals, the development of resistant microorgan-

ism in those animals, and the zoonotic spread of pathogens to humans."

228 *Many independent plants have*   Butterball, located in North Carolina, is the largest producer of turkeys in the world. While Minnesota raises more turkeys, North Carolina processes more of them.

234 *The idea of slaughtering an animal*   Awad A. Shehata and others, "The Effect of Glyphosate on Potential Pathogens and Beneficial Members of Poultry Microbiota In Vitro," *Current Microbiology* 66, no.4 (April 2013). As of this writing H5N2 has decimated over five million of Minnesota's turkeys, as I note above, in just several months. The state's five hundred turkey Concentrated Animal Feeding Operations (CAFOs) pack as many as sixty thousand birds, caged beak to tail, in one warehouse. Their diets of GMO soy and corn contain high levels of glyphosate (also found in Roundup) and are known to compromise their immune systems. Few USDA, university, or industry researchers question the relationship of these practices to bird health, however. It may be that the funding for such research has dried up or the findings are being squelched. Since 2002, leading USDA microbiologists have reported being prohibited from releasing their findings on the potential hazards to human health posed by industrial animal practices. Perry Beeman, "Ag Scientists Feel the Heat," *Des Moines Register*, December 1, 2002.

Meanwhile, health officials worry the virus may jump to humans. They have been "requiring that cullers and barn-cleaners wear the kind of protective gear that Ebola workers do. Officials have also advised that everyone who was recently in contact with affected poultry operations—workers, truckers, veterinarians—take Tamiflu, a flu preventative." Donald McNeil, Jr., "A Flu Epidemic That Threatens Birds, Not Humans," *New York Times*, May 4, 2015.

WILD RICE

238   *The Indians know how you follow*   Thomas Vennum, *Wild Rice and the Ojibway People* (St. Paul: Minnesota Historical Society Press, 1988). Vennum's book is the most complete and authoritative text on Ojibwe wild rice that I've found. It includes stories, legends, history, gathering, and nutritional and medicinal information about the Northern Heartland's most important indigenous food.

241   *those on the path given by the Creator*   Basil Johnston, Ojibway Heritage (Lincoln: University of Nebraska Press, 1990).

241   *The Anishinaabeg, writes Robin*   Robin Wall Kimmerer, *Braiding Sweetgrass: Indigenous Wisdom, Scientific Knowledge, and the Teachings of Plants* (Minneapolis: Milkweed Editions, 2013).

242   *to create a hybrid strain that ripens*   Native Harvest, "Patents and Biopiracy," http://nativeharvest.com/node/249.

246   *The debates over wild rice's*   Twin Metals and La Pointe Mining (both in Minnesota); RGGS Land and Minerals, Ltd., Houston, Texas; and Gogebic Taconite, Wisconsin.

247 *Work is underway to support* "DNR Aquatic Habitat Program, Amended ML 2011 Accomplishment Plan," *Lessard-Sams Outdoor Heritage Council Report*, January 29, 2015, http://www.lsohc.leg.mn/FY2012/accomp_plan/5a.pdf.

247 *The issues at stake, according to Pember* Mary Annette Pember, "Wisconsin Endangers a Sacred Tradition," *Indian Country Today Media Network*, January 25, 2012, http://indiancountrytodaymedianetwork.com/2012/01/25/wisconsin-endangers-sacred-tradition-73365.

248 *The area's surface and groundwater* Wisconsin John Muir Chapter, "Blocking Destructive Mining," Sierra Club, http://www.sierraclub.org/Wisconsin/issues/mining.

Further Reading

Michael Ableman, *Fields of Plenty: A Farmer's Journey in Search of Real Food and the People Who Grow It* (San Francisco: Chronicle Books, 2005)

With glorious photography and compelling prose, Ableman takes the reader on a journey across the country to explore the meaning of food and our culture.

Dan Barber, *The Third Plate: Field Notes on the Future of Food* (New York: Penguin Books, 2014)

Barber builds the case for a food system that marries good farming practices to great cooking—the kind of cooking that has established Manhattan's Blue Hill restaurant as a leader in the farm-to-table movement, and the practices that made his nonprofit farm, Stone Barns Center for Food and Agriculture, an epicenter for local food advocates.

John Bates, *Graced by the Seasons: Fall and Winter in the Northwoods* (Mercer, WI: Manitowish River Press, 2008)

A love song to winter by a local naturalist.

Wendell Berry, *Bringing It to the Table: On Farming and Food* (Berkeley: Counterpoint Press, 2009)

Along with everything Berry has written, this book belongs on everyone's shelf. Berry reminds us time and again, "A significant part of the pleasure of eating is in one's accurate consciousness of the lives and the world from which food comes."

Mark Bittman, *The Food Matters Cookbook: 500 Revolutionary Recipes for Better Living* (New York: Simon & Schuster, 2010)

Here is the essential encyclopedia for sourcing and cooking sustainable ingredients, based on the guidelines spelled out in Bittman's *Food Matters.* It's the how and why to cook local and live lightly on the earth.

Craig Cox, *Storefront Revolution: Food Co-ops and the Counterculture* (New Brunswick, NJ: Rutgers University Press, 1994)

A history of the co-op movement in the US.

Atina Diffley, *Turn Here Sweet Corn: Organic Farming Works* (Minneapolis, University of Minnesota Press, 2013)

This beautifully rendered memoir is the best depiction I've encountered of a good life on an organic farm; it's a treatise on the importance of soil, it's a love song, and it's a thriller. This original and compelling story is told by Atina—a strong, passionate woman and wise leader who lives her values, stands up to bullies, and protects all she holds dear—with great humor and joy.

Beth Dooley, *Minnesota's Bounty: The Farmers Market Cookbook* (Minneapolis: University of Minnesota Press, 2013)

A field guide to the farmer's markets of this northern Midwest.

Beth Dooley, *The Northern Heartland Kitchen* (Minneapolis: University of Minnesota Press, 2011)

The hows and whys of eating local in our region.

Beth Dooley and Lucia Watson, *Savoring the Seasons of the Northern Heartland: 200 Recipes Blending Bold, New Flavors with the Traditional Foods of the Upper Midwest* (Minneapolis: University of Minnesota Press, 2004)

The story of our local food, its history and lore, and how it plays out on our plates today.

Susan Freinkel, *American Chestnut: The Life, Death, and Rebirth of a Perfect Tree* (Berkeley: University of California Press, 2007)

The story of the perfect tree.

Harva Hachten and Terese Allen, *The Flavor of Wisconsin: An Informal History of Food and Eating in the Badger State* (Madison: Wisconsin Historical Society Press, 2009)

A complete culinary history of the state.

Richard Horan, *Harvest: An Adventure into the Heart of America's Family Farms* (New York: Harper Perennial, 2011)

Horan provides portraits of farmers and glimpses into their intelligence, diligence, and inspiring work.

Anne R. Kaplan, Marjorie A. Hoover, and Willera B. Moore, *The Minnesota Ethnic Food Book* (St. Paul: Minnesota Historical Society Press, 1986)

This is the first, and remains the most complete, book to explore the rich landscape of Minnesota's food and cultural heritage.

Robin Wall Kimmerer, *Braiding Sweetgrass: Indigenous Wisdom, Scientific Knowledge and the Teachings of Plants* (Minneapolis: Milkweed Editions, 2015)

Weaving together indigenous stories and scientific information, Kimmer engages us in the natural world with appreciation and wonder. She reveals hard facts while celebrating beauty, all to help us understand and appreciate this amazing place and our place in it.

Frederick L. Kirschenmann, *Cultivating an Ecological Conscience: Essays from a Farmer Philosopher* (Berkeley: Counterpoint Press, 2011)

This collection of essays by a farmer-philosopher lays the groundwork for much of the local-food and sustainable-farming movements. Kirschenmann, like Wendell Barry and Wes Jackson, is one of the fathers of the ethical land movement.

Marjorie Kreidberg, *Food on the Frontier: Minnesota Cooking from 1850 to 1900 with Selected Recipes* (St. Paul: Minnesota Historical Society Press, 1975)

This is both social history and cookbook.

Meridel Le Sueur, *North Star Country* (Minneapolis: University of Minnesota Press, 1998)

A brilliant maverick, Le Sueur defines the region by presenting indigenous material with a historical perspective and describes the essential character of the people whose lives are shaped by this land, this weather, and the seasons, as well as their own personal histories.

Barry Lopez, ed. *The Future of Nature: Writing on a Human Ecology from* Orion *Magazine* (Minneapolis: Milkweed Editions, 2007)

This collection of essays, gathered from the finest writing in *Orion*, explores our relationship to nature and the barriers we've created that keep us from intimate engagement with land and place.

Deborah Madison, *Vegetable Literacy: Cooking and Gardening with Twelve Families from the Edible Plant Kingdom, with over 300 Deliciously Simple Recipes* (Berkeley: Ten Speed Press, 2013)

Madison provides delicious insights into the diversity of the plant kingdom and the relationships among vegetables, flowers, herbs, wild plants, and us.

Tracie McMillan, *The American Way of Eating: Undercover at Walmart, Applebee's, Farm Fields and the Dinner Table* (New York: Scribner, 2012)

This is a haunting tale of how our food really comes to us, via Walmart, Applebee's, and our farms.

Kent Meyers, *The Witness of Combines* (Minneapolis: University of Minnesota Press, 1998)

Deeply moving stories of a joyous boyhood and the loss of a family farm.

Gary Paul Nabhan, *Coming Home to Eat: The Pleasures and Politics of Local Food* (New York: W.W. Norton & Company, 2009)

Nabhan, an internationally acclaimed ecologist and essayist, lays out all the personal, environmental, political, and spiritual reasons for eating close to home in this account of trying to eat only foods grown, fished, or gathered within two hundred miles of his house. The results provide surprising insights into our personal relationships to the land.

Marion Nestle, *Food Politics: How the Food Industry Influences Nutrition and Health* (Berkeley: University of California Press, 2002)

Relying on research, government transcripts, and corporate reports, Nestle makes the compelling argument that America's agribusiness lobby has stifled our government's regulatory power, helped create a seasonless and regionless diet, and hampered our access to essential nutritional advice.

James Norton, *Lake Superior Flavors: A Field Guide to Food and Drink Along the Circle Tour* (Minneapolis: University of Minnesota Press, 2014)

The most complete culinary guide to Lake Superior's local food.

James Norton and Becca Dilley, *The Master Cheesemakers of Wisconsin* (Madison: University of Wisconsin Press, 2009)

The stories of our country's most interesting cheesemakers.

Michael Pollan, *Cooked: A Natural History of Transformation* (New York: Penguin Books, 2013)

Readers follow Pollan on his journey to the kitchen to understand the four elements—power of fire, water, air, and earth—that transform the stuff of nature into our dinners.

Michael Pollan, *The Omnivore's Dilemma: A Natural History of Four Meals* (New York: Penguin Books, 2006)

This is *the* Bible of the local-food movement, a national best seller that changed the way we view the ecology of eating. It is the essential tome for anyone interested in our food systems—industrial, organic industrial, organic-local, and alternative.

Janisse Ray, *The Seed Underground: A Growing Revolution to Save Food* (White River Junction, VT: Chelsea Green Publishing, 2012)

A beautiful memoir and a passionate and urgent plea for saving seeds, saving our food, and saving the planet.

Philip Rutter, Susan Wiegrefe, and Brandon Rutter-Daywater, *Growing Hybrid Hazelnuts: The New Resilient Crop for a Changing Climate* (White River Junction, VT: Chelsea Green Publishing, 2015)

This is the very first comprehensive guide for farmers interested in growing a crop that will address a host of problems created by modern agriculture. It's loaded with Phil's bon mots, plus a lot of practical information. Hazelnuts will preserve and nourish soil, feed wildlife, protect water, and provide food, oil, wood, and biodiesel.

Vandana Shiva, *Stolen Harvest: The Hijacking of the Global Food Supply* (Boston: South End Press, 2000)

A world-renowned environmentalist charts the impact of globalized corporate agriculture on small farmers, the environment, and the quality of our food.

FURTHER READING

Thomas Vennum, *Just Too Much of an Indian: Bill Baker, Stalwart in a Fading Culture* (Madison: University of Wisconsin Press, 2009)

This is a rare portrait of an Ojibwe elder, Bill Baker, who teaches us all what most have forgotten, the meaning and practice of Ojibwe tradition. The story is told through events and movements relevant to Indians in the twentieth century—the boarding-school disasters, allotments, the World Wars, spear-fishing and ricing controversies. It also relays essential native practices: wild ricing, the hunt, naming ceremonies, and powwows.

Thomas Vennum, *Wild Rice and the Ojibway People* (St. Paul: Minnesota Historical Society Press, 1988)

This is the seminal work on wild rice and its importance to the Ojibwe culture. It illuminates every aspect of wild rice—botanical, historical, ethnological, ecological, and culinary. Thoroughly researched and carefully documented, it contains myths, legends, songs and ceremonies, as well as interviews with members of the various ricing tribes. It remains the most important work on wild rice today.

Gilbert Wilson, *Buffalo Bird Woman's Garden: Agriculture of the Hidatsa Indians* (St. Paul: Minnesota Historical Society Press, 1987)

This reprint of the anthropological study done by Wilson in 1917 provides stories, jokes, and personal anecdotes about village life among the Hidatsa Indians. It also includes useful gardening lore, tales of tools and structures, and descriptions of the heritage beans, corn, and squash that are being reclaimed today.

Acknowledgements

My deepest thanks to Elly Grace, for planting the seeds of this book with Milkweed Editions; to Patrick Thomas, for cultivating the initial draft; and to the unwavering support and wisdom of Daniel Slager, under whose guidance the manuscript flourished. I owe much to the collaborative efforts of Joey McGarvey, a savvy, careful, and insightful copy editor, and to Connor Lane, for shepherding the manuscript through its transitions. I'm ever grateful to the farmers and producers, professors, researchers, and authors who served as advisors and mentors: Roger Blobaum, Dan Bussey, Atina Diffley, Mary and Dave Falk, Andy Gaertner, Tom Galazen and Ann Rosenquist, Jack Hedin, Loretta Jaus, Gunnar Liden, Victor Moritz, John Peterson, Jodi Ohlsen Read and Steven Read, Greg and Mary Reynolds, Phil Rutter, Michael Stanitis, Arion Thiboumery, and Dale Wiehoff; to dear friends Bonnie Blodgett, Leslie Bush, Kathy Coskran, Sarah Evert, Patricia Hoolihan, Lisa Ide,

Randy Lebedoff, Angie Lillehei, Mary O'Brien, Megan O'Hara, Larkin McPhee, Julie Ristau, Sally Spector, Sarah Sponheim, and Charlie Wagner, for their encouragement, and to Lucia Watson, who inspired this journey and from whom I've learned so much. Thanks to my parents, Liz and Mark Anton, who believed in my work, and our sons Matt, Kip, and Tim, who literally devoured my words and cheered me on. And it's because of the steadfast faith of my lifelong partner and loving ally, Kevin Dooley—apt critic and devout fan—that I've found my way home.